MICHIGAN'S UPPER PENINSULA

*Mackinac celebrates its annual lilac festival in early June,
when the island is awash in purple blossoms.*

1ST EDITION

MICHIGAN'S UPPER PENINSULA

Amy Westervelt

The Countryman Press
Woodstock, Vermont

To my parents for instilling in me a love of travel, small towns, and good people, my brother Darren for sharing that love, and Matt Girvan for always being there.

ISBN 978-1-58157-081-6

Cover photo © Dennis Cox LLC

Interior photos by the author unless otherwise specified

Book design by Bodenweber Design

Composition by Opaque Design & Print Production

Maps by Mapping Specialists Ltd., Madison, WI © The Countryman Press

Published by The Countryman Press, P.O. Box 748, Woodstock, Vermont 05091

Distributed by W. W. Norton & Company, Inc., 500 Fifth Avenue, New York, NY 10110

Manufactured in the United States of America

10 9 8 7 6 5 4 3 2 1

GREAT DESTINATIONS TRAVEL GUIDEBOOK SERIES

Recommended by *National Geographic Traveler* and *Travel + Leisure* magazines

[A] CRISP AND CRITICAL APPROACH, FOR TRAVELERS WHO WANT TO LIVE LIKE LOCALS.
—*USA Today*

Great Destinations™ guidebooks are known for their comprehensive, critical coverage of regions of extraordinary cultural interest and natural beauty. The authors in this series are professional travel writers who have lived for many years in the regions they describe. Each title in this series is continuously updated with each printing to insure accurate and timely information. All the books contain more than one hundred photographs and maps.

Current titles available:

THE ADIRONDACK BOOK

ATLANTA

AUSTIN, SAN ANTONIO
& THE TEXAS HILL COUNTRY

THE BERKSHIRE BOOK

BERMUDA

BIG SUR, MONTEREY BAY & GOLD COAST WINE
COUNTRY

CAPE CANAVERAL, COCOA BEACH
& FLORIDA'S SPACE COAST

THE CHARLESTON, SAVANNAH
& COASTAL ISLANDS BOOK

THE CHESAPEAKE BAY BOOK

THE COAST OF MAINE BOOK

COLORADO'S CLASSIC MOUNTAIN TOWNS

COSTA RICA: GREAT DESTINATIONS CENTRAL
AMERICA

THE FINGER LAKES BOOK

THE FOUR CORNERS REGION

GALVESTON, SOUTH PADRE ISLAND
& THE TEXAS GULF COAST

THE HAMPTONS BOOK

HAWAII'S BIG ISLAND

HONOLULU & OAHU: GREAT DESTINATIONS
HAWAII

THE JERSEY SHORE: ATLANTIC CITY TO CAPE MAY

KAUAI: GREAT DESTINATIONS HAWAII

LAKE TAHOE & RENO

LAS VEGAS

LOS CABOS & BAJA CALIFORNIA SUR:
GREAT DESTINATIONS MEXICO

MAUI: GREAT DESTINATIONS HAWAII

MICHIGAN'S UPPER PENINSULA

MONTREAL & QUEBEC CITY:
GREAT DESTINATIONS CANADA

THE NANTUCKET BOOK

THE NAPA & SONOMA BOOK

NORTH CAROLINA'S OUTER BANKS
& THE CRYSTAL COAST

PALM BEACH, FORT LAUDERDALE, MIAMI & THE
FLORIDA KEYS

PALM SPRINGS & DESERT RESORTS

PHOENIX, SCOTTSDALE, SEDONA
& CENTRAL ARIZONA

PLAYA DEL CARMEN, TULUM & THE RIVIERA MAYA:
GREAT DESTINATIONS MEXICO

SALT LAKE CITY, PARK CITY, PROVO
& UTAH'S HIGH COUNTRY RESORTS

SAN DIEGO & TIJUANA

SAN JUAN, VIEQUES & CULEBRA:
GREAT DESTINATIONS PUERTO RICO

SAN MIGUEL DE ALLENDE & GUANAJUATO:
GREAT DESTINATIONS MEXICO

THE SANTA FE & TAOS BOOK

THE SARASOTA, SANIBEL ISLAND & NAPLES BOOK

THE SEATTLE & VANCOUVER BOOK

THE SHENANDOAH VALLEY BOOK

TOURING EAST COAST WINE COUNTRY

WASHINGTON, D.C., AND NORTHERN VIRGINIA

YELLOWSTONE & GRAND TETON NATIONAL PARKS AND
JACKSON HOLE

YOSEMITE & THE SOUTHERN SIERRA NEVADA

If you are traveling to, moving to, residing in, or just interested in any (or all!) of these enchanting regions, a Great Destinations guidebook is a superior companion. Honest and painstakingly critical, full of information only a local can provide, Great Destinations guidebooks give you all the practical knowledge you need to enjoy the best of each region. Why not own them all?

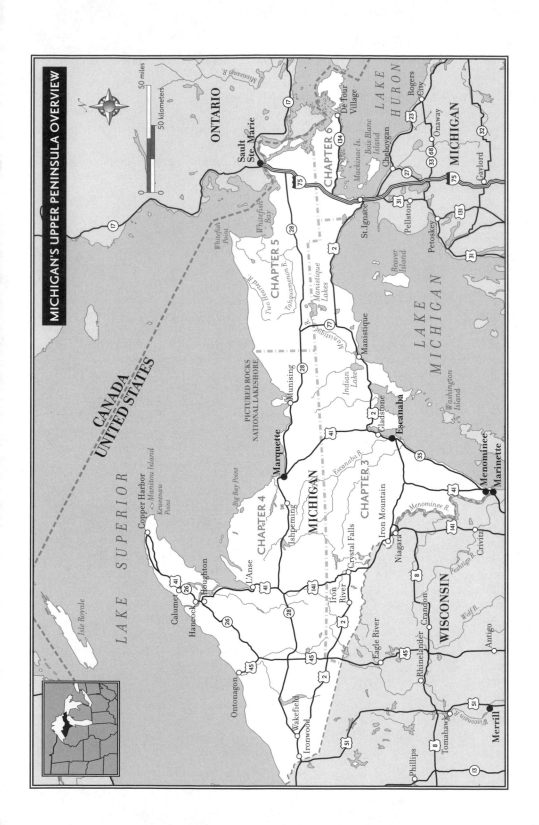

MICHIGAN'S UPPER PENINSULA OVERVIEW

Contents

7
Information
Nuts & Bolts
235

ACKNOWLEDGMENTS

Yoopers (what locals and "downstaters" call Upper Peninsula residents—the word evolved from UP-per)—are hands-down the nicest, most sincere group of people I've come across. And this in the face of nearly seven-month winters and rural living that is not always terribly easy.

Among this charming and welcoming lot, I'd like to thank a few shining stars for sharing the things they love about the place they call home: Wendy Jameson, the best damn bartender in the Straits for her spot-on recommendations, fantastic local tales, and the ability to cure hiccups; John Brown for letting me in on the remedies, rituals, and favorite retreats of the Ojibwa tribe; Georg Spuhler for teaching me how to kayak through the lakes; Phil Cook for introducing me to the wonderful world of pasties; and Karla Kingsley for directing me to the best stops along the Keweenaw Peninsula.

I am also indebted to Kim Grant for giving me the opportunity to write this book in the first place and seeing it through the editing process, Countryman Press for publishing it, and my favorite person, photographer, and travel partner Matt Girvan.

INTRODUCTION

When I arrived in Michigan from California I expected snow and lakes and friendly midwesterners. What I did not expect was that I, who had traveled the world from Brazil to Italy, Morocco to Japan, would find one of my all-time favorite vacation destinations here: the Upper Peninsula.

As I've been telling friends and family for years, the U.P. is one of the best-kept secrets in America. In the summer, swimmers, kayaks, small pleasure boats, and yachts skim across crystal-clear lake waters; cyclists ride through mountains and woods or take it easy closer to shore, enjoying the views; hikers find indescribably beautiful waterfalls and rock formations, not to mention an incredible variety of birds and wildlife. In fall, leaves turn from green to gold to fiery orange and bright red, rivaling the famous fall foliage of New England. In the winter—OK, in the winter it is freezing cold in the U.P., but you know what? It's still beautiful. The snow is always white and soft; there's none of that dirty, salty city snow up here. Cross-country skiers have mile after mile of wide-open or woodland snow at their disposal, and even with all those skiers, there's enough room for snowmobilers to tear it up for miles without anyone telling them to keep it quiet or slow it down. And there's no need to forgo the fishing in winter—ice fishing for walleye, whitefish, and trout is great fun, and the lakes freeze up enough by mid-December. When the ice begins to melt and leaves begin to sprout on the trees, April marks the start of trout-fishing season, and it's hard to imagine a better place to watch the magic of spring. Lilac runs riot over the islands, cherry blossoms explode with color, and birds sing cheerful tunes along the shore and in the woods. Though summer is warm and lovely, it is the only time of the year when crowds form in certain parts of the U.P. (Mackinac, Pictured Rocks). For those who prefer to avoid crowds, I recommend heading up in the spring, just after the first blooms (April and May) but before the summer crowds, or in September when the crowds have left but the sun is still shining and the leaves are just starting to turn.

No matter what time of year it is, visitors are always treated to a warm, friendly Yooper welcome. People still wave "hello" to strangers, and although there are certain local treasures that residents are hesitant to share, most are happy to show off their home by pointing visitors in the direction of the best local sights and eats. Perhaps even more important, they have no problem steering tourists away from sights that aren't what they're cracked up to be.

My goal is that this guide be your own personal Yooper traveling companion—friendly and knowledgeable, pointing you toward secret waterfalls and charming B&Bs, romantic dinner spots, and the best piping-hot pasties, all while entertaining you with ancient legends and juicy bits of modern history.

THE WAY THIS BOOK WORKS

Michigan's Upper Peninsula is larger than the four states of Connecticut, Delaware, Massachusetts, and Rhode Island combined, with a continuous 1,700-mile shoreline provided by Lakes Superior, Michigan, and Huron. Within these boundaries the 384-mile-long peninsula stretches from Drummond Island in the east to Ironwood in the west, reaching 233 miles wide from Menominee in the south to Copper Harbor at the tip of the Keweenaw Peninsula.

The first two chapters of this book cover the intriguing history of the U.P., from Native American tribes to French fur trappers to British and American soldiers, and transportation—getting to and getting around this large region. Then, because the Great Lakes continue to dominate local life and are the pride of all Michigan residents, but especially of Yoopers, we've used those massive bodies of water to organize the rest of the guide, starting with Lake Michigan and moving clockwise up to Lake Superior, then Whitefish Bay, Lake Huron, and the magical Straits of Mackinac. Within each lake chapter you'll find a brief characterization of the surrounding regions and what to expect when you visit, both in summer and in winter (a VERY important distinction!), along with recommendations for lodging, dining, shopping, and activities.

It is important to remember that the U.P. has many more trees than people and several more miles of isolated wilderness than developed civilization, so there will be some areas with limited lodging and dining options. Other areas, like Mackinac Island and its environs, are major tourist destinations with plenty of restaurants and resorts to choose from. Another important fact to keep in mind: Winter is considered the "off" season in the U.P., which means that a restaurant that was full of diners in June may well be boarded up in December. Some innkeepers shut their doors as well, and even those that remain open are surprised to hear from tourists outside of the main season (May–September).

I have personally tested the waters throughout the U.P. in every season and included only those establishments I enjoy myself and would recommend to a good friend. I've marked those restaurants and lodging options that exceed all expectations with a star, for those looking to plan an extra-special trip.

Lodging Prices

Within each lake chapter, lodging prices are noted in information blocks and are based on a per-room, double-occupancy rate. The price range runs from low off-season rates to higher summer and holiday weekend rates.

Dining Prices

I have included an Inexpensive, Moderate, Expensive, or Very Expensive label with each of the dining reviews. Average prices refer to a dinner consisting of an entrée, appetizer or dessert, and glass of wine or beer (tax and gratuities not included). Following is a breakdown of the dollar value range of these tags:

Inexpensive	Up to $15
Moderate	$15–$30
Expensive	$30–$50
Very Expensive	$50 or more

Credit Cards are abbreviated as follows:

AE: American Express
D: Discover
MC: MasterCard
V: Visa

A Revolutionary War–era cannon on the shores of Mackinac Island serves as a reminder of the tiny island's role as a major trade and military hub. Matt Calvani

1

History

Tribes, Timber, Mines, and Ghost Towns

Though it may seem a harsh place to live by today's standards, Michigan's Upper Peninsula has been considered an ideal home by an assortment of inhabitants, from early Native American settlers to French fur trappers, British miners, Finnish fishermen, and the all-American Henry Ford. The area was and still is rich in natural resources that lent themselves to both early rural life and modern industrialization—fresh water, lakes and streams chock-full of fish, a thriving deer population, huge forests, and large amounts of copper and iron ore. Though copper and iron mining didn't really take off until the mid-1800s, Native Americans mined for copper on Isle Royale and throughout the Keweenaw Peninsula (in the northwest of the U.P., jutting up into Lake Superior) to make tools and jewelry as early as 3000 B.C.

These very early settlers disappeared to parts unknown, replaced by the Ojibwa (also known as Chippewa) and Menominee Indian tribes, both part of the Algonquian language group, beginning in A.D. 800. The Ojibwa and Menominee lived off of fish and nuts and had the peninsula to themselves until the first European explorers discovered the area in the 1620s. French fur traders soon had a thriving beaver pelt business in the U.P., establishing Sault Ste. Marie and Mackinac Island as major trading posts. The British eventually wrested the area and the fur trade away from the French, only to be supplanted by the Americans after the Revolution.

British influence returned to the U.P. several decades later in the form of Cornish miners who immigrated to work in the iron and copper mines in the mid-to-late 1800s, bringing with them their Cornish pasties—meat and vegetable pies that made for a portable meal, easily eaten in the mines—which remain a Yooper staple to this day. Finnish, Scottish, Eastern European, Norwegian, and Italian miners all made their way to the U.P. during the mining boom, and their influence is still felt today in the regional music (it resembles Scandinavian folk music), cuisine, and architecture. By the 1880s the Keweenaw Peninsula provided nearly 90 percent of the nation's copper.

Meanwhile, farther south and east, in the Menominee Range, the Gogebic Range, and the Marquette Range, highly productive iron mines were booming, making the area the nation's largest iron supplier by the end of the century. Michigan's lumber boom also crept north during this period, clearing acre after acre of U.P. forest. This burst of industry in what had long been a quiet rural area piqued the interest of Michigan's great captain of industry Henry Ford in the early 1920s. Looking to control the source of his raw materials and to illustrate his version of the American Dream—a combination of old-fashioned rural life and hard work with modern industrial productivity—Ford established company mining towns, bought up forests, and erected sawmills throughout the U.P. Though his U.P. empire was sold off after his death, Ford's towns, with their neatly divided management and worker housing areas, community squares, and industrial complexes, can still be toured today.

Ford wasn't the only one to establish company towns in the U.P. With lumber, copper mining, and iron mining all booming at the same time, numerous towns were built throughout the peninsula in the mid-to-late 1800s. Though there are still active mining and lumber operations in the U.P. today, the boom eventually went bust, and only some of the towns made it through the downturn in all three industries. Today the area is dotted with ghost towns that stand as a life-size monument to those days.

NATURAL HISTORY

The Upper Peninsula's rich iron and copper ores are the result of volcanic eruptions, the last of which occurred roughly 3 billion years ago, creating the Keweenaw Peninsula and raising the western half of the peninsula above the eastern half. In addition to eventually creating a mining industry in the U.P., these mineral deposits and geological rumblings, combined with erosion caused by the surrounding bodies of water and the area's harsh weather, have resulted in stunning stretches of coastline. Iron, copper, and manganese have painted the shore of Lake Superior between Munising and Grand Marais, known now as Pictured Rocks National Lakeshore, with deep greens and blues, burning reds and oranges, and coal black.

The lakes and their network of rivers and streams have long dominated both the land-scape and local life in the U.P. Fish from the lakes have provided locals with food for thou-

Sable Falls, outside Grand Marais, is just one of hundreds of waterfalls throughout the Upper Peninsula.
Matt Girvan

sands of years, and the lakes—especially Superior, infamous for its unpredictable weather and swells—have claimed their fair share of fishermen in return. Rivers jump off rocks on their way to the lakes and become beautiful waterfalls all over the U.P. You can hardly drive 10 miles through the peninsula in any direction without passing a sign directing you to a nearby waterfall. One local family—the Penroses—has documented and rated all the waterfalls in the area in a popular book that puts the waterfall count at 199.

Despite decades of overfishing, and the introduction of invasive species such as the lamprey eel—a vicious carnivore that eats up to 40 pounds of fish per week and is typically found in the waters of northern Europe—the lakes and rivers of the U.P. remain full of fish, from Lake Superior whitefish to salmon, trout, and perch.

Large bodies of water and vast areas of untouched forest make the U.P. an ideal home for numerous animals, from the ubiquitous deer to the elusive wolf. Wolves are notoriously development-shy, and they thrive in the U.P. forests, where they can easily hide from humans and choose from plenty of deer for dinner. Another elusive mammal—the moose— also calls the U.P. home, especially the woods northwest of Marquette and the almost entirely undeveloped Isle Royale in Lake Superior. Moose were hunted to the brink of extinction in the U.P. during the mining boom, but in the 1980s a pack of 59 moose was introduced to the Marquette area from Canada, and their numbers grew to over 300 by the late 1990s. Now lucky visitors can spot moose grazing or slurping from ponds or marshes at dawn or dusk.

Besides being drawn by the larger wildlife, people visit the U.P. from all over the world for its unique bird population. In addition to numerous bald eagles, hawks, and herons, notoriously cagey ('scuse the pun) birds like the loon flourish here, sandhill cranes visit every year, and the Seney National Wildlife Refuge is home to countless rare birds like the yellow rail and the black-backed woodpecker.

SOCIAL HISTORY

"Old Copper Indians" to Modern-Day Tribes

Little is known about the first settlers in the U.P., except that they lived in the area approximately 5,000 years ago and they mined for copper, with which they made arrowheads and jewelry. These so-called "Old Copper Indians" mysteriously disappeared, eventually replaced by the Algonquian tribes—Ojibwa (Chippewa), Potawatomi, and Menominee—in A.D. 800. The Ojibwa and Potawatomi occupied most of the eastern U.P., and the Menominee occupied the central and western U.P. and much of what is now Wisconsin. Under the catch-all names of Ojibwa and Menominee are several distinct regional tribes including the "Soo"—the common name for the Sault St. Marie tribe of Ojibwa who are descendants of the Anishinabeg tribe.

By the mid-1500s the Ojibwa were joined in the east by the Ottawa (Odawa) and Huron tribes, both of which had fled from the Iroquois. These tribes are still active in the U.P. today; their history and culture are evident in the names of lakes, regions, streets, and parks. The tribes still hold regular powwows as well, and a real effort has been made to provide museums, tours, and events that delve into tribal culture.

Numerous "Indian casinos" have also sprung up throughout the U.P. in recent years—in some regions the casinos are the primary development for miles around.

The Ojibwa people, longtime residents of the Upper Peninsula, continue to honor their traditions in celebrations like this one on Mackinac Island, which holds a special place in the Ojibwa creation myth.
Courtesy Mackinac Island Tourism Bureau

The French Introduce Europe to the U.P.

French explorer Étienne Brûlé is generally thought to be the first European to set foot in the Upper Peninsula. Brûlé crossed St. Mary's River into the eastern U.P. in 1620, apparently looking for a trade route to the Far East. What he discovered instead were waterways teaming with beaver. Brûlé was soon followed in 1634 by Jean Nicolet, another explorer looking for a route to the Orient and finding fur instead. By the late 1600s French fur trappers were doing a booming business in the U.P., with trading posts at Sault Ste. Marie and St. Ignace. In the early 1700s, justifiably fearful of attack from the British, the French moved their fur-trading operations to a fortified village, Fort Michilimackinac, which has since been reconstructed just outside Mackinaw City. Those interested in this period of the U.P.'s history can stop by the fort today for a glimpse of how the early traders and their families lived, dressed, and entertained themselves.

In addition to the fur trade, the French brought with them new food, customs, and religion, which they attempted to share with the Ojibwa people they met in the U.P. One of the better known of these explorers was Father Jacques Marquette, who arrived in the U.P. in the late 1660s, building a mission in Sault Ste. Marie in 1668 and at St. Ignace in 1671. Marquette was not your garden-variety missionary. He had a knack for native tongues, and believed, as did other Jesuits at the time, that the native people were inherently good and already believed in God.

Distinguishing him further from other missionaries of the day was Marquette's zeal and talent for exploration. In 1673 he joined explorer Louis Jolliet and a small French and Indian crew to "discover" the Mississippi River. The Jolliet-Marquette expedition marked the first time Europeans entered the Mississippi River—the crew traveled via canoe from St. Ignace, through Lake Michigan to Green Bay, up the Fox River and over to the Wisconsin River, which led them to the Mississippi. The priest helped to map these waterways before heading back to St. Ignace via Chicago, but the weather and the long journey caught up with him and he died near Ludington, Michigan, in 1675. Marquette's statue looks over St. Ignace still; his mission and life are paid tribute to in the Marquette Mission Park there, and the Museum of Ojibwa Culture occupies roughly the same spot that Marquette's mission once did. The priest was also the namesake for the U.P.'s largest city and is memorialized in various other spots throughout the peninsula.

The British Are Coming

The British did eventually turn up, defeating the French in Montreal in 1760 and taking over Fort Michilimackinac and the fur trade in 1761 after victory in the French and Indian War. (They eventually moved the bulk of the fur trade to Mackinac Island, where it was protected by Fort Mackinac from the tribes and the rebellious American colonists.)

While the French had viewed the Native American tribes as neighbors, often working with, marrying, and having children with the Ojibwa, the British viewed and treated the tribes as conquered people. Dissatisfied with the policies of the British, the Ojibwa, Potawatomi, Ottawa, and Huron tribes revolted in 1763, led by Ottawa chief Pontiac in what was later called Pontiac's Rebellion.

The American Dream

After the Revolutionary War, all of the U.P. eventually became American soil, but otherwise it was business as usual. The fur trade continued to thrive, with Mackinac Island as its hub under the watchful eye of businessman John Jacob Astor, until the 1830s.

In 1837, after the Toledo War—really more of a squabble—was ended by President Andrew Jackson, Congress admitted Michigan to statehood, giving the disputed Toledo Strip to Ohio and offering Michigan the U.P. as a consolation prize. Though at the time the U.P. was described in the federal register as desolate wilderness, industry continued to prosper in the region. The opening of the Soo Locks at Sault Ste. Marie, connecting Lake Superior to the other Great Lakes via St. Mary's River, increased the flow of goods to and from the U.P., and though the fur trade had long since declined, mining and lumber kept the locks so full that at one point the tonnage passing through them surpassed that passing through either the Panama Canal or the Suez Canal.

Though Native Americans had been mining for copper for thousands of years, the copper industry really began to boom in the U.P. in the 1860s, with production centered on the Keweenaw Peninsula. Iron mining had begun in earnest in the 1850s after an 1842 geological report of the Marquette Range by Michigan's state geologist was published, revealing large amounts of iron ore in the range. Iron was eventually discovered in the Gogebic and Menominee Ranges as well, placing three of the six principal American iron ranges in the U.P.

Immigrants came from all over the world to work in the iron and copper mines and as lumberjacks in the emergent lumber industry, but the dominant groups were from England (mostly Cornwall), Scotland, Finland, Norway, Sweden, Italy, and Poland. The descendants of these early miners are still alive and well in the U.P. today, making for a vibrant music, food, and art scene.

Industry Gives Way to Tourism, Convicts, and Casinos

The lumber and mining industries began to decline toward the end of the 19th century, due to less expensive options elsewhere in the country and beyond. It was railroad executives who first thought to turn the U.P. into a tourist destination in the late 1800s, in order to recover profits that were slowly dropping off as the companies transported fewer and fewer loads of timber, iron, and copper. No longer a remote wilderness, the U.P. had become a viable vacation destination.

Built in 1852, the Island House on Mackinac Island was the first hotel to cater to summer visitors. Its construction was followed by that of several other hotels including the legendary Grand Hotel in 1887, and Mackinac quickly became a favorite vacation destination for visitors from "down below" and even for out-of-staters. When the Mackinac Bridge was constructed in 1957, tourism increased and began to spread beyond Mackinac Island to the rest of the U.P., just in time to employ at least some of

The opulent Grand Hotel opened in 1887. Amy Westervelt

the workers who had been laid off by mining, lumber, and railroad companies.

To keep visitors entertained and locals employed, tribe-owned casinos began springing up throughout the U.P. in the 1980s. In addition to a tourist mecca, the U.P. became home to the bulk of the state's prisons, with six prisons built between 1988 and 1993. Currently the prison system and the casinos are the top employers in the U.P. In the summer, tourism employs far more people, but the drop-off in winter leaves many people out of work for several months.

NEIGHBORS ALL AROUND

The Upper and Lower Peninsulas of Michigan could easily be considered separate states. Downstaters sometimes look down on Yoopers as unsophisticated roughnecks, while Yoopers refer to those from "down below" as everything from trolls to fudgies (due to the number of downstate tourists that crowd Mackinac's fudge shops in the summer). The factories to the south lured a large percentage of U.P. workers in the 1940s, contributing in some part to economic problems up north. And Detroit, in its heyday, was a very cosmopolitan city that thought itself better than the mining towns up north, despite the fact that, as Yoopers are quick to point out, the Calumet Theater in the Keweenaw Peninsula predates any of Detroit's landmarks.

From its large tracts of wild land to the widespread enjoyment of and respect for nature and wildlife, the U.P. actually has more in common with its neighbor on the other side of its watery borders—Canada. Even the Yooper accent sounds more Canadian than Michigan, with its Scandinavian-influenced intonations and frequent use of "eh" to punctuate both statements and questions.

People often wonder why the U.P. is part of Michigan as opposed to Wisconsin, which is closer to the peninsula and shares a long land border (lower Michigan is connected to the U.P. only by the Mackinac Bridge). In 1835, before Michigan was formally admitted to the Union, Ohio senators lobbied for a long slice of southern Michigan at the mouth of the Maumee River. Ohio prevailed easily, and Toledo is now located in that strip, but Michigan was given the U.P. as consolation. At the time, Wisconsin was not yet populated enough to apply for statehood.

In many ways the history of the U.P. mirrors that of the United States as a whole, and there are few places in the country where that past—from Native American culture to the Industrial Revolution to modern-day globalization—is so easily traced. In addition to still being one of the more beautiful, large, untouched pieces of wilderness left in the country, the U.P. stands as a sort of living American history museum—ghost towns, closed mines, national parks, and remnants of ancient Native American culture interspersed with modern-day Indian gaming casinos and grand old buildings in towns that today boast no more than a few hundred year-round residents.

It's hard to imagine the U.P. becoming much different in the future. Tourism increases a bit every year, but the long winter and long journey still keep the U.P. from becoming completely overrun, and the huge tracts of national forest ensure that it will never become overdeveloped. The state may build more prisons, but surely they can only need so many, and the locals and visitors can support only so many casinos. Still, Yoopers have always been industrious and hardworking, and it is entirely possible that a completely new industry will sweep through the region, creating new jobs and prosperity.

Before the Mackinac Bridge was built in 1957, visitors to the Upper Peninsula had to take a car-ferry.
Matt Girvan

2

TRANSPORTATION

Waterways, Freeways, and the Mighty Mack

Getting around the U.P. is pretty straightforward—there are only so many main roads, the major attractions are well marked (unlike in the rest of Michigan, road signs indicating attractions here are large, obvious, and placed at logical intervals before you need to turn off the main road), and it's fairly easy to travel between regions. Getting to the U.P., on the other hand, can be somewhat of a trek, depending on where you start. Whether you plan to take a short flight or a longer drive, plan on spending at least a week if you want to visit multiple attractions, or devote weekends to particular spots. We don't recommend trying to tackle the U.P. in one fell swoop, unless you're prepared to spend a good month or two seeing everything you need to see.

GETTING TO THE U.P.

The Mackinac Bridge is the primary route between the Lower Peninsula and the Upper Peninsula. It is so much a part of life in Michigan that state residents refer to the U.P. as "above the bridge" and the Lower Peninsula as "below the bridge."

By Car

Everyone driving to the U.P. from the south will cross the Mackinac Bridge. Even some visitors from Wisconsin will bring their cars on the ferry from Manitowoc, Wisconsin, to Ludington, Michigan, and then drive up and over the bridge. From Detroit to St. Ignace (the first U.P. town across the bridge), the drive takes approximately five hours; from Ludington to St. Ignace takes about three hours.

By Plane

Flights operated by Mesaba Air and booked by Northwest fly between Detroit and Marquette (closest to Pictured Rocks National Lakeshore), Hancock (gateway to the Keweenaw Peninsula), and Pellston (closest to Mackinac Island) daily. See www.mesaba.com.

By Bus

Indian Trails operates buses between Chicago, Milwaukee, lower Michigan, and the U.P. In the summer of 2007, Indian Trails began offering weekend package deals that include bus fare, two nights' accommodation, and ferry to Mackinac Island for $199 a person. See www.indiantrails.com for schedules, routes, and fares.

GETTING AROUND THE AREA

Getting around in the U.P. generally requires a car, with the notable exception of Mackinac Island, which is car-free. It is possible to get from the east to the west of the peninsula and vice versa by bus, but you'll still need some other form of transportation upon arrival at your destination. That said, biking is terrific throughout the U.P., with numerous rides of all lengths and difficulty levels offering terrific views and an easy way to get around town. Most of the waterfront towns also have boardwalks that are ideally suited to a sunset stroll. Ferries are abundant in the U.P. but don't operate in the winter for obvious reasons.

By Car

Traffic can get backed up on US 2 during the summer, from St. Ignace in the east moving westward, so it's best to drive during off-peak hours in the summer months (early morning, midday, nighttime). In addition to US 2, which runs along the entire southern U.P. from St. Ignace in the east to Ironwood in the west, there are a handful of other main highways in the U.P. connecting various regions. US 41 runs from Escanaba in the south-central part of the peninsula north to Marquette and then northwest all the way up to Copper Harbor on the Keweenaw Peninsula. I-75 connects the Lower Peninsula to the Upper Peninsula, taking drivers across the Mackinac Bridge and farther north and east up to Sault Ste. Marie. US 45 leads from the Wisconsin-Michigan border in the south up to Ontonagon in the northwest. MI 123 takes visitors to and from popular Tahquamenon Falls and can get fairly congested in the summer months.

Types of Roads

The U.P. is crisscrossed with various types of roads, ranging from interstate highways to unpaved country roads. Following is a list of the road types and abbreviations used here:

CR—County road. Generally paved roads, county roads tend to link major towns or provide a direct route to a popular attraction off a larger highway.

FR—Forest road. Generally unpaved roads through national forests.

H—H Roads are small, sometimes unpaved roads that either provide scenic routes between towns or connect small towns to larger roads or highways.

MI—Michigan state road. Slightly larger than county roads, state roads typically lead from a highway to either a large town or a popular landmark (MI 123, for example, leads drivers off US 28 to Tahquamenon Falls and returns to the highway in a loop).

US—U.S. highway. These highways provide the primary links between regions.

I—Interstate highway. I-75 is the only interstate highway in the U.P.; it leads up from the lower peninsula to Sault Ste. Marie in the northeast of the U.P.

By Rental Car

Cars are available for rent from Avis, Budget, Alamo, and National Car Rental at the Marquette airport, from National Car Rental at the Houghton County Memorial Airport in Hancock, and from Avis and Hertz at Pellston Regional Airport. Prices start at $48 a day and go up, but you can sometimes find a package deal with a flight and/or hotel that drives the cost down considerably.

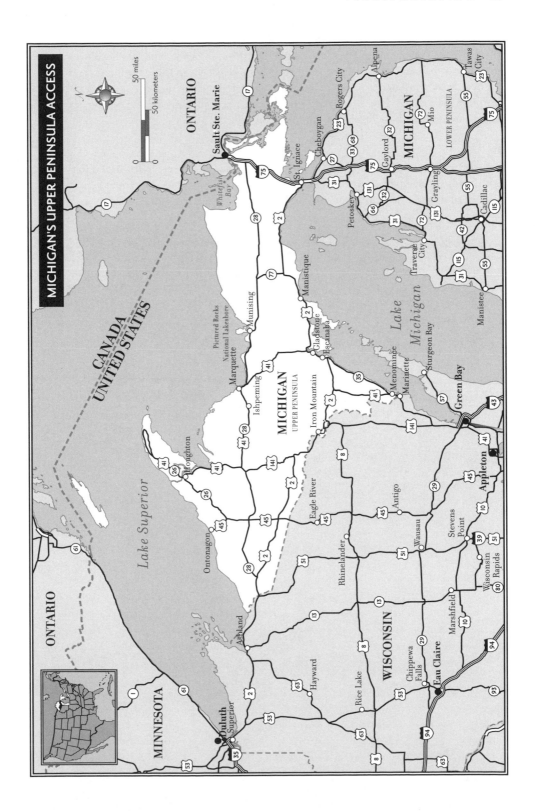

MICHIGAN'S UPPER PENINSULA ACCESS

By Ferry

Ferry service is available to Mackinac Island, Drummond Island, and Isle Royale on varying schedules. Ferries to Mackinac book up quickly in peak season (June through August) so it's best to purchase ferry tickets well in advance. Isle Royale is also very popular in the summer, so it's a good idea to buy ferry tickets at least a week in advance, although you can sometimes squeak by with a last-minute purchase.

By Bus

Bus service is available on Indian Trails from St. Ignace in the east to Ironwood in the west, with a stop at Escanaba along the way. Indian Trails also operates a bus route between Calumet, in the Keweenaw Peninsula, and Marquette. See www.indiantrails.com.

Model T in the U.P.

As with the rest of Michigan, Henry Ford and the auto industry left an indelible mark on the U.P., not only with the mines, lumberyards, and company towns he set up, but also with his vehicles. And Ford wasn't the only one. The U.P. is full of classics, both in various museums and on the roads and in the lots they once dominated. Old-timers in Eagle Harbor love to tell the story of when a shipment of new Chryslers had to be rescued and hauled in over the ice when its carrier was shipwrecked on a piece of Lake Superior ice. It's easy to imagine a new Model T hopping down the road through the middle of many a U.P. town, and spotting one of them in reality is always a treat.

3

LAKE MICHIGAN

Southern Hospitality—Ski Resorts, Beaches, Waterfalls, Landlocked Lakes, and Intriguing Ghost Towns

The large swath of the U.P. running along the coast of Lake Michigan to the Wisconsin border and then inland, from Brevort to Watersmeet, is known for its fantastic fishing and beaches in the summer, hunting in the fall, and ski-worthy mountains in the winter. During much of its past the area was also part of what was called Iron Country. Two of the six largest American iron ranges are here—the Gogebic Range and the Menominee Range (a third, the Marquette Range, is due north near Marquette)—and iron production dominated the area for several decades. Remnants of that past are still visible, particularly in the area's ghost towns. One such town—Fayetteville—has been preserved and is now part of the state's park system. Visitors can tour through the old ironworks, the town's hotel, and examples of various living quarters, and marvel at how a town of several thousand was depopulated virtually from one day to the next.

In addition to its numerous sandy beaches and lovely lake views, the shores of Lake Michigan are home to one of the U.P.'s largest cities, Escanaba. Escanaba made an appearance in the 2001 Jeff Daniels comedy *Escanaba in Da Moonlight,* which folks up here don't like to talk about much. In fact, the real Escanaba is far more citified than the movie version—it's one of the few towns in the U.P. where you don't feel like absolutely everyone knows each other, and its restaurants are well respected throughout the state.

This area also boasts hundreds of beautiful, clear inland fishing lakes, as well as the U.P.'s largest deer population, making it a popular vacation spot for avid hunters and fishermen. Though they're not as well known for skiing as the Ironwood mountains farther west, a handful of popular ski resorts clustered in the Menominee Range around Iron Mountain draw families with youngsters learning their way around the slopes in the winter.

The primary regions bordering Lake Michigan, from east to west, are: Lake Michigan Beach, Brevoort Lake, and the Manistique Lakes; Manistique and the Garden Peninsula; and Escanaba and Menominee. Farther inland along the Wisconsin border are Iron Mountain, Iron River, and Watersmeet.

Lake Michigan Beach, Brevoort Lake, and the Manistique Lakes
Eighteen miles west of St. Ignace along US 2, the Lake Michigan Campground in the Hiawatha National Forest offers one of the best slices of summer living in the country.

LAKE MICHIGAN REGION

LAKE SUPERIOR

LAKE MICHIGAN

MICHIGAN

WISCONSIN

PICTURED ROCKS
NATIONAL LAKESHORE

1. Iron River
2. Crystal Falls
3. Iron Mountain
4. Menominee
5. Escanaba
6. Peninsula Point Lighthouse
7. Fayette Ghost Town
8. Portage Bay
9. Watersmeet
10. Sylvania Wilderness Area
11. Kitch-Iti-Kipi (Big Spring)
12. Manistique
13. Seney Wildlife Refuge
14. Curtis
15. Manistique Lakes
16. Lake Michigan Beach
17. Brevort Lake
18. Cut River Bridge

25 miles

25 kilometers

Between the town of Brevort—once a popular overnight stop before the Mackinac Bridge was built and visitors from the Lower Peninsula had to ferry across the lake—and the town of Pointe aux Chenes, Lake Michigan Beach offers 8 miles of sandy shores, giant dunes, and wild blueberries. Just inland from the beaches, also in the Hiawatha National Forest, Brevoort Lake is a beautiful and popular summertime destination, with 4,000-plus acres of prime fishing and boating, and reliably warm water for swimming.

Northwest of Pointe aux Chenes, and strangely more than 20 miles from the town that bears their name, the Manistique Lakes are popular in winter and summer alike. The charming town of Curtis sits along the isthmus between Big Manistique Lake and South Manistique Lake and offers dozens of cabins, cottages, and resorts for visitors. In the summer the lakes are full of fishermen and swimmers, in the fall the fall colors and prime hunting make it a popular weekend destination, and in the winter the area's well-groomed cross-country ski and snowmobile trails are popular as well, so most of the resorts stay open year-round.

Manistique and the Garden Peninsula

An old paper mill and lumber town, Manistique is a bit plain, despite its attractive landmark water tower. Still, a pretty waterfront boardwalk and plenty of camping, cottages, and fishing at nearby lakes make it a popular summer destination. The paper mill, Manistique Papers, still employs most of the locals, but has shifted its focus to recycling millions of pounds of paper a year into fresh new stacks of recycled paper.

The Garden Peninsula has even less going on than Manistique, which is precisely why some visitors choose it over more obvious U.P. destinations. With quiet beaches and uncrowded campgrounds, the Garden Peninsula is ideal for those looking to truly get away from it all and unwind.

The bulk of visitors to this area stay here because it is an affordable, attractive place from which many of the U.P.'s attractions, including Mackinac Island, Pictured Rocks, and Tahquamenon Falls, may be visited on easy day trips. One of the peninsula's favorite spots is only a few miles from Manistique: Kitch-iti-kipi (Big Spring), a thunderous sulfur spring that bubbles up into a crystal-clear, turquoise pond surrounded by silvery logs and bright green moss. Visitors pile onto a self-propelled wooden platform boat with a large, open viewing area in the center, and move slowly over the spring, oohing and ahhing as the bubbles become clearer and pointing out the large trout that call the pond home.

Manistique is also a good home-base for those looking to explore the world-famous Seney National Wildlife Refuge. Home to numerous rare birds, the refuge sits in the middle of untouched wilderness that runs the height of the peninsula, from Manistique in the south to Grand Marais in the north.

Escanaba and Menominee

The stretch of Lake Michigan shoreline between Escanaba and Menominee is known locally as the "banana belt" for its temperate (by U.P. standards) climate and fertile farmland. The area still leads the U.P. in agricultural production, primarily producing dairy products and hay.

Escanaba's downtown actually feels larger than Marquette's, although Marquette is a much larger city. Once you get past the unappealing strip malls and fast food joints on the city's outskirts, the historic downtown is very attractive, with beautiful old buildings and numerous galleries, cafés, restaurants, and retail stores. At the east side of downtown, where the land

Manistique's landmark water tower. Matt Girvan

juts into the lake, is lovely Ludington Park, with benches looking out over Little Bay de Noc on Lake Michigan, paths, bike trails, and grassy areas just crying out for a picnic.

Menominee, sitting at the southernmost tip of the U.P. on the Wisconsin border, sits across the Menominee River from its sister city, Marinette, Wisconsin. Between the lake, the Menominee, and the nearby Peshtigo River (known as an ideal white-water rafting spot), Menominee is virtually surrounded by water. Like many towns in the U.P., Menominee has been in decline since its primary industries began drying up, but the Victorian architecture of its more successful past makes for a charming downtown, and the demise of various mills and lumberyards on the waterfront has opened up large areas of waterfront for public use. In recent years the downtown area has begun to revive a bit, with new shops and restaurants. Across the river in Marinette, the Marinette Marine shipbuilding company is still going strong, and from the vantage point of the Menekaunee Bridge, which connects the two towns, it's entertaining to watch new ships being launched into the river.

Iron Mountain, Iron River, and the Menominee Range

One of the least developed areas in a region known for its wilderness, the thick forests along this stretch of US 2 west of Escanaba and north of Wisconsin are known for their brilliant fall colors, their rivers, streams, and waterfalls, and their abnormally large wolf and deer populations. Interspersed among the forests are old iron mining towns, many of which are ghosts of their former selves. Those that have survived the departure of the iron industry are known not for attractive downtowns, of which there are few in these parts, but for shockingly good Italian restaurants run by the ancestors of Italian immigrants who moved here in the early 1900s to work the iron mines. Although the ski resorts surrounding nearby Ironwood are better known, a handful of popular family resorts are located here in the Menominee Range, and Piers Gorge, near Norway, offers some of the Midwest's most rough-and-tumble white-water.

Ludington Park at the end of downtown Escanaba. Matt Girvan

The Cut River Bridge, off US 2 between Naubinway and Epoufette, is one of the most often photographed bridges in the U.P. A trail leads under the bridge, along the river, and to the beach on Lake Michigan.
Richard Newton

Central Time
Although most of Michigan is on Eastern Time, the Michigan counties along the Wisconsin border are on Central Time—this includes the length of US 2 from Ironwood almost to Escanaba. Ironwood, Watersmeet, Iron River, Iron Mountain, and Menominee are all on Central Time, so be sure to change your watch, or you might show up an hour early for your dinner reservation.

Watersmeet

Located almost entirely within the confines of the Ottawa National Forest and known predominantly for fishing, the Watersmeet area is chock-full of lakes, the best of which are surrounded by old-growth forests in the Sylvania Wilderness Area. The Sylvania's forests are unique in the U.P. in that they were protected from the lumber industry early on, which allowed trees, wild mushrooms, and wildflowers—including some incredibly rare breeds— to flourish, and kept its 34 lakes clear of sediment and full of fish.

Though Watersmeet is an entirely unassuming little place, the town came to national attention a few years back when its high school basketball team, the Nimrods, was included in an ESPN commercial spotlighting the most unusually named U.S. high school teams, and subsequently in a Sundance Channel documentary that focused on the Native American ancestry of half the team and the school. In recent years Watersmeet, unlike most other U.P. towns, has actually grown in population, thanks to its large and popular casino (Dancing Eagle Lac Vieux Desert Resort & Casino, owned and operated by local Ojibwa) and the increasing popularity of its affordable lakefront property with retirees from southern Michigan and Chicago.

Just across the state border, a few miles away, the Wisconsin resort village of Land O'Lakes is beautiful and charming and full of the restaurants and shops that Watersmeet lacks. Plenty of visitors stay in Watersmeet for the good prices and the solitude and head over to Land O'Lakes when they feel like being more sociable.

LODGING

Although there are a number of lodging options in this area, it's not particularly overrun with hotels, and you won't find many over-the-top bed-and-breakfasts or five-star resorts here. Which is probably a good thing—who needs a resort when you can stay in a cottage on the lake or camp in a forest that's thousands of years old? That said, the ski condos and lodges around Iron Mountain can book up quickly during winter holidays, so if you're planning a trip during late December or early January, be sure to reserve lodging early.

A number of chain hotels have properties in this area, some of which offer decent rooms for good prices. We have not included reviews of specific chain properties but generally recommend the following chains in the area: AmericInn, Best Western, and Holiday Inn Express. Lodging reviews are listed by region, and regions are listed in alphabetical order. We recommend all the lodging options but have indicated special spots with a star. Camping options are included as a separate section after the regular lodging listings.

Lodging Prices

Prices listed are based on a per-room, double-occupancy rate. Price ranges run from low off-season rates to higher summer rates.

Credit Cards

AE: American Express
D: Discover
MC: MasterCard
V: Visa

ESCANABA AND MENOMINEE

House of Ludington

Owners: Edward and Suzell Eisenberger
906-786-6300
www.houseofludington.com
holf@dsnet.us
223 Ludington St., Escanaba, MI 49829
End of Ludington St., past downtown,
    across the street from Ludington Park
Price: $55–$85
Credit Cards: MC, V
Handicapped Access: None
Open: Year-round

Within walking distance to downtown
Escanaba's shops, art galleries, and cafés in
one direction, and the lakefront paths,
lighthouse, and picnic areas of lovely
Ludington Park in the other, this landmark
Queen Anne–style hotel, built in 1865, is in
an ideal location from which to explore all
that Escanaba has to offer. The location also
provides easy access to the highway, making
it a nice home base for exploring the rest of
the area as well. Half of the Ludington's 25
guest rooms boast Lake Michigan views,
and all have cable TV and private baths.
Rooms are decorated according to a variety
of themes—Lighthouse, Stars & Stripes, Log
Cabin, Honeymoon, Country Meadows,
Garden, or Victorian—and come with one
double bed, two double beds, or two separate rooms with an adjoining bath. The
hotel also houses two restaurants—a more
formal dining room with lake views, and a
casual restaurant with home cooking at reasonable prices—as well as a pub that resembles an Old West watering hole.

House of Ludington. Matt Girvan

★ The Lauerman House Inn

715-732-7800
www.lauermanhouse.com
innkeeper@lauermanhouse.com
1975 Riverside Ave., Marinette, WI 54143
Off US 41 from Menominee, just over the
    river, make a right on Riverside Ave.
Price: $90–$170
Credit Cards: AE, D, DC, MC, V
Handicapped Access: No
Open: Year-round

A huge and beautifully restored colonial-revival building complete with grand white columns, the bright red Lauerman House looks cheerily out over Riverside Avenue on the Marinette side of the Menominee River. The original wood and detailed light fixtures have been restored to their past splendor, but the rest of the decor is fairly modern, with art deco furniture, clean lines, and bright colors, not to mention Egyptian cotton sheets. All of the Lauerman's rooms are large and include a private bath and sitting room, and its two suites also include two-person Jacuzzi tubs. The Red Room and the Green Room both boast excellent river views, as do most of the inn's common rooms. A full breakfast, including a hot entrée, fresh fruit, and fresh pastries, is served every morning. The Lauerman House Café bakes bread and pastries daily and serves soups, salads, and sandwiches for lunch Monday through Friday. Less formal than its sister inn, the M&M, the Lauerman House feels like a lovely old family home, and the rooms are large and comfortable for families traveling with children.

★ M&M Victorian Inn

715-732-9531
www.mmvictorian.com
innkeeper@mmvictorian.com
1393 Main St., Marinette, WI 54143
From US 41 take Stephenson St., turn left
    on Newbury Ave., then right on Main St.
Price: $90–$165
Credit Cards: AE, D, DC, MC, V
Handicapped Access: No
Open: Year-round

M&M Victorian Inn in Menominee. Tina Allen

An absolute stunner of an inn in downtown Marinette, just over the Menominee River from Menominee, the Queen Anne–style M&M has had every ornate detail lovingly restored. It might actually look better now than it did when it was built in 1893 by a local lumber baron. Rooms strike a nice balance between Victorian and modern, with antique beds covered in Egyptian cotton and goose-down duvets. Suites include two-person Jacuzzi tubs, and all rooms have high-speed wireless Internet access, cable, private baths, and phones. The common rooms are as lovely as the guest rooms, with lots of polished wood antiques, stained-glass windows, and brightly painted walls that make all that vintage finery seem fresh and modern. In addition to its five guest rooms, the M&M houses the popular La Grappe D'Or restaurant, which specializes in French bistro fare, as well as two bars and a well-stocked wine cellar. Breakfast is a lavish affair featuring a hot entrée, fresh-baked pastries and muffins, fresh fruit, and Starbucks coffee. The M&M's sister inn, the Lauerman House (see above) welcomes families with open arms, but the M&M is more of a couple's getaway, and children under the age of 10 are not allowed.

Iron Mountain and Iron River

Edgar's Riverview Bed & Breakfast
Owner: Richard Edgar
906-875-6213
www.iron.org/biz/river/edriv
2168 MI 69 / P.O. Box 58
    Crystal Falls, MI 49920-0058
MI 69 at the Michigamme River, 6 miles
    east of Crystal Falls
Price: $85–$105
Credit Cards: MC, V
Handicapped Access: Limited
Open: Year-round

On the banks of the Michigamme River just outside charming Crystal Falls, Edgar's offers three rooms with private baths and river views. The most expensive room also includes a private Jacuzzi. Room decor is not amazing—think 1970s shag carpet and wood paneling—but the house is cozy, and the river views are lovely. The property is nestled in the woods, and its nearest neighbor is a distance away, which makes for maximum quiet and privacy and excellent wildlife spotting opportunities, including deer and eagles. Guests can fish in the river or borrow canoes in the summer, and have direct access to snowmobile trails in the winter. Edgar's also offers cross-country skis and snowshoes for guest use during winter. A central sitting room has a large stone fireplace, cathedral ceiling, and comfy couches. All guests are treated to a hot and hearty north woods breakfast every morning, no matter what time of year it is. The only potential problem with Edgar's is that it's not walking distance to much, but it is located just off the highway, making it easy to get from the B&B to various local attractions.

Lac O'Seasons Resort
Owners: Randy and Nancy Schauwecker
906-265-4881 or 1-800-797-5226
www.lacoseasons.com
176 Stanley Lake Dr., Iron River, MI 49935
7 miles southwest of Iron River, 5 minutes
    from Ski Brule
Price: $98–$120
Credit Cards: MC, V
Handicapped Access: Limited (one cabin)
Open: Year-round

A large resort, Lac O'Seasons has 14 two-, three-, and four-bedroom cottages, about half of which are located on the shores of Stanley Lake. The resort sits on nearly 40 wooded acres, and each cabin has a decent amount of space around it so visitors don't feel piled on top of each other. Popular with families, Lac O'Seasons hasn't splurged on fancy furnishings—the cottages are basic, comfortable, and clean, done up in a folksy, country style that fits well with the surroundings. Five of the cottages are traditional log cabins, and several also have fireplaces. A communal recreation building provides an indoor pool, sauna, and whirlpool hot tub. In the summer visitors fish or swim in placid Stanley Lake, lie on the lake's sandy beach, or meander along numerous wooded paths, when not making short car trips to the area's other attractions. In the winter the resort is bordered by two snowmobile trails and is within a five-minute drive of the Ski Brule lifts.

Pine Mountain Resort & Timber Stone Golf Course
906-774-2747 or 1-877-553-7463
www.pinemountainresort.com
N3332 Pine Mountain Rd.
   Iron Mountain, MI 49801
From US 2 heading west turn left on
   Stephenson Ave., which becomes
Fairbanks St., then right on Foster,
which becomes Walker St. and then
Hibbard St., then turn right onto Pine
Mountain Rd.
Price: $60–$150
Credit Cards: MC, V
Handicapped Access: Yes
Open: Year-round

Developed in the 1930s by Milwaukee brewer Fred Pabst, the Pine Mountain Ski Resort features the newly renovated 34-room Pine Mountain Lodge, two dozen condos at the base of the mountain, and the five-star Timber Stone golf course. Rooms and condos have all been recently spruced up with new carpet, paint, and linens, and the lodge includes an indoor pool, hot tub, and sauna. Two-room family suites are a great deal for families traveling with children. In addition to skiing in the winter and golf in the summer, the resort is just 2 miles from Piers Gorge, which offers some

The lodge at Pine Mountain Resort in Iron Mountain. Pine Mountain Resort

of the Midwest's best white-water rafting in summer. The resort's Famers restaurant serves decent if not delicious classics like pizza, fish-and-chips, and ribs.

Ski Brule
906-265-4957 or 1-800-362-7853
www.skibrule.com
397 Brule Mountain Rd., Iron River, MI 49935
Follow MI 189 south 6 miles from downtown Iron River to the Ski Brule entrance billboard; turn right (west) on Osterlund Rd., 2 miles to Ski Brule.
Price: $88–$412
Credit Cards: A, D, MC, V
Handicapped Access: Limited
Open: Year-round

Ski Brule is a large winter (and summer, despite the name) family resort with 16 chalets that sleep anywhere from 4 to 12 people, plus a lodge with 15 separate condos. In the summer the resort offers boating, tubing, rafting, fishing, and guided horseback rides, and in the winter seven lifts carry skiers and snowboarders all over the mountain. Each of the chalets has a completely different look, but all are very well kept, if simple. Some of the larger chalets have indoor saunas and hot tubs, and the Pioneer Lodge condos have access to two large outdoor hot tubs, but there is no pool on resort grounds (lake swimming is just a short drive away). Some of our favorite chalets include Anderson Lake Lodge, which is completely private, right down to its own private lake; Beaver Lodge Bottom for its sauna, updated kitchen, and beautiful stone fireplace; Wildwood for its almost ridiculously large stone fireplace and beautiful hardwood floors; and Heaven's Window for its groovy loft, stained-glass window, outdoor covered hot tub, and wood-burning stove.

LAKE MICHIGAN BEACH, BREVOORT LAKE, MANISTIQUE LAKES

Big Manistique Resort
Owners: Kyle and Kim Grimwood
906-586-9828 or 1-800-880-9828
www.bigmanistiqueresort.com
W18424 Hoffy Rd., Curtis, MI 49853
Follow US 2 west from Mackinac Bridge about 60 miles, then turn right on County Road H33; go to dead end, turn left into Curtis. Go through Curtis (H42) to the "T" in the road. Make a right, go down the hill, around the second curve, and look for sign.
Price: $95–$125 (extra $10 deposit for dogs)
Credit Cards: MC, V
Handicapped Access: Limited
Open: Year-round

Six two- and three-bedroom cottages on a sandy strip of shoreline surrounding Big Manistique Lake have hardwood floors, knotty pine interiors, full kitchens, new TVs, and north-woods country decor (lots of quilts and overstuffed chairs). Each cottage comes with its own 14-foot rowboat for exploring the lake. The resort also rents canoes, kayaks, and bikes, but if you bring your own, there's plenty of room to park your trailer. In the winter a heated shop provides a warm spot to fix sleds and snowmobiles. Pets are welcome for a small deposit, making this an ideal spot for family vacations.

★ Chamberlin's Ole Forest Inn
Owner: Bud Chamberlin
906-586-6000 or 1-800-292-0440
www.chamberlinsinn.com
P.O. Box 307, Curtis, MI 49820
South shore of Big Manistique Lake in Curtis on County Road H33
Price: $89–$129
Credit Cards: MC, V
Handicapped Access: No

Open: Year-round

A historic railroad hotel-turned-B&B, Chamberlin's offers five-star accommodations for two-star prices. Originally built in the late 1800s, the hotel was moved to its present-day location overlooking Big Manistique Lake in 1924 and remained a hotel until the early 1970s. When Bud Chamberlin stumbled across it in 1989 on a snowmobile ride, it had been sitting empty for over 10 years. Chamberlin bought the hotel, spent nearly two years refurbishing it, and opened it as a bed-and-breakfast in late 1990. Much of the original 1800s woodwork remained intact, and the house is furnished predominantly with antiques left over from the hotel's early days, although Chamberlin has updated the 12 guest rooms with large bathrooms, placing a Jacuzzi tub in one. While the majority of the rooms have private baths, a few do not—they are obviously priced lower, but be sure to ask for a private bath if you want one. In 1992 Chamberlin opened a restaurant in the inn, which is very popular, especially in the evening when diners can enjoy beautiful sunset lake views from the dining room or the wraparound porch. The porch is also a fantastic spot just to sit and marvel at the colors in fall. A wonderful spot for couples, Chamberlin's isn't a great fit for families with young children.

Gordon's Resort
906-586-9761
www.gordonsresort.com
P.O. Box 284, Curtis, MI 49853
In downtown Curtis on South Manistique
    Lake
Price: $86–$143
Credit Cards: D, MC, V
Handicapped access: Yes
Open: Year-round

Located on South Manistique Lake and Portage Creek in downtown Curtis, Gordon's offers two-, three-, and four-bedroom cabins for rent, overlooking either the creek or the lake. Cabins 1 and 2 are the newest and thus in the best condition, but are two-bedroom cabins. Cabin 3 offers three bedrooms, and Cabin 4 offers four; both could use a new couch and carpet but are perfectly clean and comfortable. All four cabins have knotty pine interiors, full kitchens, cable TV, decks, and spacious rooms. The resort offers picnic tables and gas grills, plus the use of several 14-foot rowboats. The only things not provided for some reason are towels. In addition to being on one of the Manistique Lakes and near the others, Gordon's is walking distance to Curtis, which is a small but charming waterfront village located on a narrow isthmus between South Manistique Lake and Big Manistique Lake.

Interlaken Resort and Burnt Island
Owners: Bill and Sherry Pew
906-586-3545
www.interlakenresort.org
minskyd@charter.net
24517 CR 98, McMillan, MI 49853
1/4 mile off of County Road H44, north of
    Curtis
Price: $85–$150
Credit Cards: No credit cards
Handicapped Access: Yes
Open: Year-round

A popular family resort with cute, funky little cabins featuring knotty pine interiors and dark wood exteriors on a huge section of Big Manistique Lake. For the slightly more adventurous, in addition to the eight main resort cabins, Interlaken offers two rustic cabins out on Burnt Island in the lake, easily accessed by boat, and also allows visitors to camp and picnic on completely undeveloped "Virgin Island." The main cabins are fully equipped with kitchens, microwaves, TV/VCR units, towels, and linens; the Burnt Island cabins have built-in bunks and wood-burning stoves. All guests have free access to canoes, paddleboats, motorboats, and pontoon boats, and the resort sits on several well-groomed cross-country ski trails and snowmobile trails for winter fun.

MANISTIQUE AND THE GARDEN PENINSULA

★Royal Rose Bed & Breakfast
Owners: Gilbert and Rosemary Sablack
906-341-4886
www.royalrose-bnb.com
rrbnb@chartermi.net
230 Arbutus Ave., Manistique, MI 49854
Downtown Manistique, north from US 2
Price: $85–$120
Credit Cards: D, MC, V
Handicapped Access: No
Open: Year-round

A stately white Dutch colonial with red accents on a tree-lined residential street in downtown Manistique houses four charming Victorian-style rooms, each with a private bath. Two of the rooms also feature fireplaces and whirlpool tubs, and all guests are treated to a hot, full breakfast, accompanied by home-baked breads and muffins and served with candles and music in a formal dining room with beautiful crystal chandeliers. Common rooms include a bright and cheery sunporch, a living room with a fireplace, and a large wraparound deck with benches. The B&B is within walking distance to downtown Manistique and day-trip distance of Big Spring, Pictured Rocks, and Tahquamenon Falls. Cookies, snacks, and beverages are on offer throughout the day, and hosts Gil and Rosemary are very knowledgeable about the area and always happy to offer suggestions for places to see and things to do.

WATERSMEET

Lac Vieux Desert Dancing Eagle's Hotel
Owners: The Lac Vieux Desert Band of Lake Superior Chippewa (Ojibwa)
Manager: Craig Mansfield
906-358-4226 or 1-800-583-3599
www.lvdcasino.com
craig.mansfield@lvdcasino.com
N5384 US 45, Watersmeet, MI 49969
Located on US 45 North in Watersmeet, about 8 miles north of the Wisconsin-Michigan border
Price: $70–$150
Credit Cards: AE, D, MC, V
Handicapped Access: Yes
Open: Year-round

A 132-room hotel connected to the large and popular 25,000-square-foot Lac Vieux Desert Casino, the Dancing Eagle's Hotel is nice in the way that not-quite-budget hotels like the Holiday Inn or Best Western are nice—basic rooms with a faintly musty smell, those quilts that you know a machine has made thousands of, a cable system with $12 pay-per-view movies on it. If you splurge a bit, the suites are fitted out with hot tubs and fireplaces. The indoor heated pool is a plus, especially in the winter, and easy access to the casino is what you make of it. There's also an adjacent golf course for those not interested in the slots, and Lac Vieux is within easy driving distance of the Sylvania Wilderness Area, Land O'Lakes, Wisconsin, and Agate Falls.

★Vacationland Resort
906-358-4380
www.vacationlandresort.com
E19636 Hebert Rd., Watersmeet, MI 49969
Off CR 535 / Thousand Lake Rd., about 10 miles south of the US 2 Sylvania turnoff
Price: $85–$240
Credit Cards: Not accepted
Handicapped Access: Limited—one cabin
Open: Year-round

A picturesque resort with several independent cabins on Thousand Island Lake, along the Cisco Chain of Fifteen Lakes, Vacationland looks like a perfect photograph taken out of someone's family vacation photo album. Each of the lovely pine cabins has a huge picture window looking out on the lake, a full kitchen, and a 14-foot fishing boat. Some cabins also have fireplaces, and tree-shaded RV spaces are available as well. In addition to a sandy beach, grills, and picnic tables for each cabin, the resort provides docks, boat rentals, and a great floating swimming platform out in the lake. Fishermen will love the access to 15 great fishing lakes, kids will love the lakes' 270 miles of shoreline, and everyone will love the idyllic permanent vacation feel of the appropriately named Vacationland.

CAMPING

Camping areas abound in the U.P., thanks in large part to the region's extraordinary number of protected nature areas, from state parks to wildlife refuges to enormous national forests. In this area, the Hiawatha National Forest, the Ottawa National Forest, and the Sylvania Wilderness Area provide a variety of options, as do numerous smaller parks. Whether you prefer to camp in untouched wilderness, in a shady camp-ground with modern conveniences, or on the beach, you'll find plenty of options here.

Camping Information

We have listed our favorite campgrounds here. For detailed information about all the campgrounds in the federal- and state-main-tained parks of the region, visit the following Web sites:

Hiawatha National Forest:
www.fs.fed.us/r9/forests/hiawatha/
Ottawa National Forest and Sylvania
Wilderness Area: www.fs.fed.us/r9/ottawa/

ESCANABA AND MENOMINEE

Little Bay de Noc Recreation Area
www.fs.fed.us/r9/forests/hiawatha/
From US 2 in Rapid River (between

Manistique and Escanaba) take CR 513 south for 6 miles.
Amenities: Campground host in summer, some showers, grills, boat launch, swimming beach, picnic area. No flush toilets.
Fee: $11 a night single; $12 a night single for premium sites; $40 a night group
Reservations: Accepted (and required) only for group site
Sites: 36
Open: May–Sep.

Fantastic waterfront camping in the Hiawatha National Forest, with large rustic sites arranged around the shore of Little Bay de Noc, on the north end of Lake Michigan. Each site has a view of the water and a trail to the shore, and sites are separated by trees for privacy. Fishing in the bay is excellent, particularly for walleye, and sunsets here are spectacular. The campground can get very busy in summer, and reservations are accepted only for group sites.

LAKE MICHIGAN, BREVORT LAKES, AND THE MANISTIQUE LAKES

Brevoort Lake Campground
From US 2 turn north on the Brevort Camp Rd. (FR 3108), then right at FR 3473 to the campground entrance.
Amenities: Fire rings, picnic tables, fish-ing, toilet facilities, potable water, dumping station, convenience store, boat and canoe rentals
Fee: $16 (plus $9 processing fee if you reserve ahead)
Reservations: Accepted and suggested; call 1-877-444-6777, $9 processing fee
Sites: 70
Open: May–Sep.

A large and popular campground with all the amenities, including water, flush toi-lets, and even a convenience store on-site. Sites are scattered throughout the sandy peninsula between Boedne Bay and

Brevoort Lake, and most have direct water access to the 4,000-plus-acre lake. In addition to several short trails, the North Country Trail and the Route of the Sand Dunes pass through the campground, providing two excellent hiking opportunities. Fishing is fantastic here—a walleye spawning reef in the lake ensures a near-constant supply of walleye, but smallmouth bass, crappies, sunfish, perch, northern pike, and muskellunge are also caught here. In addition to a sandy swimming beach with access to the usually warm waters of Brevoort Lake, campers can take an easy 2-mile hike to nearby Lake Michigan Beach.

Flowing Well
From US 2 at Nahma Junction (about 25 miles west of Manistique), take FR 13 north for 3 miles.
Amenities: Fire rings, picnic area, canoeing, fishing, toilet facilities, potable water
Fee: $9
Reservations: Not accepted, but space is usually available
Sites: 10
Open: Mid-May to Nov.

Ten large sites along the banks of the Sturgeon River are ideal for fishermen—the river is known for trout fishing (brook and steelhead) and salmon—and for travelers looking to avoid the crowds but still stay within reasonable driving distance of the U.P.'s big attractions. Sites are extra large, and there are plenty of trees and space between them, so privacy is not a problem here. Some sites are on the bank, overlooking the river, others are placed farther back in the forest. In the springtime wildflowers take over the forest, making the site even prettier than usual.

Lake Michigan Campground
Off US 2, 5 miles east of Brevort
Amenities: Running water, flush and vault toilets, parking for RVs and trailers
Activities: Swimming, surfing, hiking, bird-watching
Fee: $16 a night

Calm, swimmable Brevoort Lake is just 2 miles inland from Lake Michigan Beach. June Hymas

Reservations: Not accepted; very popular in
summer
Sites: 35
Open: May–Sep.

This very popular campground on Lake
Michigan offers several large campsites and
spectacular views of the lake. Some sites are
placed between 20- to 30-foot-high stabi-
lized dunes for maximum privacy. Sites are
available for RVs and trailer tents as well.
Swimming is allowed in the lake, but the
water can be cold, and when the wind picks
up the surf can get rough. The wind has
actually been known to produce surf-wor-
thy waves, but with no lifeguard on duty and
a strong undercurrent, it's not a good place
for beginners. For calmer, warmer waters
and good fishing, campers can hike an easy
2 miles to nearby Brevoort Lake.

MANISTIQUE AND THE GARDEN PENINSULA

Portage Bay Campground

From US 2 at Garden Corners take MI 183
    south, past Garden, and turn on Portage
    Bay Rd., then follow the dirt road 6
    miles to the park.
Amenities: Potable water from hand pump,
    vault toilets
Fee: $15
Reservations: Not accepted, but space is
    usually available
Sites: 23
Open: May–Nov.

This is a lovely secluded campground in a
state forest, with sites placed throughout
the forest surrounding dunes, wetlands,
and a quiet cove. Arriving at Portage Bay
down a long dirt country road feels like dis-
covering a beautiful new corner of the
world. In the spring the wildflowers and
birds are a sight to see. Swimming is pleasant at the sandy cove, and two walking loops
through the forest explain the significance
of the surrounding plants to Ojibwa life.

Although a popular spot, Portage Bay's
remote location keeps it from getting over-
crowded, even in the summer.

WATERSMEET

Clark Lake Campground

From US 2, 4 miles west of Watersmeet,
    head south on CR 535 for 7 miles. The
    turnoff is clearly signed.
Amenities: Hot showers, running water,
    flushable toilets, dumping station,
    kayak/canoe launch, drive-up sites
Fee: $12
Reservations: Not accepted, but space is
    usually available
Sites: 48
Open: May–Sep.

For those who want access to the Sylvania
Wilderness without the wilderness camping, Clark Lake offers drive-up sites in the
forest with all the amenities, including the
rarest: hot showers. Close to a lovely swimming beach on Clark Lake and a pleasant
stretch of the Clark Lake Trail surrounded
by old-growth forest, the campground truly
offers the best of all worlds.

Sylvania Wilderness Area

From US 2, 4 miles west of Watersmeet,
    head south on CR 535 for 7 miles. The
    turnoff is clearly signed.
Amenities: fire ring, vault toilets
Fee: $10 May–Sep.; free Oct.–Apr.
Reservations: Accepted via Web site
    and phone (www.reserveusa.com;
    1-877-444-6777); walk-in sites also
    available
Sites: 29
Open: Year-round

This is wilderness camping at its finest and
purest. Sites are well placed around the 34
pristine lakes and acres of old-growth forest that make Sylvania the treasure it is,
which means that even on a crowded summer weekend, campers feel like they've got

The Sylvania Wilderness Area in the Ottawa National Forest offers mile after mile of wilderness camping.
Aaron Landry

the forest to themselves. In addition to viewing various other wildlife and birds of all kinds, campers should remember that this is bear country—black bears are a regular sight, and campers should prepare accordingly. If handled appropriately, of course, a bear sighting could be the highlight of your trip. Fishing in the lakes is spectacular, but highly regulated—be sure to visit the Ottawa National Forest's Web site for details. Canoeing, kayaking, and swimming are all absolutely amazing here; no mechanized items of any kind (that includes bicycles and sailboats) are allowed.

RESTAURANTS AND FOOD PURVEYORS

As with the rest of the U.P., you cannot go wrong with whitefish in this area, but the dozens of inland lakes provide numerous other fresh seafood options as well, including walleye, trout, and perch. The shores of Lake Michigan have also benefited gastronomically from the influence of numerous immigrants. From handmade pastas to house-cured meats, some of the best Italian food in the state is available in Iron Country (Iron Mountain, Iron River, and the Menominee Range), and the mix of French, German, Scandinavian, and Italian immigrants in the town of Escanaba has created a delicious dining scene known throughout the peninsula.

Prices are generally very reasonable throughout the U.P., and this region is no exception, although there are a couple of splurges worth indulging in. Restaurants reviewed here are organized by region, and regions are listed alphabetically. All these restaurants are recommended, but particularly great spots are noted with a star.

Dining Price Codes

Restaurant prices are described as Inexpensive, Moderate, Expensive, or Very

Expensive in each of the dining reviews. These tags refer to the average price of a dinner consisting of an entrée, appetizer or dessert, and glass of wine or beer (tax and gratuities not included).

Following is a breakdown of the dining price code:

Inexpensive	Up to $15
Moderate	$15-$30
Expensive	$30-$50
Very Expensive	$50 or more

Credit Cards

AE: American Express
D: Discover
MC: MasterCard
V: Visa

ESCANABA AND MENOMINEE

The Buck Inn

906-786-7453
www.buckinnrestaurant.com
6696 US 2, Wells, MI 49894
Open: Daily
Price: Inexpensive—Moderate
Cuisine: American
Serving: L, D
Credit Cards: MC, V
Handicapped Access: Yes

A longtime local favorite, especially during the hunting season, the Buck Inn is a good ol' all-American steakhouse with thick juicy cuts and seriously good burgers. Don't be afraid to bring non-meat-lovers here, though, at least not on account of the menu; the game heads decorating the place may be a different story. The expansive menu includes an assortment of salads, soups, wraps, seafood dishes, and even a few Mexican favorites. That said, the best thing going at the Buck, and what the restaurant has built its reputation on, are the steaks and the burgers, both of which are on offer with a wide selection of toppings and sides.

The Delona Restaurant

906-786-6400
7132 US 2, Gladstone, MI 49829
US 2 East toward Gladstone, north of the Escanaba River
Open: Daily
Price: Inexpensive
Cuisine: American
Serving: B, L, D
Credit Cards: None
Handicapped Access: Yes
Special Features: Home-baked pies

Very popular for hearty, delicious breakfasts, the Delona has an atmosphere as warm and comforting as its food. Located in an old house overflowing with charm, the Delona also has a bakery that churns out delicious pies that locals rave about and visitors drive many miles for. Though breakfast is by the far the most popular meal here, home-cooked dinner classics like roasted turkey and mashed potatoes, and warm and delicious homemade soups made fresh daily and paired with sandwiches on fresh-baked bread for lunch make it a great choice any time of day.

Ferdinand's

906-786-8484
1318 Ludington St., Escanaba, MI 49829
Open: Mon.–Sat.
Price: Inexpensive
Cuisine: Mexican
Serving: L, D
Credit Cards: MC, V
Handicapped Access: Yes
Special Features: Gift store, full bar, good for large groups

Known for its friendly service, its jumbo margaritas, its pork enchiladas, and its tasty salsa (sold in jars at the restaurant's gift shop), Ferdinand's has been an Escanaba favorite for decades. The food is surprisingly good despite the near-total absence of Mexican immigrants in this part of the state. For those in your group not

Downtown Escanaba is home to some of the U.P.'s most popular eateries. Marjorie O'Brien

ready to venture beyond meat and potatoes, Ferdinand's menu includes a few midwestern standards such as hamburgers and steak as well. If you've still got room after a plate of enchiladas or fajitas, the Mexican fried ice cream is definitely worth a try. Watch out—the fresh fruit margaritas are dangerously delicious, and it's easy to forget that they're packed with alcohol.

★ Hereford & Hops
906-789-1945
www.herefordandhops.com
624 Ludington St., Escanaba, MI 49829
Open: Daily
Price: Moderate
Cuisine: American
Serving: L, D
Credit Cards: D, MC, V
Handicapped Access: Yes
Special Features: Grill your own steaks, outdoor patio, on-site microbrewery

Escanaba is home to the first of three Hereford & Hops restaurants, a combination grill-your-own-steak restaurant and microbrew pub started by two local couples. The restaurant, brewery, and pub are housed on the ground floor of a former hotel built in 1914 and restored when the restaurant's owners purchased the building in 1994. The dining room is pleasant and simple, with white tablecloths and lots of exposed brick. In addition to the grill-your-own-steaks (your choice of sirloin, rib eye, filet, T-bone, or New York strip), which are incredibly popular, the restaurant offers an expansive menu, including its take on the Outback "Bloomin' Onion," pork chops, pastas, pizzas, slabs of delicious BBQ ribs, prime rib, and a wide selection of seafood dishes that includes fresh walleye from nearby Fayette and a popular Fish Fry Friday. All the grill-your-own dinners come with a trip to the restaurant's legendary salad bar, plus baked potato and Texas toast. The brewery's microbrews are good and go really well with the

steaks. In fact its Whitetail Ale was a gold-medal winner at the 2006 World Beer Cup. In the summer diners can sit outside on the patio, grill their own steaks, and enjoy some microbrews—almost like having a BBQ at home, except without the clean-up.

Pacino's Food & Spirits
906-786-0602
www.bestwesternescanaba.com/
    restaurant.asp
2635 Ludington St., Escanaba, MI 49829
Open: Daily June–Oct.; closed Sun. and
    Mon. in the off-season, Nov.–May
Price: Moderate
Cuisine: Italian
Serving: B, L, D
Credit Cards: AE, D, MC, V
Handicapped Access: Yes
Special Features: Reservations recommended

You wouldn't expect to find the finest dining in town at the Best Western on the highway, but that is exactly what has happened here. With a respected chef and a very solid Italian menu built around daily fresh seafood specials, inventive pastas, and perfectly cooked steaks, Pacino's is a popular spot for special-occasion dining. The decor is a bit over the top—more like the Italy you might find at Epcot Center than the old country—but the service is great and the food is consistently good. The daily specials take advantage of local fresh seafood and are always a good bet. Dinner is really the star here; at lunch, entrée-size salads and pasta dishes are tasty and filling but nothing spectacular, and the breakfast buffet is downright bad, with undercooked bacon and biscuits with lumpy gravy.

Schloegel's Bay View Restaurant
906-863-7888
2720 10th St., Menominee, MI 49858
Open: Daily
Price: Inexpensive

Cuisine: American and Swedish
Serving: B, L, D
Credit Cards: AE, D, MC, V
Handicapped Access: Yes
Special Features: Bakery, gift shop, water-front views

A favorite family restaurant on the water overlooking Green Bay, Schloegel's specializes in the local classics—walleye, whitefish, pasties, and brats—with some popular Swedish favorites like Swedish pancakes and Swedish meatballs thrown in. The bakery bakes delicious pies fresh daily, as well as bread and a number of giant pastries. The restaurant is a sort of stand-in for the U.P. itself: The atmosphere is friendly and casual, and the views are great.

★ Serving Spoon Café

906-863-7770
821 First St., Menominee, MI 49931
Open: Daily
Price: Inexpensive
Cuisine: American
Serving: B, L, D
Credit Cards: MC, V
Handicapped Access: Yes
Special Features: Focus is on healthy cooking

A 145-year-old house across from the park on First Street is home to one of Menominee's favorite eateries, the Serving Spoon. With its porch, windows looking out on the waterfront, old hardwood floors, and charming quirks, the house feels more like that of an old friend than a restaurant. Despite its strict no-fryer policy, the Serving Spoon has become a popular spot for breakfast, lunch, and increasingly dinner. Though it places an emphasis on healthy cooking, the restaurant always puts taste first, and it shows. Cakes, pastries, and pies are handmade daily, as are breads and soups. Lured by veggie sandwiches and traditional Reubens, Greek gyros, a popular portobello mushroom sandwich (sliced, seasoned portobellos, grilled on tomato focaccia with sun-dried tomato pesto and fresh parmesan cheese), and arguably the town's best burgers, the Serving Spoon's loyal fan base always returns for more. Breakfast options include breakfast burritos, omelets, and a tasty Veggie Benedict, as well as Menominee's best coffee. In the summer, when it stays open later, the café also serves pasta dishes and at least one special entrée per night, typically a fresh seafood dish.

★ Swedish Pantry

906-786-9606
www.swedishpantry.com
819 Ludington St., Escanaba, MI 49829
Open: Daily
Price: Inexpensive
Cuisine: Swedish
Serving: B, L, D
Credit Cards: D, MC, V
Handicapped Access: Yes
Special Features: Bakery and gift shop; very busy for breakfast

A delightful kitschy Swedish restaurant, the Swedish Pantry is almost always as full of people as it is chock-full of clocks from the motherland—none of them are set to the right time or even the same time, so at least one clock's chimes are usually ringing. The clocks and the bustle only make the place more fun, and the fact that the food is terrific only adds to the draw. From Scandinavian classics such as Swedish pancakes or Swedish meatballs with lingonberries to down-home American standards such as pot roast and meatloaf, absolutely everything here is homemade and delicious. And cheap! The restaurant hasn't raised its prices in years. Though breakfast is served all day, the restaurant is very busy most mornings and absolutely crammed on Sunday. If you're in a hurry, consider opting for something from the attached bakery—everything in it is oversize for some reason, from the muffins to the cookies, but it's all good, and the Swedish *limpa* bread is great for sandwiches.

IRON MOUNTAIN AND IRON RIVER

★ Alice's
906-265-4764
402 W. Adams / US 2, Iron River
Open: Tue.–Sun.
Price: Inexpensive
Cuisine: Italian
Serving: D
Credit Cards: Not accepted
Handicapped Access: Yes
Special Features: Reservations recommended in summer

Fantastic Italian restaurants like this one are what give this area its reputation for quality Italian food. Alice's menu revolves around home-cooked Italian specialties passed down from generation to generation in the owner's Italian family. Everything is handmade, from the pasta and gnocchi to the delicious *cappelletti* soup. Though the restaurant touts chicken Valdostanna as its specialty, it's actually an Americanized version of an Italian dish. Stick instead with the traditional dishes—meat or cheese ravioli with meat sauce, or handmade gnocchi served with portobello mushrooms (delicious!), and a grilled pork chop or steak on the side for the very hungry. The wine list includes a number of great and affordable choices from the old country, and Alice's lounge is a pleasant place to relax and try a few. Save room for the chef's infamous three-chocolate mousse—it's well worth it.

★ Damian's Pasta Works
906-774-3058
909 S. Stephenson / US 2
    Iron Mountain, MI 49801
Open: Mon.–Fri.
Price: Inexpensive
Cuisine: Italian
Serving: L, D

Credit Cards: Not accepted
Handicapped Access: Yes
Special Features: Takeout only

Hungry customers wait in their cars or in the tiny front room and salivate over fresh-baked breads and sweets while hints of their meal waft through from the back of this terrific hole-in-the-wall takeout favorite. Locals know this place is amazing, and visitors are consistently blown away by just how good it is. Located in an old house east of downtown Iron Mountain, Damian's is strictly takeout, and the owner-chefs make everything—pasta, 10 different sauces, lasagna, bread, roasted and cured meats for sandwiches—from scratch. Though it's all delicious here, there are a few standouts: gnocchi, ravioli, lasagna, and the *porchetta* (spicy, slow-roasted pork) sandwiches are all favorites. Fresh pastas are ready from three in the afternoon onward, and the lunch menu includes an assortment of salads. Portions are enormous, and prices are so low they're actually hard to believe.

Fontana Supper Club
906-774-0044
115 S. Stephenson / US 2
Iron Mountain, MI 49801
Open: Mon.–Sat.
Price: Inexpensive–Moderate
Cuisine: Italian
Serving: L, D
Credit Cards: MC, V
Handicapped Access: Yes
Special Features: Entrance and parking in back of restaurant

Good, straightforward Italian fare similar to what you'd find in the south of Italy served up in a blast-from-the-past supper club, complete with dim lighting, cavernous booths, and big leather menus. Fontana's is a longtime local favorite, particularly for family meals out. Homemade pasta dishes and steaks are the specialties of the *casa*, and one order of pasta, which comes with soup and salad, is more than enough for two, particularly if you order the Italian Holiday (gnocchi, cheese ravioli, and spaghetti with meatballs), which we did one night and lived to regret once the heavy food coma set in. Our favorite is the cheese ravioli with a meatball on the side for good measure. Service can be a little slow here, but it sort of adds to the charm. The bar, with its sports memorabilia and beer signs, is a fun place to hang out of a night, with regular drink and appetizer specials.

Romangnoli's

906-774-7300
1603 N. Stephenson Ave.
Iron Mountain, MI 49801
Open: Mon.–Sat.
Price: Inexpensive–Moderate
Cuisine: Italian
Serving: L, D
Credit Cards: MC, V
Handicapped Access: Yes

Another classic Iron Mountain Italian family restaurant, Romagnoli's has been family-owned and operated for more than 20 years. House specials include homemade pasta (made fresh daily), ribs with a secret family sauce, roasted chicken, local fresh seafood specials, and steaks. The meat, chicken, and seafood entrées are all served with a salad, a warm loaf of homemade crusty bread, and your choice of spaghetti, gnocchi, or french fries. It's a lot of food. The lounge offers a full bar and appetizer menu, and the dining room is pleasantly nondescript. The restaurant's slogan is "Come as you are!" and they mean it—this is a casual dinner spot with friendly, excellent service.

LAKE MICHIGAN BEACH, BREVOORT LAKE, MANISTIQUE LAKES

★ Chamberlin's Ole Forest Inn

906-586-6000 or 1-800-292-0440
www.chamberlinsinn.com
H33 County Road, P.O. Box 307

Guests, locals, and other Curtis visitors gather at the restaurant at Chamberlinn's Ole Forest Inn for good food and great views. David Friar

Curtis, MI 49820
Open: Mon.–Sat.
Price: Inexpensive–Moderate
Cuisine: American
Serving: B, L, D
Credit Cards: MC, V
Handicapped Access: No
Special Features: Connected to inn

The food is decent at Chamberlin's (especially the planked whitefish—yum!), but the reason people come here is the view—a spectacular panorama of Big Manistique Lake from the dining room windows and the porch of the restored 18th-century railroad hotel that houses the restaurant. This is also one of the few games going in town. Curtis is home to a number of cabins and resorts, but restaurants are in short supply. Breakfast and lunch here are solid as well, particularly the homemade biscuits and gravy at breakfast, and homemade soup at lunch.

★ Cut River Inn
906-292-5400
W 5962 US 2, P.O. Box 233
Epoufette, MI 49762
Open: Daily
Price: Inexpensive
Cuisine: American
Serving: B, L, D
Credit Cards: MC, V
Handicapped Access: Yes
Special Features: Closed early
Dec.–Christmas

Just a mile from the picturesque Cut River Bridge, the Cut River Inn has been popular with summer visitors for years, but the simple dining room is also a local favorite, with folks driving from far and wide for its broiled or fried whitefish and perch, and delicious apple dumplings with ice cream and rum sauce. Fairly tasty, if bland, breakfast burritos and filling lunchtime wraps and sandwiches make it a good bet no matter what time of day you happen to be passing through.

MANISTIQUE AND THE GARDEN PENINSULA

Garden House Bar & Grille
906-644-2844
6342 State St., Garden, MI 49835
Open: Daily
Price: Inexpensive
Cuisine: American
Serving: L, D
Credit Cards: MC, V
Handicapped Access: Yes

Once a rowdy bar and local hangout, the Garden House has become much more of a real restaurant in recent times. The all-you-can-eat Friday fish fry is popular, and the fish is always fresh and good. Homemade chili is tasty, as are the homemade soups, but our favorite is the prime rib sandwich with grilled mushrooms, onion, and cheese added on—it's one of the best lunches we've had in a while. The Garden House still features a full bar as well, and what a bar it is—an antique wooden beauty stocked with various microbrews and a super-tasty old-fashioned root beer.

Pizza Stop
906-586-6622
W17162 Main St., Curtis, MI 49820
Open: Daily except Friday
Price: Inexpensive
Cuisine: Italian, American
Serving: L, D
Credit Cards: MC, V
Handicapped Access: Yes
Special Features: No alcohol; call ahead for pizza pick-up

The tiny Pizza Stop's chef-owners make the sauce and the dough fresh every day, churning out delicious pizzas that are generally considered the best within a number of miles. Locals and regular summer visitors call ahead to order and run over to pick up their pies or grab one of a handful of tables to eat in. Toasted sandwiches and salads are also on offer, as are specialty coffee drinks, and ice cream in the summertime. Located in tiny "downtown" Curtis, the Pizza Stop is the only casual restaurant within walking distance of the town's resorts and residential areas, so the owners make an effort to provide whatever the community wants, resulting in a well-loved and popular spot.

Three Mile Supper Club
906-341-8048
8555W County Road 442
Manistique, MI 49854
Open: Daily
Price: Inexpensive
Cuisine: American
Serving: D
Credit Cards: Not accepted
Handicapped Access: Yes

Don't let the somewhat institutional feel scare you off. The Three Mile Supper Club actually has some of the best whitefish around, and a surprisingly good salad bar to boot. In fact, this may be the only Manistique restaurant that is consistently recommended by locals. Soups and salad dressings are all homemade, and the BBQ items and steak are also very good if you're not in the mood for whitefish. Steaks are cut to order and always cooked perfectly. The restaurant was a roadside disco of some kind at some point, and the full bar is still there, which can be good or bad. Because the dining room and the bar are in the same big room, and smoking is allowed in both, it can get very smoky, which can sometimes put a bit of a damper on dinner.

★ The Upper Crust Bakery & Deli Café
906-341-2253
www.uppercrustdeli.com
375 Traders' Point Dr.
Manistique, MI 49854
Open: Daily
Price: Inexpensive

Cuisine: American
Serving: L, D
Credit Cards: MC, V
Handicapped Access: Yes
Special Features: Outdoor deck; closed Sunday during winter

A fantastic place flooded with natural light and blessed with pleasant river views from its many windows and its outdoor deck, the Upper Crust is every Manistique local's favorite lunch spot. Occupying the same space as the popular Tamarack Books, Traders' Point Antiques, and the River Shack Antiques Annex, the café features a handful of salads and 40-odd sandwich choices, all made with bread baked on the premises every morning. Two soups are made fresh daily as well, and could include chicken noodle, Wisconsin cheese, or the popular potato bacon. The bakery portion of the Upper Crust churns out tasty pies, cookies, pastries, and cakes daily. Aside from its wall of windows, the Upper Crust is decorated simply, with wooden café tables on hardwood floors, and Tamarack Books on one side, which lends the place a pleasant literary vibe. In the summer the café serves dinner on Saturday, offering a surprisingly large and varied menu for an establishment that serves dinner only one day a week for three months out of the year. Homemade pastas are a favorite, as are the delicious, fall-off-the-bone country ribs.

WATERSMEET

The Bear Trap Inn
715-547-3422
Two miles west of Land O'Lakes, WI, on Highway B (look for 2B sign on snowmobile trail)
Open: Tue.–Sun. in summer, Thu.–Sat. in winter
Price: Inexpensive–Moderate
Cuisine: American
Serving: D

Credit Cards: AE, MC, V
Handicapped Access: Yes
Special Features: Spring and winter closing breaks, call for details

A quaint log cabin with red trim and knotty pine interior, the Bear Trap has been serving hearty north-woods meals to happy customers for several decades. Walleye is delicious here, and the Friday fish fry is a terrific deal. Other favorites include the garlic-stuffed tenderloin, the pork chops, and the duck, and the Bear Trap offers a long and decent wine list as well. From some tables diners can watch deer feeding outside or check out the fish in the restaurant's back pond.

★ Bent's Camp

715-547-3487
www.bents-camp.com
6882 Helen Creek Rd.
Land O' Lakes, WI 54540
Open: Daily; closed Tue. in winter
Price: Inexpensive–Moderate
Cuisine: American
Serving: L, D
Credit Cards: AE, MC, V
Handicapped Access: Yes
Special Features: No reservations accepted; dock space available for boaters

A former logging camp has been turned into a popular fishing resort with an outstanding restaurant, famous for its Friday fish fry, Saturday prime rib, juicy roast duck, and homemade pizzas. Located in the main lodge of the resort, Bent's Camp restaurant features wood tables in a large wooden, open-beam interior decorated with Native American trinkets and local hunting trophies. The restaurant has its own dock for those boating in for a meal. The Friday fish fry is renowned throughout the region, so plan on getting there early or waiting awhile if you want to find out what the big fuss is about—it's worth it. If you don't feel like braving the crowds, order up one of their famous deep-dish pizzas for takeout. For lunch the burgers are great, but they also offer an assortment of large fresh salads if the Midwest meat diet is getting to you. And save room for dessert— homemade pies baked fresh daily are delicious. The adjoining bar is always a good time, though it can get very smoky; it's almost always packed in summer, and some sort of event or live music is often scheduled.

People boat in from all over the area for the legendary Friday fish fry at Bent's Camp. Bent's Camp

Friday Fish Fry

If you didn't grow up in the Midwest, or you're not Catholic, Friday fish fries might seem a touch unusual, but it's a widespread tradition in the U.P., and nearly every restaurant worth its salt has a version of it. The custom sprang out of the Catholic tradition to avoid meat on Friday, particularly during Lent, and it remains popular, especially in Michigan, Wisconsin, and Minnesota—more so up north than in the southern regions of those states. Irrespective of religion, everyone loves the fish fry tradition in the U.P., where whitefish, walleye, and perch are caught locally and fried to perfection.

Picnic Provisions

Angeli's Central Market (906-265-7103; www.angelifoods.com, 426 W. Genesee St., Iron River, MI 49935) An extraordinary market with great fresh produce, homemade local foods, and bread baked fresh daily, lots of organic options, high-quality meats, imported cheeses, a fantastic wine selection, and various tasty treats from the infamous **Zingerman's Deli** down south. It seems entirely out of place in tiny Iron River, but the locals aren't complaining, and neither are savvy visitors. This is the best place for miles around to stock up on picnic provisions.

RECREATION

The U.P. is as much a nature lover's dream as it is an outdoorsman's paradise, equal parts wildlife refuge and hunter's haven. This particular region is especially popular with sportsmen for its dozens of inland lakes, which are incredible for fishing in the summer, and its large deer population, which makes for excellent hunting in the fall. Meanwhile, bird-watchers will love the Sylvania Wilderness and the Seney National Wildlife Refuge, both home to numerous species, many of them rare. Wild mushroom picking is also popular around these parts, as is blueberry season. Of course Lake Michigan's beaches are always popular as well—a day spent lying on the lake's shores and dipping into its cool blue waters is just about perfect.

In the fall visitors flock to view the beautiful colors as the leaves turn and to hunt various deer and fowl; and in the winter the well-groomed cross-country ski trails, mile after mile of snowmobile trails, and family-friendly ski resorts bring almost as many visitors in December as the summer sun brings in July.

Beware of the Blackflies

One word of caution—when the snow finally melts away and the ground defrosts, the U.P. is home to legions of blackflies, which are extremely unpleasant. And we're not just talking annoying, buzzing flies—these guys bite. And swarm. Though it shifts a bit from year to year, depending on how long the winter was, a general rule is that if you're going to the U.P. from mid-May to mid-June, bring insect repellent, leave your cologne and perfume at home, and wear long pants and sleeves in light colors. The popular mosquito repellent DEET doesn't really work on blackflies, but some people swear by Avon's Skin So Soft and B_1 vitamins. The blackflies tend not to bite indoors, and they disappear at night, but staying inside all day and coming out at night isn't why most people come to the U.P.

Beaches

Thanks to its assortment of inland lakes, islands, and peninsulas, and its long, unbroken stretch of Lake Michigan shoreline, this region of the U.P. offers more beaches than any other. Following are some of the best, from east to west:

Lake Michigan Beach, off US 2 near Brevort. This long stretch of perfect white-sand beach is backed by low dunes, with Hiawatha National Forest in the background. The beach is also part of the national forest—to get to it you need to pay the $5 day-use fee.

Cut River Gorge, off US 2, 4 miles west of Brevort, near Epoufette. This is an excellent spot for a picnic and a swim. Turn off and park by the charming Cut River Bridge. Pathways on the east and west sides of the bridge lead down into the Cut River Valley, to the mouth of the river and then out to Lake Michigan. The river has carved out a beautiful limestone gorge on its way to the lake. The walk out to the beach on Lake Michigan takes about 15 minutes.

Scott Point, west of Naubinway. Turn south off US 2 at Gould City and follow Gould City Road to a dead end at the park. About 10 miles off US 2, Scott Point feels miles away from anywhere, and because it's not an obvious turnoff, you've got a good chance of having this beautiful, seemingly endless white-sand beach all to yourself.

Rogers Park, off US 2, 4 miles west of Manistique. Great, sandy Lake Michigan swimming beach surrounded by pine forest.

Fayette Historic State Park, south of Garden. From US 2 in Garden Corners take MI 183 to Fayette, next to the ghost town. This is a lovely, secluded beach surrounded by trees, a great place to camp or just to take a picnic and a walk before or after checking out the ghost town.

Portage Bay, east of Garden. Past Garden, turn east on Portage Bay Road. The road is a little rough, but you'll be rewarded with a lovely white-sand beach surrounded by low dunes and shade trees; the bay is calm and pleasant for swimming, and in spring the area is awash with wildflowers.

Ludington Park, off Ludington St., Escanaba. This is a fantastic 120-acre lakeside park with lots of bright green grass, a jogging trail, shade trees, playgrounds, tennis courts, concert area, and benches and picnic tables overlooking the water. The bridge to Arnson

Ludington Park encompasses several miles of beachfront property adjacent to downtown Escanaba. Matt Girvan

Island leads to an idyllic sandy swimming beach.

Red Arrow Park, in Marinette, Wisconsin. Across the First St./Ogden St. bridge from Menominee in Marinette, turn east onto Leonard, and east again on Bay View, which leads to the park. With both river and lake access, this park is a local favorite. Grills, picnic tables, boat launch, and playground are available. The sandy swimming beach is unsupervised.

Henes Park, off MI 35, north Menominee. This 50-acre city park has a playground, lily pond, and pleasant sandy beach.

Bewabic State Park, off US 2, 4 miles west of Crystal Falls. This very large, beautiful state park comprises several lakes, footbridges, walkways, sandy beaches, and tennis courts. Fishing is great in several of the lakes, and canoes and kayaks are available for rent.

Clark Lake, Sylvania Wilderness Area, near Watersmeet. A sandy beach in a national park filled with jewel-toned, crystal-clear lakes. Stay here as long as you can.

Bicycling

There are numerous cycle routes for every type of rider in this region, from rough-and-tumble mountain bike rides to gentle scenic shoreline jaunts.

Top Rides

Ludington Park, Escanaba. Ludington Park and the city of Escanaba are perhaps best explored by bicycle, and you can rent bikes at the Escanaba Marina, located within the park. Five miles of concrete bike paths swerve through the 120-acre lakeside park at the end of Ludington Street, downtown Escanaba's hub. This is an easy, scenic ride.

George Young Recreational Complex, off CR 424 at the southwest end of Chicaugon Lake between Iron River and Crystal Falls. In addition to a golf course and a pool, this lush and beautiful 3,000-plus-acre recreational complex includes 7.5 miles of mountain-bike trails that wind through woods, up and down hills, and beside the lake that adjoins the recreation area.

Fumee Lake Loop, Iron Mountain. An easy 9-mile ride made much more difficult by occasional steep ascents and descents, the Fumee Loop visits two beautiful inland lakes, perfect for a quick swim to break up the ride.

Agonikak Trail, from Watersmeet to Land O'Lakes. An easy-to-moderate 12-mile ride that begins in the Ottawa National Forest near Watersmeet and meanders through dense forest and past inland lakes to Land O'Lakes. Head out in the late morning, stop in Land O'Lakes for lunch, and then take it easy on the flat return route to Watersmeet. For a longer but flatter version of this ride, stick to the Watersmeet Rails-to-Trails, an old railroad line converted to a biking, hiking, and ATV path, which begins at the U.S. Forest Service Visitor Center in Watersmeet and ends at the public library in Land O'Lakes.

Bird-Watching

The U.P. is world-renowned for bird-watching, thanks in large part to the Seney National Wildlife Refuge. With its thousands of acres of protected woodland, there are few places on Earth better suited to bird-watching. In this region, the southern section of the Seney refuge, the Sylvania Wilderness Refuge, and the Hiawatha and Ottawa National Forests all attract numerous species. The region's many inland lakes are also home to the notoriously edgy loon, as well as osprey, bald eagle, and the sandhill crane.

Bewabic State Park, off US 2, 4 miles west of Crystal Falls. This large state park, with its chain of five Fortune Lakes surrounded by acres of mature birch-maple forest, is a great place to see a variety of U.P. birds, particularly during the spring migration. Warblers are often in full view, some of the lakes are quiet enough for loons, and eagles build their nests around two of the five lakes (First and Third).

Deer Marsh Interpretive Trail, south of Sidnaw. From US 2 in Crystal Falls take US 141 north to Covington, then MI 28 west to Sidnaw. Drive south on Sidnaw Road about 8.5 miles to Lake Ste. Kathryn Campground. Turn right (west) and proceed about 100 feet to the site entrance on the left side of the road. An easy 3-mile hike loops through wetlands and around Deer Marsh, which is positively brimming with interesting wildlife. Osprey, bald eagles, hooded mergansers, great blue herons, and American bittern are all common here, and you may also spot black-backed woodpeckers, boreal chickadees, and the ever-elusive trumpeter swan.

The majestic osprey is one of many birds seen often in the Upper Peninsula. Steve Ryan

Gene's Pond, north of Felch. From US 2 in Escanaba, take MI 69 to Felch; turn right on CR 581, and after about 5 miles turn left at "Public Access" sign and follow the road about 1 mile to parking lot. Thanks in part to their remote location, these flooded woodlands created by the Sturgeon River are a fantastic place to spot rare large birds. Loons and cormorants hover near the shore and make quick dives for fish in the shallow pond, while bald eagles and osprey make big powerful plunges in from high above, and great blue heron nest in the tops of nearby trees. Beyond the main pond, a large cedar and pine swamp hides numerous warblers and other songbirds. Be careful venturing too far into the swamp, as it is also home to bobcat, bear, and the occasional gray wolf.

Peninsula Point, Stonington. From US 2 east of Rapid River, take CR 513 south approximately 18 miles. With its historic lighthouse, this remote point jutting out into Lake Michigan is a favorite resting spot of various migrating birds, and permanent home to gulls, duck, geese, heron, and various other shorebirds and songbirds. Though a bit off the beaten path, this spot is especially popular with birders in the spring and fall when migrating owls, hawks, and eagles land here. Thousands of migrating monarch butterflies also stop here every fall on their way to Mexico. Between the fall colors, the lake, the various birds, and the huge swaths of beautiful butterflies, it's hard not to be completely enchanted by this spot in autumn.

Portage Marsh, near Escanaba. From Escanaba, take MI 35 south to Portage Point Lane. Turn left (east) and drive to the parking lot at the end of the road. The protected bay and interconnected network of coastal wetlands created by Portage Creek provide shelter to a huge variety of shorebirds, songbirds, waterfowl, and migratory birds. According to the Department of Natural Resources, state-threatened birds like bald eagles and Caspian and common terns are commonly spotted here.

Rainey Wildlife Viewing Area, 5 miles north of Manistique off MI 94 in Thompson. Wooden boardwalks lead into a quiet maple and birch forest, then over Smith Creek and surrounding wetlands to an observation platform. Songbirds are plentiful here, especially warblers, and a nearby bald eagle nest makes for prime viewing in the spring and early summer.

Sylvania Wilderness Area, less than 5 miles west of Watersmeet, off US 2 on CR 535. If you needed any more reasons to visit the pristine lakes and stately hushed forests of the 21,000-acre Sylvania Wilderness Area, how about the fact that a pair of loons nests at nearly every lake, or that barred owls are out in abundance at night, only to be replaced by pileated woodpeckers, blackburnian warblers, black-throated green warblers, red-eyed vireos, and ovenbirds in the morning? The area is also home to bald eagles, broad-wing hawks, and osprey, which stick around for the abundance of fish in the lakes.

Canoeing and Kayaking

In addition to Lake Michigan, the region's vast network of inland lakes and rivers makes it ideally suited to canoeing and kayaking, whether you're an expert paddler or just testing the waters. Kayak and canoe outfitters abound in this region as well, with affordable rentals and well-trained guides.

Rentals

Northwoods Wilderness Outfitters (906-774-9009 or 1-800-530-8859; www.northwoodsoutfitters.com; N-4088 Pine Mountain Rd., Iron Mountain)
Big Cedar Campground and Canoe Livery (906-586-6684; 7936 MI 77, Germfask)

Sylvania Outfitters (906-358-4766; www.sylvaniaoutfitters.com; E23423 US 2, Watersmeet) The only Special Use Permit holder for providing canoe trips into the Sylvania Wilderness and Recreation Area and the surrounding Ottawa National Forest.

Top Paddles

Brevoort Lake. From US 2 turn north on the Brevort Camp Road (FR 3108), then right at FR 3473 to the campground entrance. Easy paddling, and canoe rentals available at this 4,000-plus-acre lake.

Manistique River, Germfask, along MI 77 north of US 2. Easy-to-moderate paddle; launches near Germfask, flows into Seney National Wildlife Refuge.

Menominee Watershed, with various launches on Brule, Michigamme, and Menominee Rivers. The Menominee creates a boundary between Michigan and Wisconsin; part of the Menominee also includes Piers Gorge, a white-water for experienced paddlers only. The National Park Service (www.nps.gov) produces canoe trail maps for the region. A variety of trips are possible here, ranging from easy to advanced.

Flowing Well and Sturgeon River. From US 2 at Nahma Junction take FH 13 about 3 miles north to Flowing Well. Easy 4-mile trip.

Sylvania Wilderness Area. Includes 34 named lakes, plus 25 miles of portages, waiting to be explored. Canoe launch at Clark Lake is simple and straightforward; get a map from the Ottawa National Forest Service for details on other lakes and portages. Due to the area's vast size and the remote location of some lakes, we highly recommend a guided trip with Sylvania Outfitters, or at least stopping in to talk to those guys before heading out on your own.

Clark Lake, in the Sylvania Wilderness Area of the Ottawa National Forest, provides excellent paddling.
Aaron Landry

Fishing

As you might suspect, with all its lakes and streams, this region boasts some absolutely phenomenal fishing spots. Whitefish are plentiful in Lake Michigan and several of the inland lakes, trout abound in the rivers and streams, and fishermen come from far and wide to catch salmon, bass, perch, pike, and muskellunge ("musky") as well. To fish in the state parks and national forests, you must have a Michigan fishing license if you're over the age of 17. Visit www.michigan.gov for details.

Charters and Rentals

Full Moon Charters (906-497-4106; www.fullmoonguide.net; N16465 Township Line G Rd., Wilson) Seven-time master angler Captain Dan Linder shares tips to help fishermen of all levels catch salmon, trout, bass, musky, walleye, perch, you name it. Children 16 and under are welcome aboard for free, provided each child is accompanied by an adult.

    Delta Dawn Charter (906-428-9039; www.deltadawnchartersup.com; Escanaba Municipal Marina, Loren W. Jenkins Memorial Dr.) Comfortable 24-foot 232 Gulfstream Grady-White, captained by avid local fisherman Captain Bill Myers, who focuses on catching walleye, salmon, and trout. Operates out of Escanaba, Manistique, and Gladstone.

    Sylvania Outfitters (906-358-4766; www.sylvaniaoutfitters.com; E23423 US 2, Watersmeet)

The Sturgeon River is known for great trout fishing. Heidi Hansen

Places to Fish
Roughly east to west:

Brevoort Lake. From US 2 turn north on the Brevort Camp Road (FR 3108), then right at FR 3473 to the campground entrance. Large managed and stocked lake with walleye, small-mouth bass, crappies, sunfish, perch, northern pike, and muskellunge.

Big Manistique Lake. East of MI 77, near Curtis. Large, deep lake best known for yellow perch. Also good for ice fishing in winter.

South Manistique Lake. East of MI 77, near Curtis. Smaller, shallow lake, great for muskellunge, walleye, and bass.

Flowing Well and Sturgeon River. From US 2 at Nahma Junction take FH 13 about 3 miles north to Flowing Well. River fishing for trout and salmon.

Haymeadow Creek. US 2 east from Rapid River 1.6 miles, then turn left on CR 509 and go north 9.4 miles to the entrance. High-quality trout stream known for brook trout.

Bays de Noc, Escanaba. The "walleye capital of the world" and home to numerous pro-fessional walleye fishing competitions, Bays de Noc are also full of salmon, bass, perch, and pike. Little Bay de Noc has made numerous top-10 fishing lists.

Sylvania Wilderness Area. Less than 5 miles west of Watersmeet, off US 2 on CR 535. Comprising 34 lakes, all great for fishing, Sylvania is well known for its catch-and-release bass program. All the lakes in the tract except for Crooked Lake abide by a set of regula-tions specific to Sylvania, which can be picked up at the park's entrance. Motors are allowed only on Crooked Lake, where the regular state of Michigan fishing regulations apply and not the Sylvania regulations.

Golf
Golf has really taken off in the U.P. over the last several years, and visitors are typically just as surprised by the quality of the courses up here as they are by the low greens fees. Many of the 18-hole courses here today started out as 9-hole courses, and there are still several public 9-hole courses in the region, including the Crystal View Golf Course in Crystal Falls and the Country Meadows Golf Course in Escanaba.

Escanaba Country Club (906-786-4430; www.escanabacc.com; 12th Ave. South, Escanaba) The oldest course in Delta County, the Escanaba Country Club was built in 1915 as a 9-hole course and expanded to a full 18-hole course in 1991. It now includes tree-lined fairways as well as several challenging water holes. 18 holes, 6,233 yards, par 71. Pro shop, driving range.

Highland Golf Club (906-466-7457; www.highlandgolfclub.net; P.O. Box 773, Escanaba) Wide-open fairways and a mellow atmosphere make this a great course for beginners, with a few challenges thrown in for good measure. 18 holes, 6,237 yards, par 71.

Terrace Bluff Golf Club (906-428-2343; www.terracebay.com; 7146 P Rd., Gladstone) One of the most respected courses in the area and rated No. 1 in the U.P. more than once, Terrace Bluff is a championship course cut into the woods on a bluff overlook-ing Terrace Bay. The course is both scenic and challenging, with narrow fairways bounded by beautiful birch and maple forests, and panoramic views of the bay below. 18 holes, 7,008 yards, par 72. Pro shop, cart rental, driving range, putting green, bar, restaurant.

Oak Crest Golf Course (906-563-589; www.oakcrestgolf.com; 1N1475 US 8, Norway) Surrounded by the large oak trees that give it its name, Oak Crest is a moderate course, made more difficult by the rolling hills on which it is built. 18 holes, 6,158 yards, par 72. Pro shop, driving range, cart rental, bar, restaurant.

Timber Stone at Pine Mountain (906-774-2747; www.pinemountainresort.com; N3332 Pine Mountain Rd., Iron Mountain) Rated a five-star course by *Golf Digest*, Timber Stone is a championship course designed by Jerry Matthews and draws as many visitors to Pine Mountain in the summer as the ski runs do in winter. The sort of manicured beauty you'd expect golf magazines to rave about, Timber Stone is surrounded by birch and maple trees and takes advantage of its panoramic Pine Mountain views. Though the course has a 300-foot vertical drop, golfers only have to contend with two uphill holes. 18 holes, 7,000 yards, par 72. Pro shop, driving range, putting green, cart rental, bar, restaurant.

Pine Grove Country Club (906-774-3493; www.pinegrovecc.com; 1520 W. Hughitt St., Iron Mountain) A semiprivate club founded in 1902, Pine Grove is surrounded by dense virgin stands of white and red pine, maple, and oak and features a challenging hilly terrain with an 84-foot elevation change. Another course that began life as a 9-holer, Pine Grove was expanded and redesigned by Roger Packard in the 1960s. A bit swankier than some of the other clubs because of its semiprivate status, Pine Grove is nonetheless incredibly affordable and friendly when compared to private or semiprivate clubs elsewhere in the country. 18 holes, 6,600 yards, par 70. Pro shop, driving range, cart rental, bar, restaurant.

George Young Recreational Area (906-265-3401; www.georgeyoung.com; 159 Young's Lane, Iron River) Fantastic 18-hole course in the middle of a 3,000-plus-acre recreational area donated to the public by a Chicago millionaire in the early 1990s. Young built the course himself, one hole at a time, modeling each after a personal favorite hole of his at various courses throughout the country. It's no wonder that the resulting course is the longest in the U.P.! With its narrow fairways and large greens, hills and panoramic views, the course was awarded four stars by *Golf Digest*, which called it "a gem off the beaten track." In addition to the design of the course itself, its surroundings make George Young very pleasant to play, with acre after acre of undeveloped forest, woodland wildlife, and a neighboring lake. The colors in the fall are vivid and beautiful. The main lodge is well designed, with plenty of windows and open beams that create a perfect blend of north country rustic style and modern architectural design. 18 holes, 7,041 yards, par 72. Driving range, putting green, restaurant, indoor pool, spa, sauna.

Hiking

Bay de Noc to Grand Island. Two miles east of Rapid River on US 2. Turn left onto CR 509 and travel 1.5 miles north. Parking lot is on the west side of the road. This 40-mile trail, from Bay de Noc near Rapid River up to Grand Island near Munising, roughly follows the route historians believe the Ojibwa used to portage goods between Lake Superior and Lake Michigan. Although there are no loops, there are three trailheads, and views of the Whitefish River Valley coupled with pretty streams and mature forests make the trail interesting enough that hiking just a section of it back and forth is well worth doing.

Pine Marten Run. In the Hiawatha National Forest, accessible from CR 440, approximately 30 miles northwest of Manistique. A 26-mile system of hiking and horseback riding trails with five distinct loops, the Pine Marten Run offers several different experiences in one. Although all the trails are lovely, our favorites are the Triangle Lake Trail (7.2 miles), which passes by active Indian River beaver communities, and Ironjaw Lake for its lake views. Still, the Swan Lake Trail passes close enough to the water for an afternoon swim, making it the obvious choice on a warm summer day.

Piers Gorge. From US 2 at Norway, near the Wisconsin border, take US 8 south and turn onto Piers Gorge Road. If you haven't got the experience or the courage to brave the white-water of Piers Gorge by boat, you can still enjoy it from a safe distance on a wonderful trail that goes from cedar forest to a ridge 70 feet above the river, with a view of Misicot Falls. The gorge's namesakes are actually outcroppings of rock that look a bit like piers and create small waterfalls as the water rushes over them. Adventurous hikers can make their way down closer to the river and sit on the rocks near the third pier to catch the spray off the white-water, or even dip into some of the river's quieter sections. In addition to the river and the white-water, the wildflowers are especially beautiful here in the late spring and early summer.

Clark Lake Loop. In the Sylvania Wilderness Area of the Ottawa National Forest. From US 2, 4 miles west of Watersmeet, head south on CR 535 for 7 miles. The turnoff is clearly signed. Although most people believe that the Sylvania is best experienced by canoe, there is something absolutely magical about walking through the immense peace and silence of trees that are hundreds of years old. That section of the trail alone would be enough to make it memorable, but add to it the delight of happening upon rare wildlife or flowers, and possibly a swim in the crystal blue quiet of Clark Lake, and you've got yourself a day you'll never forget.

North Country Trail

The North Country National Scenic Trail is the longest scenic trail in the United States—to date only four hikers have completed successful end-to-end trips. The trail spans 4,600 miles and seven states, from New York to North Dakota. You can hike the North Country Trail across the entire breadth of the U.P., from the Mackinac Bridge in the east to Ironwood in the far west, before heading down into Wisconsin. The trail was first envisioned in the late 1960s as part of the National Scenic Trails program, was eventually completed in the early 1970s, and finally officially designated in the early 1980s. While trekking across the entire peninsula may sound like a bit much, many hikers take advantage of pleasant sections of the trail running through both the Hiawatha and Ottawa National Forests. For information on the trail, visit www.northcountrytrail.org.

Hunting

Game/Season
White-tailed deer—Bow: Oct. 1–Nov. 14 and Dec. 1–Jan. 2; regular firearm: Nov. 15–30; muzzle loaders: Dec. 2–18
Russian boar—Year-round (hunters can hunt boar with any valid hunting license)
Black bear—Sep. 10–Oct. 26
Elk—Aug. 25–29; Sep. 15–18; Dec. 11–18
Wild turkey—Oct. 8–Nov. 14
American woodcock—Sep. 22–Nov. 5
Pheasant—(Males only) Oct. 10–Nov. 14
Ruffed grouse—Sep. 15–Nov. 14; Dec. 1–Jan. 1
Ducks and mergansers—Sep. 29–Nov. 27
Canada geese—Sep. 18–Nov. 1

Guides and Outfitters
U.P. Wide Adventure Guide (906-430-0547; www.upwideadventureguide.com; W6508 Epoufette Bay Rd., Naubinway)
Wild Spirit Guide Service (906-497-4408; www.wildspiritguide.com; N15107

A white-tailed buck. Sarah Steffens

Township Line Rd., Powers (US 2, 30 miles west of Escanaba)

Greenwoods Outfitting (906-863-5033; www.greenwoodsoutfitting.com; W6216 2.5 Rd., Menominee)

Northwoods Wilderness Outfitters (906-774-9009 or 1-800-530-8859; www.northwoodsoutfitters.com; N-4088 Pine Mountain Rd., Iron Mountain)

Public Land Hunting Locations

Hiawatha National Forest near Stonington, south of Rapid River, on CR 513 off US 2.
Indian Lake State Park, 8970W CR 442, Manistique
Fayette Historic State Park, 13700 13.25 Lane, Garden. Thirty miles south on MI 183 off US 2.
Ottawa National Forest, 906-932-1330, E6248 US 2, Ironwood

Cross-Country Skiing

(The trails listed here are solely for cross-country skiing. All three of the downhill skiing resorts listed farther below also offer cross-country ski trails and snowmobile trails.)

Rapid River National Cross Country Ski Trail (Hiawatha National Forest, off US 41, 6 miles north of Rapid River) One of the best cross-country ski trails in the U.P., because it is probably the most varied, both in terms of the skill level of the various trails and in terms of the scenery and topography. Five Nordic ski loops and two skating loops are available, and the trails meander in and out of dunes, lowland swamps, and pine forests.

Fumee Lake Natural Area (1-800-236-2447; www.fumeelakes.org; US 2 west of

Norway and east of Quinnesec) A few quiet, well-groomed trails make this 1,800-acre "no motors allowed" park surrounded by trees and hills a great place to spend a winter's day. Groomed trail loops wrap around Fumee Lake, Little Fumee Lake, and Indiana Mine Pond, as well as up the hill and through the forest to the north of Fumee Lake on the Fumee Mountain Trail. In addition to the groomed trails, several single-track trails run through the park. Be careful away from the lakes, as trails in these areas are near the designated hunting area and a handful of snowmobile trails.

Iron River Nordic Cross Country Ski Center (906-265-3401; www.georgeyoung.com; 159 Young's Lane, Iron River) Located in the George Young Recreational Complex, the Iron River Nordic Cross Country Ski Center includes 6 kilometers of groomed cross-country ski trails that head to nearby Wagner Lake or through the hills and woods of the recreational complex. After skiing, relax your muscles and warm up at the complex's indoor pool, spa, and sauna complex.

Downhill Skiing and Snowboarding

Ski Norway Mountain (906-563-9700 or 1-800-272-5445; www.norwaymountain.com; off US 2 east of Norway) 500-foot vertical drop, 16 runs, three lifts, terrain park, ski and board rentals, ski school, restaurant, bar, lodging.

Ski Pine Mountain (906-774-2747; www.pinemountainresort.com; N3332 Pine Mountain Rd., Iron Mountain) 500-foot vertical drop, 26 runs, four lifts, two terrain parks, ski and board rentals, ski school, restaurant, bar, lodging.

Ski Brule (906-265-4957 or 1-800-362-7853; www.skibrule.com; 397 Brule Mountain Rd., Iron River) 500-foot vertical drop, 18 runs, five lifts, terrain park, half pipe, restaurant, bar, lodging, opens early in season (by early November) and stays open late (May).

Snowmobiling

The U.P. is extremely popular with snowmobilers—its trails get written up in snowmobiling magazines, and the sport manages to get people excited about the prospect of a long

Snowmobiling draws almost as many visitors to the U.P. in winter as the beaches and waterfalls do in summer.
Paul T.

winter. The state actually maintains over 6,000 miles of groomed snowmobile trails, not out of the goodness of its heart, but because the sport generates a lot of tourism revenue. Several areas that are calm lakeside retreats in summer turn into buzzing centers of activity in the winter. Maps of the state-maintained snowmobile trails are available online from the Michigan Department of Natural Resources (www.michigan.gov/dnr).

Rentals

Fish and Hunt Shop (906-586-9531; www.fishandhuntshop.com; W. 17148 Main St., Curtis) $139–$229 a day

Trails

Nahma Grade Snowmobile Trail. Trailhead is on US 40 near CR 509, 2 miles east of Rapid River. Located in the Hiawatha National Forest, the Nahma trail is a beautiful ride that combines easily with other trails in the forest for rides of varying distances.

Curtis (1-800-OK CURTIS for trail report and information) Including 140 miles of groomed snowmobile trails around the Manistique Lakes, the Curtis system connects to the 6,000-plus-mile state snowmobile trail system, as well as other local systems, making it possible to ride between towns and areas.

Watersmeet. State Trails 2 and 3 intersect at Watersmeet, making it possible to go any direction you like from the town. The surrounding Ottawa National Forest is full of trails, but the forest's Sylvania Wilderness Area does not allow snowmobiles.

FAMILY FUN

Kitch-iti-kipi (Big Spring), Palms Book State Park (906-341-2355; from Manistique take US 2 to Thompson, then MI 149 north approximately 8 miles to park entrance) Kids and adults alike are delighted by this, one of the U.P.'s most popular attractions. The fun

Large trout congregate around the viewing boat at Big Spring, waiting to be fed by families. Matt Girvan

begins with a big wooden barge, self-propelled by a wheel in the back. Stay to the back right if you want to play captain, but make sure someone in your crew gets a spot around the center viewing area—a big hole cut in the center of the barge. As the barge creeps out over beautiful turquoise waters, giant brown trout swimming by will garner the first "wow!" followed soon thereafter by "oh wow!" as the barge approaches the bubbling spring below. Michigan's largest freshwater spring, Kitch-iti-kipi is 200 feet across and 40 feet deep. According to the state's Department of Natural Resources, over 10,000 gallons a minute gush from fissures in the underlying limestone, and the flow continues throughout the year at a constant 45 degrees Fahrenheit. Trout food is available for sale in the convenience store at the park entrance, which is probably why those trout are so big.

Fayette Historic State Park (906-644-2603; 13700 13.25 Lane, Garden) Well worth the detour off the beaten path, Fayette Historic State Park is a real-live ghost town, or at least as close as you can get to one inside a state park. Much of the former booming iron town has been carefully restored and preserved. Visitors can check out the old mine and ironworks, the former hotel, the town's tiny school, living quarters, and a giant model of Fayette as it once was. The rest of the park is well-suited to a picnic—a half-moon bay on one side is bordered by towering cliffs, and there's a pleasant and quiet sandy swimming beach next door.

Ludington Park (906-786-4141; in Escanaba, from the end of Ludington St. to 7th Ave.) A great place to spend an hour, an afternoon, or an entire day, depending on how much time you've got. Ludington Park occupies 5 miles on Little Bay de Noc at the southern end of downtown Escanaba and includes a large playground, a sandy swimming beach on a charming little island (Arnson), tennis courts, and a marina that rents bicycles. In addition to playing, picnicking, biking, or just hanging out, you might be able to catch a

The Upper Peninsula's boom and bust mining industry resulted in the creation and abandonment of several towns. Today, ghost towns like Fayette, pictured here, are tourist attractions. Matt Girvan

summer concert in the park's outdoor band shell, and the shoreline is a decent fishing spot as well.

Iron Mountain Iron Mine (906-563-8077; www.ironmountainironmine.com; US 2 in Vulcan, 9 miles east of Iron Mountain) Though it might not have been much fun to work in the mines, it sure is cool to tour them now. Armed with raincoats and hard hats—and who doesn't get a kick out of a hard hat?—families can tour the 2,600-foot East Vulcan Mine, marveling at the life the miners must have had. An underground train takes visitors into the mine in much the same way the miners would have ridden to work back in the late 1800s and early 1900s. Experienced guides point out various rocks, recount the history of the mine, and guide visitors to large man-made mine chambers called "stopes." The mine feels a bit like a Disneyland attraction now, with a huge "Big John—the world's largest miner" statue and sign out front, a gift shop selling toy pickaxes, and folksy blues mining songs playing on a loop, but it's a blast for kids, and it's interesting to learn a bit about the mining history of the area.

Pine Mountain Ski Jump (906-774-2747; www.pinemountainresort.com; N3332 Pine Mountain Rd., Iron Mountain) The best time of year to visit the ski jump is in February, during the Pine Mountain Ski Jumping tournament, when jumpers fly down the mountain and fling themselves off it, but in summer it's still fun to climb up to the top of the jump and check out the view. Just keep an eye on the little ones around the vertical drop!

Humongous Fungus (US 2, about 7 miles south of Crystal Falls) This bizarrely large honey mushroom was labeled the world's largest and possibly oldest living organism when it was discovered back in the early 1990s. Although Crystal Falls' fungus was soon sur- passed by other, larger fungi, it's still an impressive sight. The mushroom extends over 30 acres south of Horserace Rapids, just south of Crystal Falls, and is celebrated every year at

The Humongous Fungus is sometimes incorporated into local advertising, as it is here on the side of a U- Haul. The writing at the top reads: "Michigan: 37-acre Humongous Fungus." Aaron Landry

the Humongous Fungus Fest. Some people are just grossed out by a 'shroom this size, but kids usually get a real kick out of it.

Paulding Mystery Light (from US 2 at Watersmeet take MI 45 north toward Paulding; in about 5 miles the road will begin a slow bend to the right; watch for Robbins Pond Rd.—old MI 45—on the left; turn down Robbins Pond Rd. and follow it about 3/8 mile to a dead end) Even the local chamber of commerce and the National Park Service have gotten in on this piece of folklore—a mysterious light is seen in the woods here, which some believe to be supernatural, while others insist it's just headlights from a nearby road. Everyone has a different explanation for the light. The National Park Service posts a sign every summer that reads, "This is the location from which the famous Paulding Light can be observed. Legend explains its presence as a railroad brakeman's ghost, destined to remain forever at the sight of his untimely death. He continually waves his signal lantern as a warning to all who come to visit." Whether you believe in ghost stories or not, it's great fun to take the kids out to the forest for a glimpse of a friendly ghost and his mysterious light. Face north and look for the light in the distance along the power line right-of-way.

People huddle together and watch intently for the Paulding Mystery Light. Aaron Landry

SHOPPING

The U.P. isn't famous for its shopping, but that doesn't mean there's nothing worth buying up here. Many of this region's towns—Escanaba, Menominee, Manistique—are particularly good for antiques, and there are local galleries and bookshops in towns along each section of Lake Michigan's shoreline that sell items unique to the area.

Antiques

Bargain Barn Antiques (906-875-3381; 60 Superior Ave., Crystal Falls) This is a huge shop occupying an old hotel in charming downtown Crystal Falls. You could easily spend all day here—the Bargain Barn sells both the store's own collection and has stalls filled with collectibles from outside dealers as well. The name is no mistake; they actually do have a number of bargains here.

    Timeless Treasures Antiques & Collectibles (906-864-2412, 902 2nd St., Menominee) It seems fitting that an antiques mall should occupy a 1920s theater. A trip to Timeless Treasures is worth it just to check out the building, but you're bound to find at least some small trinket in the mountains of collectibles for sale here from dozens of dealers.

    Traders' Point Antique Mall (906-341-7500; www.traderspointantiques.com; 375 Traders' Point Dr., Manistique) A high-quality antiques mall in Manistique, adjacent to a bookshop and the popular Upper Crust Café, Traders' Point is just as jam-packed full of stuff as the average antiques mall, but it's smaller and feels less cluttered. You get the feeling that everything here has been placed where it is for a reason, not just thrown together in the usual antiques jumble. And the prices are generally very good. Traders' Point also sells a number of antiques available only in this neck of the woods, including local artwork and Munising woodenware.

Bookstores

Aurora Books (906-863-5266; www.aurorabooks.com; 625 First St., Menominee) A fantastic independent bookstore housed in a charming old brick building on the waterfront in downtown Menominee, Aurora sells both new and used books and a few collectible rare books as well. Even if you're not in the market for a new book, the store is worth a visit just to check out the local art and historical photographs lining its walls.

    Canterbury Bookstore (906-786-0751; 908 Ludington St., Escanaba) A small, independent, and locally owned bookshop selling new books in a variety of categories, Canterbury is a good stop if you're looking for a regional history or nature book. The shop also carries a number of regional hiking and nature guides and a unique assortment of Scandinavian books.

Gift and Specialty Shops

Art & Décor (906-864-7243; 601 First St., Menominee) Occupying a historic building on a corner of downtown Menominee, this spacious, light-filled gallery and home gift shop is full of unique finds, from local and international painting, sculpture, ceramics, and photography to cool home finds like recycled glass tumblers, unusual lamps, and handmade candles.

    Central Arts & Gifts (906-265-2114, 216 W. Genesee St., Iron River) This cute store in quaint and sleepy downtown Iron River offers a really wide variety of things—a good assortment of north country gifts, a gallery with sculpture and artwork from around the world, various collectibles (Beanie Babies, glass ornaments, and the like), some jewelry, and a few shelves full of books written by local authors and poets, as well as an assortment of cookbooks.

    Noc Bay Trading Company (906-789-0505; www.nocbay.com; 1133 Washington Ave., Escanaba) It is highly unlikely that you've ever set foot in a store similar to the Noc Bay Trading Company. A regular stop for local Native Americans in preparation for the regional powwows, the shop is full of everything that goes into the dance costumes, music, and revelry of a powwow, from buckskin and beads to drum parts to traditional Native American music, with plenty of history and information to make it an absolutely fascinating shop. The store's "Learning Circle" has compiled detailed instructions for various costumes and items and made them available to its customers both in the store and on its Web site. Visiting the store is an experience not to be missed!

Sayklly's Confectionery and Gifts (906-786-1524; www.saykllyscandy.com; 1304 Ludington St., Escanaba) That fantastic smell that candy stores have only gets better with age, as evidenced by the overpoweringly delicious aroma emanating from Sayklly's in downtown Escanaba. A local tradition since 1906, the shop's hand-dipped chocolates and chewy saltwater taffy are popular gifts both locally and beyond. Although you can get the same quality sweets at the family's other location in the Delta Plaza Mall, shopping at the original storefront downtown is a far more enjoyable affair.

Vintage Sundries (906-774-1324; 101 W. A St., Iron Mountain) An electric blue shop with orange trim selling fun and funky retro-styled gifts and, well, sundries in surprisingly groovy downtown Iron Mountain.

CULTURE

Although the U.P. is prized today for its natural beauty and vast array of outdoor sporting options, it is not a land devoid of museums or libraries. In fact, the U.P. is surprisingly diverse, culturally, for a region that is a bit removed and not incredibly developed. Owing to its industrial past, a lot of money was spent at one point on architecture in various parts of the peninsula. In the Lake Michigan region, lumber, iron, and fishing barons built mansions on the waterfront and contributed to picturesque downtowns complete with well-designed libraries and city halls.

The industrial era also brought immigrants to this part of the U.P. from all over the world, which resulted in a lively ethnic mix that continues to color the cultural landscape, as descendants of Italian, Scandinavian, German, and Eastern European iron and lumber workers celebrate their heritage today with museums, restaurants, events, and traditional folk music.

And of course before industry or immigrants shaped the local culture, a large Native American population called the shores of Lake Michigan home. Their rituals, celebration, and artwork continue to have a prominent place in the region today.

Historic Buildings and Sites

Escanaba Carnegie Library (First Ave. and Seventh St., Escanaba) We're not listing this under libraries because it is now a private home, but this 1902 beauty was originally built as a Carnegie Library, one of the over 2,000 public libraries donated by Scottish industrialist and philanthropist Andrew Carnegie. Visitors are not allowed inside, but there's no law against gawking at its neoclassical columns from the street and wondering what it would be like to live in a 106-year-old library.

Fayette Historic State Park (906-644-2603; 13700 13.25 Lane, Garden) The preserved and restored buildings of this iron-boom-town-turned-ghost-town are a fascinating glimpse into life as it was. See "Recreation: Family Fun" for more details.

Lighthouses

Peninsula Point Lighthouse (from US 2 east of Rapid River take CR 513 south approximately 18 miles to Stonington) After the keeper's quarters burned in 1959, Hiawatha National Park officials decided to remove the debris and any glass around the remaining

Sand Point Lighthouse, Ludington Park, Escanaba. Heidi Hansen

light tower and open it to the public. Visitors can climb the spiral staircase to the top for terrific 360-degree views of the lake, the bay, various islands, and the nearby Garden peninsula. In August and September thousands of migrating monarch butterflies stop here to rest on their way to Mexico. It's also a good spot for migrating birds to take a breather, which makes bird-watching here spectacular in the spring.

Sand Point Lighthouse (Ludington Park, Escanaba) A picturesque New England–style lighthouse, painted bright white with a red roof, the Sand Point Lighthouse was decommissioned in 1939 and completely restored by the county historical society in the 1980s. Now, summertime visitors can check out the restored keeper's quarters and climb the stairs to the top of the tower for a view across Little Bay de Noc that includes Escanaba's marina and a glimpse of the Peninsula Point lighthouse across the bay.

Museums and Galleries

East Ludington Gallery
906-786-0300
www.eastludingtongallery.com
619 Ludington St., Escanaba
Open: Mon.–Sat. 11–5
Admission: Free

Housed in a pleasant redbrick building, this co-op gallery showcases the work of 35 local artists, including everything from photography to painting, wood carving, pottery, glass, jewelry, and ceramics. Although pleasant just to browse through, this is also a great place to look for unique gifts from the area, priced in a wide range from completely affordable to big splurge.

(William) Bonifas Fine Arts Center
906-786-3833
www.bonifasarts.org
700 First Ave. South, Escanaba
Open: Tue.–Fri. 10–5:30, Sat. 10–3
Admission: Free

Located in a former church school and gymnasium donated by the Irish-born widow of William Bonifas, a lumberman from Luxembourg who made his fortune in the U.P., the Bonifas Fine Arts Center hosts a rotating schedule of exhibits focused predominantly on local artists, with the occasional international exhibit thrown in. The center also offers numerous art classes, ranging from beginning-level classes in a variety of media to youth art classes to advanced classes for working artists. Members of the center get a discount on classes, but they're very reasonably priced to begin with. The design of the center itself is reason enough for a visit—the original Romanesque-style exterior of the church school and gym has been restored, and the interior has been completely renovated and modernized to house the center's administrative offices, climate-controlled galleries, artist studios, a pottery studio, and a theater.

Menominee County Heritage Museum
906-863-9000
www.menomineehistoricalsociety.org
904 11th Ave., Menominee
Open: Memorial Day to Labor Day, Mon.–Sat., 10–4:30
Admission: Donations welcome

This popular history museum's ornate eaves and stained-glass windows seem better suited to a church than a museum, which makes sense—the building, which is on the National Register of Historic Buildings, was formerly St. John's Catholic Church. Today this large red and white structure houses the summer-only museum's collection of photographs, paintings, artifacts, and ephemera. Popular exhibits include an animated model circus, dugout canoes from the Menominee Indians, and photos of early Polish, Scandinavian, and German immigrants to the area.

Menominee Range Historical Museum
906-774-4276
www.menomineemuseum.com
300 E. Ludington St., Iron Mountain
Open: Memorial Day to Labor Day, Mon.–Sat., 10–4
Admission: $4 children, $8 adults for both Menominee Range Historical Museum and Cornish Pump Museum

A stately Carnegie library built in 1901 is now home to over 100 exhibits showcasing life in Iron Country during the 1800s and 1900s, including an exact replica of an 1800s classroom, a full livery stable complete with horse carriages, and a hands-on general store stocked with typical goods from a bygone era. In addition to its permanent exhibits, the museum hosts a series of rotating exhibits. The building itself is large and beautiful, with imposing white columns and a balcony overlooking the front lawn. Next door, its sister Cornish Pump Museum contains the largest steam-driven pumping engine built in the United States.

Native American Art and History

Harbour House Museum
906-875-4341
17 N. 4th St., Crystal Falls
Open: Memorial Day to Labor Day, Tue.–Sat., 11–4
Admission: $3 person / $6 family

Open only in the summer, this painstakingly restored Victorian house is a lot of fun to explore. Surprisingly, although it does hold a few steamer trunks filled with *Great Gatsby*–style garments of the area's ladies, the most complete collection in the house is in the Ojibwa room, where the traditional handicrafts and clothing of a local Ojibwa family are on display.

   Pentoga Park (www.pentogapark.net; 1630 CR 424, Crystal Falls) A pretty park on the south shore of Chicaugon Lake is also a preserved Ojibwa burial ground, complete with traditional wooden burial structures known as spirit houses. Dedicated in 1922 in honor of the Ojibwa tribe, the park is named, sort of, after the wife of the local tribal chief at the time, Chief Edward (his real name was Mush-Quo-No-Ns-Bi). His wife's name was Biindigeyaasinokwe, shortened to Biindige and mispronounced by the newcomers as Pentoga, meaning bullhead.

NIGHTLIFE

8th Street Coffeehouse (906-789-9174; www.8thstreetcoffeehouse.com; 720 Ludington St., Escanaba) If you leave the 8th Street Coffeehouse feeling anything short of enchanted, go back inside awhile—you need some more of their medicine. In addition to fantastic coffee that puts Starbucks to shame, 8th Street is a buzzing, happy hub for everyone from local retirees to young artists and writers. On weekends and Tuesday nights, the coffee shop is also a live music venue, and in fact with so many local musicians hanging out here, it's not unusual to hear live music that hasn't been scheduled. The café keeps a well-stocked game shelf as well, and the service revolves around the motto "Come as a stranger, leave as a friend."

Escanaba's 8th Street Coffeehouse is a popular meeting place, with live music most weekends. Marjorie O'Brien

SEASONAL EVENTS

JANUARY
Portage Anglers' Ice Fishing Derby, Curtis; 906-586-3700

FEBRUARY
Continental Cup Ski Jump Competition, Iron Mountain
Jig-It Ice Fishing Extravaganza, Gladstone; 906-786-2192
Winter Carnival, Curtis; 906-586-3700

MAY
Walleye Jamboree, Curtis; 906-586-3454

JUNE
Michigan Free Fishing Weekend. U.P.-wide, all lakes, fishing license fees waived.
Pine Mountain Music Festival, Iron Mountain; 906-482-1542
U.P. Championship Rodeo, Iron River; 906-265-5954

JULY
Art Impressions Art & Craft Show, Land O'Lakes, WI; 906-358-9961
Bass Festival, Iron River; 906-265-3822
Brown Trout Derby, Menominee; 906-863-8498
Folk Fest, Manistique; 906-341-5010

AUGUST
Dickinson County Fair, Norway; 906-774-2002
Fayette Historic State Park Heritage Days, Garden; 906-644-2603
Humongous Fungus Fest, Crystal Falls; 906-265-3822
Iron County Fair, Iron River; 906-265-3822
Upper Peninsula State Fair, Escanaba; 906-786-4011
Waterfront Art Festival, Escanaba; 906-786-3102
Waterfront Festival, Menominee; 906-863-8498

SEPTEMBER
Art on the Lake, Curtis; 906-586-3700
Cabela's Last-Chance Walleye Tournament, Gladstone; 906-786-6992
Great North Winds "Honor Our Warriors" Traditional Pow-Wow, Manistique; 906-359-4645
Harvest Festival, Crystal Falls; 906-265-3822
Menominee River Bass Tournament, Iron Mountain; 1-800-236-2447
U.P. Steam & Gas Engine Show, Escanaba; 906-474-9247

OCTOBER
Country Fair Craft Show, Escanaba; 906-786-8537
Potato Fest, Crystal Falls; 906-265-3822

NOVEMBER
Calico Christmas Craft Show, Escanaba; 906-786-8537
Christmas Tree Galleria, Caspian; 906-265-2617
Old-Fashioned Christmas, Gladstone; 906-399-5651

DECEMBER

Christmas in the Village, Escanaba; 906-786-2192
Downtown Christmas Walk, Iron Mountain; 877-324-5244
Holiday Lights Parade, Iron River; 906-265-3822
Sandpoint Lighthouse Holiday Open House, Sandpoint; 906-789-6790

Pictured Rocks National Lakeshore is one of Michigan's most visited sights. Matt Girvan

4

Lake Superior

Northern Exposure—Mountains, Moose, Woods, and Pictured Rocks

In the Ojibwa language, Lake Superior is not "Gitche Gumee" as Henry Wadsworth Longfellow called it in his celebrated poem "The Song of Hiawatha," but rather "Gichigami," which means "big water." No matter what language you're using . . . or misusing . . . there has never been a lake so aptly named—Lake Superior and its shores are superlative in every way. With the largest surface area of any freshwater lake in the world, Lake Superior inspires awe even in those who have lived their whole lives on its shores. But don't let its clear, blue, and sometimes-placid waters fool you: Superior has claimed no fewer than 350 boats, and counting, many of which make for fascinating scuba dives today.

In addition to Superior's infamous shipwrecks, the lake's shores are also home to the U.P.'s most-visited national park (the vividly beautiful Pictured Rocks National Lakeshore), the U.P.'s largest city (Marquette), and the U.S.'s least-visited national park (the wild and magical Isle Royale). Deer are as plentiful here as they are throughout the U.P., but the Lake Superior hinterland is also known for more elusive woodland animals—gray wolves and moose. Catching sight of either is a rare gift.

Sprawling west past Wisconsin to touch Minnesota's eastern shore and north all the way up to Ontario, Lake Superior touches no fewer than 9 of the U.P.'s 13 counties, forming a watery northern border for the state of Michigan. This chapter covers the shores of Lake Superior from west to east—Ironwood and the Gogebic Range, Ontonagon and the Porkies, Isle Royale, the Keweenaw Peninsula, Marquette and the Marquette Range, and Au Train, Munising, and Pictured Rocks—stopping short of where the lake does to leave the attractions surrounding Whitefish Bay and the Straits of Mackinac for other chapters. As with the lake itself, the shores that surround it are too expansive and varied to cover in one fell swoop.

Ironwood and the Gogebic Range

Promoted as Big Snow Country in the winter, the westernmost region of the U.P. is also known, understandably, as Waterfall Country in the summer when all that snow melts. According to the local tourism bureau, the region boasts 22 easily visited waterfalls, the most remarkable of which include the Presque Isle and Black River Falls in the Ottawa National Forest, and the Superior Falls on the Montreal River, which forms a border between Michigan and Wisconsin. The sister cities of Ironwood, Michigan, and Hurley, Wisconsin, on either side of the Montreal River are the most lively towns in the area—both

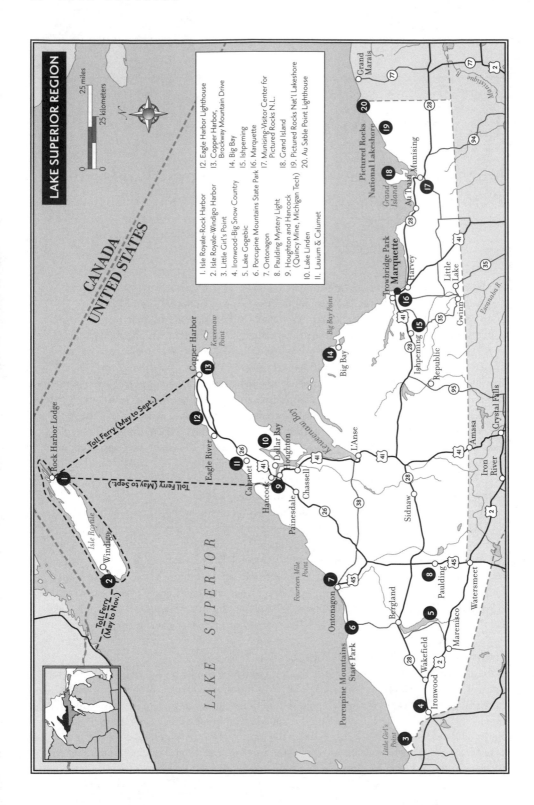

LAKE SUPERIOR REGION

25 miles
25 kilometers

1. Isle Royale-Rock Harbor
2. Isle Royale-Windigo Harbor
3. Little Girl's Point
4. Ironwood-Big Snow Country
5. Lake Gogebic
6. Porcupine Mountains State Park
7. Ontonagon
8. Paulding Mystery Light
9. Houghton and Hancock
   (Quincy Mine, Michigan Tech)
10. Lake Linden
11. Lauium & Calumet
12. Eagle Harbor Lighthouse
13. Copper Harbor,
    Brockway Mountain Drive
14. Big Bay
15. Ishpeming
16. Marquette
17. Munising-Visitor Center for
    Pictured Rocks N.L.
18. Grand Island
19. Pictured Rocks Nat'l Lakeshore
20. Au Sable Point Lighthouse

CANADA
UNITED STATES

Toll Ferry (May to Sept.)
Toll Ferry (May to Sept.)
Toll Ferry (May to Nov.)

Rock Harbor Lodge

Isle Royale

Windigo

LAKE SUPERIOR

Fourteen Mile Point

Little Girl's Point

Keweenaw Point

Copper Harbor

Eagle River

Keweenaw Bay

Dollar Bay
Houghton
Hancock
Calumet
Painesdale
Chassell
L'Anse

Big Bay Point

Big Bay

Grand Marais

Pictured Rocks National Lakeshore

Grand Island

Au Train
Munising

Trowbridge Park
Marquette
Harvey

Little Lake
Gwinn

Ishpeming
Republic

Sidnaw

Amasa

Iron River

Crystal Falls

Escanaba R.

Menominee R.

Porcupine Mountains State Park

Ontonagon

Bergland

Paulding

Wakefield

Marenisco

Watersmeet

Ironwood

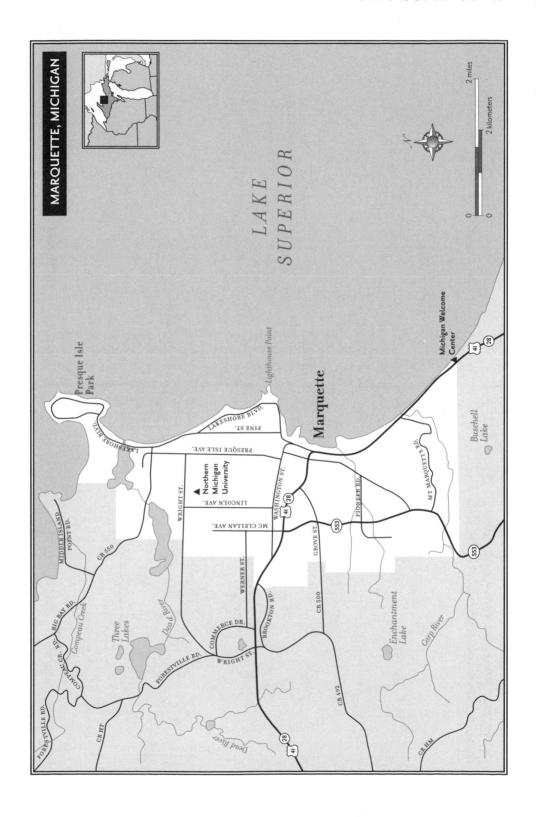

MARQUETTE, MICHIGAN

LAKE SUPERIOR

Presque Isle Park

Lighthouse Point

LAKESHORE BLVD.

Marquette

Michigan Welcome Center

Buschell Lake

2 miles
2 kilometers

LAKESHORE BLVD.

PINE ST.

PRESQUE ISLE AVE.

Northern Michigan University

WRIGHT ST.

LINCOLN AVE.

WASHINGTON ST.

MC CLELLAN AVE.

MT MARQUETTE RD.

PIONEER RD.

GROVE ST.

MIDDLE ISLAND POINT RD.

CR 550

Compeau Creek

Dead River

WERNER ST.

BROOKTON RD.

CR 500

Enchantment Lake

Carp River

553

Three Lakes

COMMERCE DR.

WRIGHT ST.

FORESTVILLE RD.

COMPEAU CR. RD.

BIG BAY RD.

CR HT

FORESTVILLE RD.

Dead River

CR 492

CR HM

553

41 28

41 28

41 28

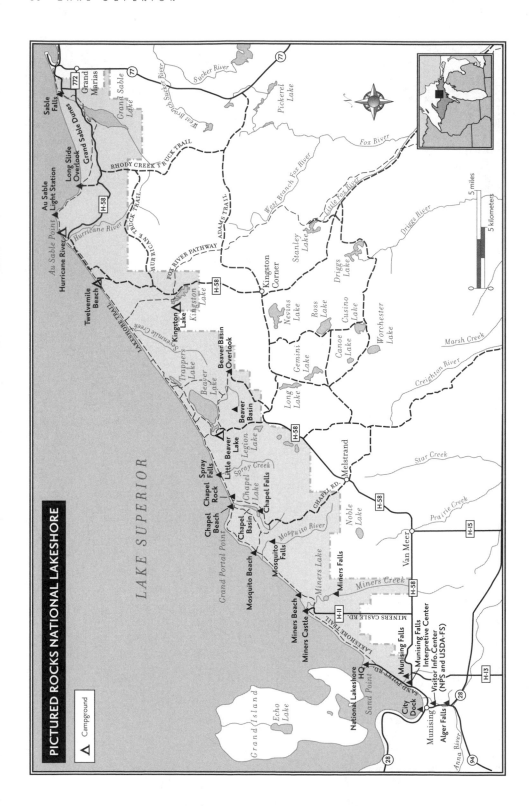

PICTURED ROCKS NATIONAL LAKESHORE

△ Campground

LAKE SUPERIOR

are populated primarily by the Finnish, Italian, and Eastern European ancestors of various immigrant mine workers. With the mines closed, their offspring have found their livelihoods in restaurants, stores, and cafés that are kept afloat by locals but are more than welcoming to visitors as well.

Inland from Lake Superior, Lake Gogebic is the U.P.'s largest inland lake. Warm and swimmable much earlier in the year than Superior, Lake Gogebic is also a prime fishing lake, which explains why it is ringed with cottages and campgrounds that draw regular visitors every summer. In the fall the colors surrounding the lake rival even those of New England, and in winter snowmobilers have free rein of hundreds of miles of snowmobile trails.

Ontonagon and the Porkies

Possibly the most underappreciated region of the U.P., Ontonagon and Porcupine Mountain State Park ("the Porkies") are often passed over by visitors in favor of more popular sights such as Pictured Rocks, Tahquamenon Falls, and Mackinac Island. Locals, however, know better. The park is Michigan's largest, with 60,000-odd acres of forest, over half of it virgin. Some of the U.P.'s most beautiful views can be had here; the region's mountains contain dozens of fantastic hikes; the lakeshore is sandy, pleasant, and rarely crowded; and there is no better spot in the U.P. to see fall color. In the winter, cross-country skiers are delighted by woodland paths and panoramic lake views, while skiers and snowboarders get a kick out of some of Michigan's highest mountains. The only real town in the area is sleepy, pleasant Ontonagon. If you're looking for a wide selection of restaurants, hotels, and entertainment options, this probably isn't the spot for you. If, however, you're looking to head off the beaten path a bit, hike, backpack, and immerse yourself in nature, look no further.

Falls along the Black River. Matt Girvan

Isle Royale

There's wilderness and then there's wilderness. Isle Royale, which holds the dubious honor of being the least visited park in the National Park System, is a six-hour, 73-mile journey from Houghton Harbor at the base of the Keweenaw Peninsula, and a three-hour, 56-mile voyage from Copper Harbor, at the northernmost tip of the Keweenaw Peninsula. Once you dock, however, this 45-mile-long, 10-mile-wide island is essentially all yours. Visitors are welcome to explore as much or as little of the island as they like—hard-core backpackers head for the farthest corners of the island, exploring its shores, caves, falls, streams, forest, and wildlife. Tent campers set up camp at one of the campgrounds near Rock Harbor, or hike farther into the woods for more privacy. And, for those who require a real bed and a hot shower, the Rock Harbor Lodge offers 60 guest rooms, each with two beds, a private bath, and a choice view of Lake Superior. Boaters and paddlers love Isle Royale almost as much as hikers and backpackers do—the island's many inland lakes, bays, and streams provide countless miles of paddling, and kayakers can just bring their camps along with them, making their way around and through the park easily.

Because of its remote location and near-total lack of development, Isle Royale is an ideal place to study nature and wildlife. The longest-running large mammal predator study on earth is the ongoing study of the gray wolves on Isle Royale. You may come across one of the subjects of this study if you're very quiet and catch it off-guard. Equally elusive moose abound on Isle Royale to such an extent that they have become a sort of mascot for the island. Head to one of the bays in the early morning for the best chance of spotting one. Keep in mind that it gets cold here even in the summer months, especially the closer you get to Lake Superior. It is not uncommon to need long pants and a fleece on Isle Royale in July.

Isle Royale's wilderness was once home to copper mines, first excavated by so-called "Old Copper Indians."
Matt Girvan

The Keweenaw Peninsula

This is the heart of Copper Country, and all those early copper millionaires sure did know how to put a town together. From Houghton and Hancock at the base of the peninsula, to Calumet and Laurium in the middle, to Copper Harbor at the northernmost point, the Keweenaw is chock-full of darling towns, beautifully designed buildings, and great views.

At one point the Keweenaw was the world's largest supplier of copper, a fact that drew to its mines thousands of immigrants, primarily of Finnish, Italian, and Eastern European descent. As with the U.P.'s various other former mining regions, the descendants of those immigrants still call the Keweenaw home and have woven their food, music, and culture into the fabric of the remaining towns.

Houghton—which is so close to nearby Hancock that most people just run the names together and think of them as one town—is the U.P.'s "other" university town. Though Northern Michigan University in Marquette is better known, Michigan Technological University in Houghton is well respected for producing world-class engineers. It was established to train mining engineers but quickly broadened its scope and has grown into a highly regarded university. And Houghton is the better for it—the students have given the town a young, but smart, vibe that's enjoyable and has a way of making the small town seem much more urban than it is.

Marquette and the Marquette Range

Though the area farther south of Marquette is known as Iron Country, this is where iron was truly king, pumping money and people into the area for years and producing some of the world's highest-quality iron. The town of Marquette was once a busy shipping port for both iron and sandstone from local quarries, tinged red by the iron ore and called "brown-stone" when it arrived to builders in Boston and New York. As with the other mining centers throughout the U.P., Marquette's iron business drew immigrant laborers from all over

Lake Superior beach near Marquette. Marjorie O'Brien

Europe, with a high proportion of British (mostly from Cornwall), Finnish, Canadian, Scandinavian, and Italian immigrants. The descendants of those miners have created a lively and unique culture in modern-day Marquette.

And, though the mines are mostly closed, this is one of the few areas of the U.P. that has remained economically prosperous. Northern Michigan University's campus in Marquette draws just under 10,000 young people to the town every fall. As in most college towns, the students keep a number of bars, cafés, restaurants, and stores open in downtown Marquette. The campus isn't the only draw—the area's lakeshore is one of the loveliest in the U.P., with 3-billion-year-old rock outcroppings and long stretches of white sand backed by large forests and rolling dunes that make it popular with families in the summer months and cross-country skiers in winter.

Au Train, Munising, and Pictured Rocks

This little stretch of Lake Superior's coast may be the highlight of a spectacular lakeshore—world-class trout fishing in Au Train, world-famous wildlife viewing in the Seney National Wildlife Refuge, and the unparalleled beauty of Pictured Rocks National Lakeshore.

Of course, because of all its charms, this area is inundated with visitors in the summer, but even still there's plenty of space. In addition to being the home base for the Pictured Rocks boat cruises (the only real way to see the Pictured Rocks is from the water), Munising offers several great beaches, hikes, and waterfalls, and a charming little downtown.

Birders come from all over the world in the hopes of spotting a rare species in the Seney National Wildlife Refuge, and a large portion of the Munising area is within the boundaries of the Hiawatha National Forest. In winter, a number of cross-country and snowmobile trails bring a second tourism season to the area, and those same trails are popular with mountain bikers in the summer months.

LODGING

Lodging options really vary throughout this region. Ontonagon and the Porcupine Mountains are best experienced on a camping trip, but there are a handful of hotels available as well. The Keweenaw Peninsula is loaded with historic homes that have been converted into B&Bs and lodges. Marquette offers everything from backwoods cross-country ski lodges to a swank downtown boutique hotel. And although Munising, despite its proximity to Pictured Rocks, has a bizarre shortage of charming lodging options, better options abound within a few shoreline miles in either direction from the town. Despite its reputation as the ultimate wilderness escape, Isle Royale offers a pleasant 60-room lodge in addition to its various campgrounds.

Lodging options are listed here by region in alphabetical order. We recommend all the lodging options included here but have indicated particularly special spots with a star. Camping options are included as a separate section at the end of the regular lodging listings.

Lodging Prices

Prices listed are based on a per-room, double-occupancy rate. Price ranges run from low off-season rates to higher summer rates.

Credit Cards

AE: American Express

D: Discover

MC: MasterCard

V: Visa

AU TRAIN, MUNISING, AND PICTURED ROCKS

★ Falling Rock Lodge on Powell Lake

Owners: Jeff and Nancy Dwyer

906-387-1623

E9004 Powell Lake Rd., Wetmore, MI 49895

From Munising take MI 28 south, turn right on National Forest Road 13, then right on Powell Lake Rd.

Price: $125 a night, two-night minimum

Credit Cards: Not accepted

Handicapped Access: Yes

Open: Year-round

Owned and operated by the owners of the popular Falling Rock Café and Bookstore in nearby Munising, the Falling Rock Lodge is a lovely, newish red cedar two-bedroom with a green metal roof and a deck looking out over spring-fed Powell Lake in the Hiawatha National Forest. The house is as cozy and delightful as the Dwyers' café, with a large picture window overlooking the lake, handmade quilts on all the beds, big overstuffed armchairs, and a delightful tree house in the backyard. The Dwyers have stocked the lodge with bicycles for exploring the forest, along with a kayak, a rowboat, and fishing equipment. Satellite TV, a DVD player, and high-speed wireless Internet will keep anyone from missing the modern world too much, and the lodge comes with a basket full of coffee from the Dwyers' café, along with baked goods for breakfast and coupons for use at the café.

★ Pinewood Lodge

Owners: Jerry and Jenny Krieg

906-892-8300

www.pinewoodlodgebnb.com

pinewood@tds.net

P.O. Box 176, Au Train, MI 49806

MI 28, 2 miles west of Au Train

Price: $120–$165

Credit Cards: D, MC, V

Handicapped Access: Yes

Open: Apr.–Nov.

A lovely log cabin resort on the shores of Lake Superior, the Pinewood Lodge caters to adults, primarily couples looking to get away. In addition to seven rooms, all with knotty pine interior, large and comfy pine-log beds, private baths, and TV/VCR units, and most with lovely Lake Superior views, the resort boasts a bright and cheerful garden full of flowers, adjacent to a gazebo on the bluff overlooking the lake. There are few better places in the area to watch the sun set over the lake. Even hammocks and pillows are supplied. Pinewood is also in the enviable position of being spitting distance from the deservedly famous Brownstone Inn, the best restaurant for several miles.

Rock River Beach Resort

Owner: Peter Braamse

906-892-8112

E4002 MI 28, Au Train, MI 49806

On MI 28, 6 miles west of Au Train

Price: $80

Credit Cards: Not accepted

Handicapped Access: Limited

Open: Apr.–Nov.

Eight large and pleasant summer cottages frame a small beach where the Rock River flows into Lake Superior. All but one of the cottages face Lake Superior, with terrific views, and a large shared patio is outfitted with rocking chairs for guests to watch the sunset or the northern lights. The cottages themselves are finished in knotty pine and feature modern country furnishings—very comfortable, but don't expect things like TV and wireless here. Rock River is all about getting outside. The resort's beach is half sandy, half rocky, with great fishing and kayaking available a few steps out your front door. In addition to immediately available recreation, the resort is conveniently close to Pictured Rocks, Au Train, and Munising.

Timber Ridge Motel Suites and Lodge

Owners: The Nolans—Terry, Janice, Mike, and Mary Sue
906-387-3790
N4045 Buckhorn Rd., Munising, MI, 49862
On Hovey Lake south of MI 94 West and less than 10 miles from Munising
Price: $59–$89
Credit Cards: D, MC, V
Handicapped Access: Limited
Open: Year-round

Although built with snowmobilers in mind—Timber Ridge is located on a trail and provides access to over 300 miles of other trails—these large and comfy suites in the Hiawatha National Forest are a real find during other seasons as well. Called motel suites, the rooms are really more like condos, each with its own private deck overlooking Hovey Lake. The view is pretty spectacular any time of year, but especially when framed by the fiery red and glowing gold leaves of fall. Though the place feels completely cut off from the rest of the world, it's only a quarter mile to the nearest restaurant, and 10 miles to Munising, making it an ideal home base for summer travelers looking to take in some of the local sights. In the winter, in addition to snowmobiling, one of the region's best cross-country ski trails is within walking distance, and Timber Ridge provides a

heated repair shed, plus a sauna to warm and soothe muscles at the end of the day.

IRONWOOD AND THE GOGEBIC RANGE

★ Black River Crossing B&B

Owners: Stan and Sue Carr
906-932-2604
www.blackrivercrossing.com
info@blackrivercrossing.com
N11485 Hedberg Rd.
Bessemer, MI 49911-9733
From Bessemer (just east of Ironwood) drive 1 mile west on US 2 and turn right (north) onto Powderhorn Rd. Follow Powderhorn Rd. north for 3 miles—the road ends at Black River Rd. (CR 513). Turn right and travel about 1 mile east, down a steep hill. At the bottom of the hill turn left (north) onto Hedberg Rd. Cross the Black River. Look for the log house one block up the hill on the left.
Price: $125–$159
Credit Cards: MC, V
Handicapped Access: Limited (two of three rooms)
Open: Year-round

This is about as swanky as log cabins get. Three rooms, each with a private bath, occupy this large and beautiful log home just a short walk away from the Black River. Rooms are lovely, with log walls, big comfy custom wood beds decorated with the dark greens and cranberries typical of the north woods. High-quality handmade wooden furnishings add to the coziness. Bathrooms are all done in marble, and two of the three rooms (Black River Waterfalls Room and Black River Pines Room) have whirlpool tubs. The same two rooms also feature private fireplaces, and two more fireplaces are located in the house's shared areas. All the rooms also have wireless Internet access and TVs with cable and DVD—a nod to the high-tech side of the computer consultant owners. In addition to sitting rooms with fireplaces, the B&B has a game room with foosball and board games, a wood-fired Finnish sauna, a landscaped garden with a waterfall pond, and bikes, snowshoes, and cross-country skis for rent. Breakfast is a warm and hearty, home-cooked affair, and the Carrs also invite their guests for evening drinks every night. In addition to its proximity to its namesake Black River, where trout fishing and kayaking are great, the B&B is in a great bird-watching zone, and within short driving distance to the popular Big Powderhorn ski resort, as well as nearby waterfalls and the many attractions of the Ottawa National Forest.

Historic Copper House

1-800-822-7768
www.sandcounty.com
sandcnty@midplains.net
Bessemer, MI (call for directions upon
    booking)
Price: $200–$400 (three-night minimum)
Credit Cards: MC, V
Handicapped Access: No
Open: Year-round

This darling restored five-bedroom Victorian painted bright blue with white trim is a private home vacation rental available all year round. An ideal hub for a group ski vacation or a family summer vacation, the house is located in the town of Bessemer, just three minutes from Big Powderhorn ski resort, five minutes from Indianhead ski resort, and 15 minutes from the popular ABR cross-country ski trails. The Copper House has four full bathrooms, four porches, a wood-burning fireplace, and rooms full of antiques, ranging from early Victorian to retro 1960s. Copper is worked into various design details throughout the house. Visitors can walk to a variety of stores and eateries in downtown Bessemer, and it's just a half hour's drive to the Porkies.

Indianhead Mountain Ski Resort and Conference Center

1-800-346-3426
www.indianheadmtn.com
info@indianheadmtn.com
500 Indianhead Rd., Wakefield, MI 49968
Off US 2 in Wakefield
Price: $58–$215
Credit Cards: AE, D, MC, V
Handicapped Access: Yes
Open: Year-round

Indianhead is a large, modern full-service ski resort with a wide variety of lodging options. In addition to the 22 runs and nine lifts on the mountain, Indianhead has a 46-room main lodge with fairly large rooms decorated in the usual north country colors (dark green and cranberry) with a number of Native American design accents. The resort also has several free-standing chalets available for rent that sleep anywhere from 4 to 12 people and a complex of fairly new, modern condos in one-, two-, three-, and four-bedroom layouts. For the best blend of value and comfort, we suggest the Trailside Condos for their spacious layout, updated decor, saunas, and hot tubs. Neither the condos nor the chalets get maid service, but guests at both have access to all of the lodge amenities, including an indoor pool, fitness club, sauna, and game room. The Lodge Restaurant, popular with locals and guests alike, serves dinner nightly in a large renovated swayback barn, while Dudley's Saloon serves as an après-ski or sun hot spot. In addition to the ski slopes, Indianhead provides a number of activities for guests, especially for families with children. In the summer the resort maintains numerous bike trails, a nine-hole golf course, and outdoor tennis courts.

ISLE ROYALE

Rock Harbor Lodge

906-337-4993 or 1-888-644-2003
www.rockharborlodge.com
Rock Harbor, Isle Royale
Price: $209–$360
Credit Cards: MC, V
Handicapped Access: Limited (some
 ground-floor lodge rooms)
Open: May 25–Sep. 7

Rock Harbor Lodge is the only lodging facility on Isle Royale (campgrounds are listed under "Camping"), which goes a long way toward explaining why its room rates are some of the highest in the U.P. Fortunately it's also a very pleasant, well-kept lodge, the best aspect of which is the Lake Superior views from every one of its 60 rooms. All-inclusive packages that include room, three meals a day, and half-day use of a canoe are available. In addition to the views, each lodge room has two beds and a private bath. Twenty duplex house-keeping cottages are also available. Each cottage sleeps up to six people and comes equipped with a kitchenette, dishwasher, utensils, electric heat, double bed and bunk bed, linens and towels, and private bath.

THE KEWEENAW PENINSULA

★ Bella Vista Motel & Cottages

Hosts: Rebecca Braun, Mike and Judy Jukuri
1-877-888-8439
www.bellavistamotel.com
info@bellavistamotel.com
P.O. Box 26, Copper Harbor, MI 49918
Price: $48–$89
Credit Cards: MC, V
Handicapped Access: Cottages and ground-
 floor motel rooms
Open: Mid-May through mid-Oct.

A quaint red-with-white-trim motel that fits exactly with Copper Harbor's whole vibe, the Bella Vista offers cute, basic rooms in one of the loveliest settings on the Keweenaw Peninsula. Most of the motel rooms offer a view of a lovely rock garden dotted with bright wildflowers in the spring and summer that stand out nicely against the deep blue of the lake just beyond. Even those without a view of the garden have a harbor view, and all have windows and slid-ing doors leading out to decks—sometimes shared, sometimes private. All guests also have access to free wireless Internet serv-ice. The cottages are darling vintage num-bers, some of which have been renovated recently, others of which could probably use an overhaul. Only some of the cottages face the water—others are closer to the road and have no real view, so be sure to ask for a lakefront cottage if you opt for the privacy of the cottages over the motel. The Bella Vista is within walking distance of the Isle Royale Ferry dock and various Copper Harbor restaurants. A picnic area on the lake side of the motel is probably the most picturesque picnic spot in Copper Harbor.

★ Dapple-Gray Bed & Breakfast

Owners: Ole and Ruth Van Goor
906-289-4200
www.dapple-gray.com
ruth@dapple-gray.com
13640 MI 26, Eagle Harbor, MI 49950
Price: $209–$360
Credit Cards: MC, V
Handicapped Access: Limited (some
 ground-floor lodge rooms)
Open: May 25–Sep. 7

A bed-and-breakfast is the perfect natural outgrowth of an antiques business, or at least it seems so in this case. Having run Dapple-Gray Antiques for three decades, hostess Ruth Van Goor knows a thing or two about decorating, particularly the sort of vintage decorating that B&Bs seem to natu-rally warrant. Now she and her husband, Ole, run this large, beautiful log B&B, and Ruth's antiques shop occupies one of the ground-floor rooms. The inn and the shop's namesake, a dapple-gray steeple-chase horse, greets visitors to both. Four suites are each decorated according to a theme that infuses everything from the style of furniture to the pattern on the comforters—Americana, North Woods, Seashore, and Lincoln (as in Abe). Each suite has its own bathroom and its own private lake-view deck. Antiques displays are dotted through the house, but guests also have access to modern amenities like satellite TV and high-speed Internet. Common rooms include a sitting room with cathedral ceiling and a 28-foot fireplace and well-stocked library, laundry room, kitchen, and a free-standing wood sauna. Breakfast is warm and usually a notch above, with eggs Benedict, Michigan blueberry pancakes, and Midwest corn fritters all making an appearance. The Van Goors also rent a private two-bedroom summer cabin in the woods on 27 acres of forest with 600 feet of private rocky shoreline.

Keweenaw Mountain Lodge
906-289-4403 or 1-888-685-6343
www.atthelodge.com
info@atthelodge.com
US 41, Copper Harbor, MI 49918
Price: $95–$165
Credit Cards: MC, V
Handicapped Access: Limited
Open: Year-round

Built in the 1930s as part of the government's public works program, the Keweenaw Lodge gave dozens of out-of-work miners a purpose for a few months: hand-building several lovely log cabins, a log lodge, and a rolling golf course in the woods on a hillside a mile south of Copper Harbor. Since then the lodge has added an eight-unit motel. Though the motel offers large, newer rooms, nothing beats the vintage architecture of the cabins, most of which also include hand-built stone fire-

places. The main lodge itself is equally special, with its Alpine-inspired dark logs and rows of white-trimmed windows. The lodge's dining room turns out consistently good meals and has become somewhat of a "special occasion" restaurant locally.

★ Laurium Manor Inn
Owners: Dave and Julie Sprenger
906-337-2549
www.lauriummanorinn.com
innkeeper@laurium.info
320 Tamarack St., Laurium, MI 49913
Price: $99–$179
Credit Cards: D, MC, V, only if reservation is made with less than a seven-day advance. Otherwise, payment in full by check or money order is expected within seven days of reserving a room.
Handicapped Access: No (there are some ground-floor rooms, but none of the restrooms are handicapped accessible)
Open: Year-round

Built in 1908 as the opulent, 45-room mansion of a Keweenaw copper baron, the Laurium Manor Inn now delights guests with its grand columns, ornate moldings, clawfoot tubs, and tales of Theodore Roosevelt having slept in their bed. The folks at the Laurium have become preservation experts in the course of restoring the inn to its former glory, so much so that they went ahead and bought the Victorian across the street too and have also turned it into a B&B (see Victorian Hall listing below). Ten guest rooms with private baths offer guests 10 totally different experiences. Room 1, where Teddy Roosevelt is said to have stayed, boasts a stately private balcony, a huge fireplace, and is large enough to accommodate up to five guests. Each room has been restored to a version of its former self, and the Sprengers provide a description of what each room was and whom it once housed. Still, though all have been fitted out with the antique furnishings

Laurium Manor Inn is a restored 45-room mansion that has been beautifully converted into a popular B&B.

Laurium Manor Inn

(sometimes original items from the manor) befitting their former lives, they also include modern luxuries such as LCD TVs with cable and free wireless Internet access, and some of the rooms also include whirlpool tubs and DVD players. The Keweenaw Suite, housed in the manor's carriage house, is one of the loveliest structures we've ever seen—it is architectural perfection wrapped in a neat package of classic French doors and beautiful hardwood floors offset by sage green walls with crisp white trim and furniture of rich, dark brown leather. The suites are over-the-top beautiful, but even the former maids' quarters here are something special, and the common areas are jaw-droppingly beautiful, partly because of the quality of the materials that have gone into this house— stained glass, marble, beautiful woods, gilded and embossed elephant leather wall covering—and partly for the sheer larger-than-life scale of everything, from the 100-foot wraparound tile balcony to the grand triple staircase flanked by a 9-by-14-foot

stained-glass window. A full buffet breakfast is served in the formal dining room every morning for all guests, but the Laurium Manor Inn is also within walking distance of a handful of local eateries.

Michigan House

906-337-1910
www.michiganhousecafe.com
mihouse@michiganhousecafe.com
300 Sixth St., Calumet, MI 49913
Price: $55–$75
Credit Cards: Not accepted
Handicapped Access: No
Open: Year-round

A former 26-room hotel constructed by the Bosch Brewing Company in 1905, the Michigan House now houses two delightful apartments, both decorated with vintage furniture and retro kitchens that will make visitors feel like they've traveled back in time 40 or 50 years. Located in historic downtown Calumet, the hotel is in walking distance to a few great eateries and shops and is conveniently close to the highway, making it easy to head north to Copper Harbor or south to Houghton and Hancock. The smaller of the two suites, called the Corner Walk-Up, accommodates up to two people comfortably with a bedroom and sitting area, a kitchen with a half-size Wedgewood stove, and a bathroom with a clawfoot tub. The larger Angler Suite is decorated in vintage fishing decor and includes a separate living room and bedroom, a full kitchen, and a private bath with a shower. Both suites have free wireless Internet access. The popular brewpub on the first floor serves lunch and dinner every day but Wednesday, when the cooks are busy brewing their Red Jacket Oatmeal Espress microbrew.

★ Sand Hills Lighthouse Inn

Owner: Bill Frabotta
906-337-1744
www.sandhillslighthouseinn.com
Five Mile Point Rd., P.O. Box 298, Ahmeek, MI 49901
From Houghton take US 41 north to Ahmeek and turn left at the first street. Immediately upon turning, you'll see signs directing you to Five Mile Point Rd. Stay on Five Mile for 8 miles to the lighthouse.
Price: $135–$200
Credit Cards: Not accepted
Handicapped Access: No
Open: Year-round

The largest and last manned lighthouse on the Great Lakes is now a fantastic bed-and-breakfast with eight lovely rooms and stunning Lake Superior views. Listed on the

Sand Hills Lighthouse once housed three keepers; it is now a beautiful B&B. Paul Emaus

National Historic Register, the lighthouse was built in 1913 to house the keeper and his family and was painstakingly restored in the mid-1990s by its warm and very proud owner. Decorated in a Victorian style that fits with the original details and moldings, all of the rooms are lovely, but the two standouts feature private balconies with sweeping Lake Superior views, king beds, and whirlpool tubs. It really doesn't get much more romantic than escaping to an old lighthouse, lighting a fire in the fireplace, and watching the moon twinkle on Lake Superior.

Victoria Hall

906-337-2549
www.lauriummanorinn.com
Innkeper@lauriummanorinn.com
305 Tamarack St., Laurium, MI 49913
Price: $79–$159
Credit Cards: D, MC, V, only if reservation is made with less than a seven-day advance. Otherwise, payment in full by check or money order is expected within seven days of reserving a room.
Handicapped Access: No (there are some ground-floor rooms, but none of the restrooms are handicapped accessible)
Open: Year-round

Also built as a mansion for a wealthy copper baron, and just as well-preserved as its sister property across the street (the Laurium Manor Inn), the Victoria Hall is all dark wood and candlelight, where the Laurium is vaulted ceilings and windows. It just depends on whether you're in more of an Edgar Allen Poe sort of mood or a Walt Whitman flight of fancy. Either way, you can't help but be delighted by these grand old houses. Four of the eight guest rooms at Victoria Hall are blessed with ornately carved fireplaces, and elaborate molding and stained glass abound. As with Laurium Manor, Victoria Hall's crown jewel is its former carriage house, which has been transformed into a darling private cottage complete with wood-burning fireplace, hardwood floors, clawfoot tub, four-poster bed, and private porch. Victoria Hall guests are also treated to a full buffet breakfast every morning, served in the dining room of Laurium Manor across the street. Something to keep in mind: There are no phones at Victoria Hall, although most people get decent cell phone service.

MARQUETTE AND THE MARQUETTE RANGE

Big Bay Lighthouse B&B

Hosts: John Gale, Jeff Gamble, and Linda Gamble
906-345-9957
www.bigbaylighthouse.com
keepers@bigbaylighthouse.com
3 Lighthouse Rd., Big Bay, MI 49808
Price: $105–$187
Credit Cards: Not accepted
Handicapped Access: No
Open: Year-round

Perched atop a cliff overlooking Lake Superior, the redbrick Big Bay Point Lighthouse is a prime location for a cozy B&B. Sticking with a nautical theme befitting the architecture and location, each of the inn's seven guest rooms is named after a different keeper of the lighthouse, or one of their assistants or helpers. Many of the rooms face Lake Superior for fantastic views. Because of the inn's remote location out on the point, surrounded by nearly 50 acres of wilderness, guests are also likely to spot various wildlife, including deer and fox. In addition to sitting by the fire and reading in the inn's shared sitting room, guests can hike from the lighthouse to various sights, including waterfalls. Breakfast includes fresh-baked breads and muffins, fruit, juice, coffee, and a hot entrée every morning.

★ **Landmark Inn**

906-228-2580

www.thelandmarkinn.com

230 N. Front St., Marquette, MI 49855

Downtown Marquette, two blocks north of
  Washington St.

Price: $124–$269

Credit Cards: AE, DC, D, MC, V

Handicapped Access: Yes

Open: Year-round

Not just cleverly named, the Landmark Inn
is the pride and joy of Marquette's lodging
industry. Just a few short blocks from
downtown, the Landmark was originally
opened in 1930 as the Northland Hotel.
From the 1930s to the 1960s it was a popular local hub and a destination for well-
known visitors, including Amelia Earhart,
Abbot and Costello, Duke Ellington, and
Louis Armstrong. After falling into disrepair throughout the 1970s, the hotel closed
in the 1980s. A massive renovation started
in 1995 and was completed in 1997, after
which the hotel became Michigan's first to
be awarded membership in Historic Hotels
of America. Today the Landmark has
regained its position in Marquette society.
Capers, the lobby restaurant, is popular
with guests and locals alike for its American
take on Spanish tapas and its inventive
Sunday brunch, while the more casual
Northwoods Pub draws a beer and nachos
crowd most nights, and the more intimate
upstairs cocktail lounge is popular with
Marquette professionals catching up over
after-work drinks. Half the hotel faces Lake
Superior, giving a fair percentage of the
rooms nice lake views. Rooms have been
decorated in a pleasant, modern take on
Victorian, dominated by bold colors and
simple stripes, as opposed to the over-the-
top frill you see at many historic inns.

Another lighthouse-turned-inn, Big Bay is in a prime location on a cliff overlooking Lake Superior.

Darrell Harden

Some of the rooms, such as the Amelia Earhart Room, have private fireplaces, and walls dotted with information about the room's well-known guest.

Nordic Bay Lodge

906-226-7516
www.nordicbay.com
stay@nordicbay.com
1880 US 41 South, Marquette, MI 49855
From Marquette follow US 41 as it turns south to bypass the city. Stay on US 41 South for 1.3 miles. Nordic Bay Lodge will be on your right toward the bottom of the hill, just before the Carp River Bridge.
Price: $75–$375
Credit Cards: AE, D, MC, V
Handicapped Access: Yes
Open: Year-round

A bastion of Scandinavian modernity in an area that tends to lean more toward Victorian, the Nordic Bay Lodge is all bleached woods, crisp white sheets, and simple, modern furniture. At least on the inside. On the outside, the place looks like a groovy Alpine ski lodge that probably serves fondue and mulled wine. Convenient during the summer for its proximity both to Marquette and the shores of Lake Superior, Nordic Bay is ideal in winter for its easy access to the 75-kilometer network of cross-country ski trails that make up the Noquemanon Trail network. The hotel's restaurant is one of, if not the, best in Marquette. That's a bold statement, but we'll stick by it. Delicious fresh meats and fish are prepared in simple yet inventive ways. It's a restaurant that people would drive several miles to eat at, so it's good luck to be staying right next door. Parking is nice and simple as well—most of the rooms are drive-up motel style. Two separate villas occupy the wooded hills behind the main lodge—the Alpine House is large and beautiful, with

The Victorian-themed lobby of Marquette's Landmark Inn. Naoko M.

plenty of windows to take advantage of spectacular Lake Superior views, while the Edelweiss Villa is small and quaint and feels like a little woodsy hideaway.

ONTONAGON AND THE PORKIES

★ Kaug Wudjoo Lodge
906-885-5275
www.michigan.gov/dnr
Porcupine Mountains Wilderness State Park
Price: $1,225 a week, plus $8 reservation
    fee. Park may consider less than one-
    week stays during low season.
Credit Cards: AE, D, MC, V
Handicapped Access: Yes
Open: Year-round

Constructed in 1945 as the park manager's residence, the lodge is now available to park guests for weekly rentals, providing an ideal spot from which to explore Porcupine Mountains Wilderness State Park, the state's largest park. A charming dark brown lodge with stone base and wood trim, Kaug Wudjoo (Ojibwa for "place of the crouching porcupine") has hardwood maple floors, a large stone fireplace, and a giant picture window overlooking Lake Superior. It sleeps up to 12 and is furnished with locally made cedar log beds. A fully equipped kitchen makes it easy for families to move right in for a week of incredible experiences.

Northern Light Inn
Innkeeper: Dianne O'Shea
906-458-0803
www.northernlightinn-vacationhomes.com
info@northernlightinn-vacation-
    homes.com
701 Houghton St., Ontonagon, MI 49953
Entering Ontonagon on MI 64, turn right
    on River St. and left on Houghton.
Price: $82–$129 B&B; $165 a night for vaca-
    tion home
Credit Cards: D, MC, V
Handicapped Access: Separate vacation

home is handicapped accessible.
Open: Year-round

A cheery and bright large white clapboard house, just two blocks from Lake Superior in Ontonagon, Northern Light offers four rooms with private baths, three of which feature Jacuzzi tubs. Rooms are fairly large and comfortable, decorated in a slightly flowery style that's too simple and modern to be called Victorian. Guests are treated to a full breakfast every morning and have free use of the large downstairs living room, with fireplace and games. The Northern Light also has a pleasant three-bedroom vacation home for rent, not too far from the B&B. Both properties are walking distance to downtown Ontonagon, which offers a handful of shops and eateries.

CAMPING

AU TRAIN, MUNISING, AND PICTURED ROCKS

Au Train Lake Campground
Located in the Hiawatha National Forest.
    West of Munising, at Au Train, travel
    south on FR HO3 for about 4 miles, then
    go 1 mile east on FR 2276 and then 2
    miles north on FR 2596.
Amenities: Picnic tables, fire pits, drinking
    water, flushable toilets, boat launch nearby
Fee: $14
Reservations: Not accepted
Sites: 37
Open: May 15–Sep. 30

A fantastic home base for the area, within easy driving distance of Pictured Rocks, Munising Falls, and Miner's Castle, this spacious wooded campground also has the benefit of being on the shores of the largest inland lake in the area, and right next door to the scenic Au Train River as well. In addition to providing pleasant scenery and swimming, both bodies of water are chock-

The Lake Superior coastline near the campsite at Hurricane River. Devon Akmon

full of fish, and the lake is popular for water-skiing as well. Campsites are large and well spaced throughout the trees for privacy. The Au Train Songbird Trail, popular among bird-watchers, also starts and ends at this campground.

Hurricane River

Located within the Pictured Rocks National Lakeshore, 12 miles west of Grand Marais off Alger County Road H58. The campground is accessible both by kayak and by car.

Amenities: Picnic tables, solar-powered water wells, vault toilets, fire grate, tent pad
Fee: $12
Reservations: Not accepted
Sites: 36
Open: May 10–Oct. 31

A pleasant wooded campground with 21 large sites arranged in two loops around the Hurricane River. Picnic tables are set up around the area where the river flows into Lake Superior, and campers can take an easy 1.5-mile hike to the Au Sable Lighthouse. Listed on the National Register of Historic Places, the lighthouse was constructed in 1874 and still operates, now with a solar-powered lamp. Hurricane River provides a put-in point to Lake Superior for kayakers wishing to get a closer look at the Pictured Rocks.

Little Beaver Lake Campground

Located within the Pictured Rocks National Lakeshore, 3 miles north of Alger County Road H58 and 20 miles northeast of Munising

Amenities: Picnic tables, solar-powered water wells, vault toilets, small-boat ramp, fire grate, tent pad
Fee: $12
Reservations: Not accepted
Sites: 8
Open: May 10–Oct. 31

This is a small, serene campground in the Pictured Rocks national park. Large sites are well spaced for privacy, and each provides a view of Little Beaver Lake below. A small boat ramp is available at the site, and fishing in the lake is great for pike, perch, walleye, and bass. Because of its size the campground fills up quickly, so get there in the morning to score a spot.

Pictured Rocks Back Country Camping

906-387-3700
Fee: $4, plus $15 fee for reservations
Reservations: Accepted 14 days or more in advance. Backcountry campers without reservations can check with the visitor center in Munising (400 E. Munising Ave., junction of MI 28 and County Road H58 in Munising) for available backcountry sites and to obtain a permit upon arrival.
Sites: 12 (7 group sites)
Open: May 10–Oct. 31

A 42-mile section of the North Country Trail runs through Pictured Rocks National Lakeshore from Munising to Grand Marais. This particularly picturesque section of the trail is very popular with backpackers and hikers, and the National Lakeshore has graciously provided numerous backcountry campsites along the trail to accommodate both trail hikers and kayakers making their way along Superior's shore. Backcountry permits are required for all backcountry campers, and reservations can be made for any one of the 12 backcountry sites, 7 of which offer group backcountry camping.

Twelvemile Beach

Located within the Pictured Rocks National Lakeshore, Twelvemile is 15 miles west of Grand Marais off Alger County Road H58. The campground is accessible both by kayak and by car.

Amenities: Picnic tables, solar-powered water wells, vault toilets, fire grate, tent pad
Fee: $12
Reservations: Not accepted

Sites: 36
Open: May 10–Oct. 31

This is a popular Pictured Rocks National Lakeshore campground, located on a sandy plateau over Twelvemile Beach. Three sets of stairs lead to the beach, which is a popular launch point for kayaks heading for the Pictured Rocks. Sites are fairly large and well-spaced, with small groves of trees separating sites for privacy. The campground is also located on the North Country Trail, making it popular with hikers.

IRONWOOD AND THE GOGEBIC RANGE

Lake Gogebic State Park
1-800-447-2757
On MI 64, 10 miles north of US 2 near Marenisco
Amenities: Running water, flush toilets, showers, boat launch, fire pits, picnic tables
Fee: $10–$16, depending on whether site is rustic, semi-modern, or modern.
Reservations: Accepted at www.mi.gov.dnr
Sites: 127
Open: Mid-May to late Sep.

Located on the west shore of the largest inland lake in the U.P., this large campground includes a mile of shoreline, and almost a quarter of the sites are right on the lake—a pretty choice spot when you consider that the rest of the shoreline has been gobbled up by private cottages. Thanks to its shallow waters, Lake Gogebic is great for swimming, and the campground includes a large sandy beach, as well as a boat launch for fishermen eager to test the lake's famed waters. Taken purely on its own, the campground is not amazing—there are few trees, which means not a lot of privacy, and the proximity of the campground to the state highway isn't ideal—but the location and modern conveniences like showers and flushing toilets more than make up for what any of the individual sites lack.

Little Girl's Point County Park
906-932-1913
From US 2 in Ironwood turn on Hemlock Rd., follow it as it become CR 505 and leads to the park.
Amenities: Picnic tables, fire pits, flushable toilets, electric hookups, boat launch
Fee: $14 for nonresidents, $12 for residents
Reservations: Accepted by phone; call early for summer reservations
Sites: 32
Open: May 15–Sep. 30

A popular local campground situated on a bluff overlooking Lake Superior, Little Girl's Point has it all—sandy beach, boat launch, wildlife, large wooded campsites, electrical hookups, bike trails that connect with the Powers Trail System, and proximity to local sights. The only slight drawback is that the trees between sites aren't tall enough or thick enough to provide privacy.

MARQUETTE AND THE MARQUETTE RANGE

Craig Lake State Park
1 mile west of Michigamme to Craig Lake Rd. Follow signs 8 miles north to parking lot.
Amenities: Boat launch, kayak portages, picnic tables, some fire pits, vault toilets. The yurt has a wood-burning stove, indoor table, and outdoor picnic table, fire ring, two wooden bunk beds, and a vault toilet. The cabins have a hand pump for water, a vault toilet, a cooking grill, and a fire ring. Firewood for heat is provided by the park staff.
Fee: $10 campsite, $60 yurt, $60–$80 cabin
Reservation: www.midnrreservations.com/
Open: May 15–Oct. 15

One of the largest and most remote state parks in the U.P., Craig Lake State Park spans nearly 7,000 acres, including six full lakes and multiple ponds and rivers that make it very popular with fishermen and kayakers. The park's namesake lake is 374 acres, surrounded by high granite bluffs and containing six wooded islands. The park is teeming with wildlife, giving visitors the opportunity to view beaver, black bear, deer, loons, and moose, especially from its various hiking trails. The park is also open to hunters and trappers during the state-regulated seasons. Fishing is very good at all six lakes—no motorized boats are permitted except on Keewaydin Lake, and the park has a catch-and-release policy for northern pike, muskellunge, and bass. In addition to numerous backcountry rustic campsites, Craig Lake State Park offers two rustic cabins built by Fred Miller of the Miller Brewing Company, and a recently constructed yurt (a step up from a tent, but not quite a cabin, yurts are domed circular tents built on top of wooden decks).

ONTONAGON AND THE PORKIES

Porcupine Moutain Yurts & Wilderness Cabins

906-885-5275
Amenities: Yurts—bunk beds, mattresses, cookstove, woodstove, ax, bow saw, cooking and eating utensils, outhouse, wood for heat. Cabins—single-size beds or bunks with mattresses, table, chairs, brooms, and a propane heater or wood-stove for heat.
Fee: $60
Reservation: www.midnrreservations.com/
Sites: 3 yurts, 19 cabins
Open: Year-round

Accessed only by trail, the new yurts are sturdy dome-shaped tents built on top of wood platforms, with built-in bunk beds. The fabric walls are so durable and pulled so snugly to the platform that the weatherproof yurts can accommodate campers in all seasons. The park's 19 rustic cabins are also accessed by trail—anywhere from 1- to 4-mile hikes—and have long been popular with visitors, especially the seven cabins that overlook Lake Superior. Even without the Lake Superior views, all of the cabins are located near the park's most scenic points. The cabins and yurts get booked up quickly, so it's best to book as far in advance as possible, especially if you're hoping to score one for a summer trip.

Presque Isle River Campground

906-885-5275 or 1-800-447-2757
West end of Porcupine Mountains Wilderness State Park. From US 2 go north at the Wakefield stoplight to the junction of CR 519 and S. Boundary Rd.
Amenities: vault toilets, water hand pumps
Fee: $14
Reservation: www.midnrreservations.com/
Sites: 50
Open: May 15–Oct. 15

This fantastic campground is in one of the area's most picturesque (and popular) settings, just a quarter mile from the mouth of the Presque Isle River on a bluff overlooking Lake Superior. Four nearby waterfalls are easily reached via a 2-mile trail loop. The sites themselves are large and well-placed. Many have lake views, while others are tucked back into the forest.

Trout Bay and Murray Bay on Grand Island

Amenities: Vault toilets, picnic areas, fire rings, boat launch near Murray Bay
Fee: None required; no permits required either
Reservation: Not accepted; first come, first served
Sites: 6
Open: May–Oct.

Two fantastic campgrounds are available on Grand Island, reachable by kayak or by an easy three-minute ferry ride from the MI 28 dock west of Munising (near the town of Christmas). Four Trout Bay sites (maximum

Grand Island. Matt Girvan

two tents each) are on a sandy beach near 200-foot sandstone cliffs and centuries-old sea caves. The two Murray Bay sites are also near to a sand beach and good swimming and fishing. This is a great spot from which to kayak to the Pictured Rocks. Backcountry camping is also permitted, but be aware that Grand Island does have some private property and don't trespass. There are black bears on the island, so campers should take all precautions to secure their tents and food to avoid meeting up with a hungry one.

RESTAURANTS

Dining options vary greatly as you make your way around Lake Superior's shore, dominated by locally available fish, produce, and meats, and influenced by the various immigrant groups that flocked to the U.P. to work the mines.

Ironwood, like nearby Iron Mountain, is known for its great Italian food, the welcome result of the large number of Italians who once worked the area's iron mines and whose children still live here. Italians also introduced the area to delicious *porchetta* (also spelled "porketta")—a spicy, slow-roasted pork roast—and *cudighi,* a spicy sausage patty sandwich.

Pasties—warm savory pies filled with meat, gravy, potatoes, and other vegetables—are popular throughout the U.P., but especially so here where thousands of iron and copper miners made their home. Though pasties have become inextricably linked to Yoopers, they are actually an import from Cornwall, England, courtesy of all those Cornish miners. The warm, portable pies were perfect sustenance for working the mines in Cornwall, and when those collapsed, the Cornish brought their tools and their pasties across the Atlantic to the U.P.

As with the rest of the U.P., restaurants

in this region tend to be casual, down-home affairs with friendly service. A few more upscale, special-occasion options exist along the Keweenaw Peninsula and in Marquette, but even at these spots it would be strange to see someone in formal wear.

Dining Price Codes

Restaurant prices are described as Inexpensive, Moderate, Expensive, or Very Expensive in each of the dining reviews. These tags refer to the average price of a dinner consisting of an entrée, appetizer or dessert, and glass of wine or beer (tax and gratuities not included). All the restaurants included here are recommended, but the real standouts have been marked with a star. Restaurants are grouped by region, and regions are listed alphabetically.

Following is a breakdown of the dining price code:

Inexpensive	Up to $15
Moderate	$15-$30
Expensive	$30-$50
Very Expensive	$50 or more

Credit Cards

AE: American Express
D: Discover
MC: MasterCard
V: Visa

AU TRAIN, MUNISING, AND PICTURED ROCKS

★ The Brownstone Inn

906-892-8332
E4635 MI 28, Au Train, MI 49806
Open: Daily; closed Mon. in off-season
Price: Inexpensive–Moderate
Cuisine: Fusion
Serving: L, D
Credit Cards: AE, MC, V
Handicapped Access: Yes

The popular Brownstone Inn is known for inventive takes on classic north-woods fare. Matt Girvan

Special Features: Takeout available; dinner service from 3 PM on; full bar

Far and away the best restaurant for several miles around, the Brownstone Inn specializes in inventive twists on north-woods classics. The owners are California transplants, which could have something to do with the introduction of tropical salsas and Caribbean spices to the usual Lake Superior whitefish. From Mexican quesadillas and burgers to filet mignon topped with crab, the Brownstone covers multiple culinary bases and does it well. Desserts are homemade and delicious, with options changing regularly, and the wine list is also excellent, with several bottles from the California wine country making an appearance alongside local Michigan wines and beers. The inn is not an inn, but it certainly looks like one from the road, with its stonework and chimneys. Built in the 1940s from locally found stones and salvage materials, the Brownstone sits right on MI 28, beckoning hungry motorists. The interior is cozy and warm, and service is extremely friendly. One night when we were too tired to drive after taking our time and enjoying a two-hour meal, we asked our waitress to recommend a nearby hotel and she not only called around to get a reservation for us (not easy on Fourth of July weekend at the last minute!), but drew us a map and gave us her phone number to call her if we ran into any trouble.

Camel Rider's Restaurant
906-573-2319
16887 42.5 Rd., Wetmore, MI 49895
From Munising take MI 28 south to
    Hiawatha National Forest entrance in
    Wetmore
Open: Tue.–Sat.; open Sun. as well in winter (this is a popular stop for snowmobilers)
Price: Inexpensive
Cuisine: American
Serving: L, D
Credit Cards: MC, V
Handicapped Access: Yes

Close-up of the strange but entertaining murals at Houghton's popular Ambassador restaurant. Matt Girvan

Special Features: Located in national forest

Attached to the Camel Rider's Resort in the Hiawatha National Forest, the restaurant overlooks a beautiful chain of lakes, which produce plenty of fresh fish for the menu. Perch, trout, whitefish, and walleye are all available in season, and delicious. The kitchen is big on drawn butter and deep frying, but you can ask to have your fish broiled instead if you like. On the meat front, they serve a decent steak (including one monster that's big enough for two) and offer special extra-thick 1-pound stuffed pork chops that are delicious, if entirely unhealthy. The food is consistently good here, but the restaurant is made great by its unique and beautiful surroundings.

★ Falling Rock Café and Bookstore

906-387-3008
www.fallingrockcafe.com
104 E. Munising Ave., Munising, MI 49862
Open: Daily; closed Mon. in off-season
Price: Inexpensive
Cuisine: American
Serving: B, L, D
Credit Cards: AE, MC, V
Handicapped Access: Yes
Special Features: Old-fashioned fountain drinks, ice cream sodas and egg creams; takeout; gift shop

It's easy to imagine spending many hours sitting in this spot, reading a book on one of the couches or catching up with friends at a table in the café. Falling Rock is the hub of social life in Munising, with outstanding coffee, gourmet sandwiches made fresh on the spot, homemade soups made daily, and an old-fashioned soda fountain of polished chrome that serves the local favorite Jilbert's Dairy ice cream. The café also provides free high-speed wireless, although last time we were in they were collecting donations to keep that service going. In addition to deli sandwiches for lunch, the café serves excellent egg sandwiches for breakfast, along with bagels and homemade muffins and pastries. CDs from local musicians are on sale, as are the handicrafts of various local artisans, making Falling Rock a good place to look for gifts as well. This is one of those special places that draws a town together—so much so, in fact, that in 2006, when the owners announced that they were thinking of closing during the off-season because it was just too hard to stay afloat financially as a small bookstore in a feast-or-famine economy like Munising's, the local community banded together to convince them otherwise. The café created a "Friends of Falling Rock" program, asking local patrons to donate $100 a year to keep the business open, and the public responded enthusiastically, raising over $13,000. It just goes to show how important a community gathering place is to people, especially during the harsh winter months in a remote place like Munising.

IRONWOOD AND THE GOGEBIC RANGE

Don & GG's Food and Spirits

906-932-2312
1300 E. Cloverland Dr., Ironwood, MI 49938
Open: Daily
Price: Inexpensive
Cuisine: American
Serving: L, D
Credit Cards: MC, V
Handicapped Access: Yes
Special Features: Outdoor deck, extensive beer list

One of the most popular restaurants in Ironwood, Don & GG's serves good classic north-woods fare with just enough twists to make the menu feel unique. It's also one of the few restaurants in the area that really makes an effort to offer an assortment of vegetarian dishes. Fresh whitefish and trout are always on offer, homemade soups are outstanding, the nachos are delicious, and they serve sandwiches and inventive entrée-size salads all day along, with a dinner menu of pastas, fish, chicken, steaks, and a rotating assortment of specials. The outdoor deck is a huge bonus during the summer.

Manny's
906-932-0999
316 E. Houk St., Ironwood, MI 49938
Open: Daily
Price: Inexpensive
Cuisine: Italian
Serving: B, L, D
Credit Cards: Not accepted
Handicapped Access: Yes
Special Features: Daily lunch buffet; smoking permitted in dining room

To be honest, Manny's doesn't have the most amazing food in town, mostly because it specializes in decent Italian food in a town and area full of great Italian food. Nevertheless, it's worth dining here for a number of reasons: First, it's in a neighborhood that you would never just stumble upon; second, it's next to the "World's Tallest Indian" statue, which is an experience in and of itself; then there's its excellent old-school neighborhood restaurant atmosphere; then there's the fact that their breakfast menu includes a noodle omelet, which you're not likely to see anywhere else; and lastly there's the handmade ravioli, which are actually delicious. All of which conspire to transform Manny's from a so-so spot into a must-try.

Tacconelli's Downtown Towne House
906-932-2101
www.tacconellis.com
215 S. Suffolk St., Ironwood, MI 49938
Open: Daily
Price: Inexpensive
Cuisine: Italian
Serving: L, D
Credit Cards: AE, D, DC, MC, V
Handicapped Access: Yes
Special Features: Buffet lunch; takeout

A very popular Ironwood restaurant, especially during its famous Sunday lunch buffet, which includes a great salad bar, plus pizzas, pastas, and the restaurant's popular BBQ ribs, Tacconelli's is a typical old Ironwood spot with brick exterior and dark green interior. The restaurant's bar is almost as popular as its dining room. In addition to the ribs, the gnocchi, homemade soup, and lasagna are all standouts. Tacconelli's To-Go will also deliver food, including full dinners, not just pizza, which is handy if you're camping and don't feel like cooking out of a can.

ISLE ROYALE

Greenstone Grill and Dining Room
906-337-4993 or 1-888-644-2003
www.rockharborlodge.com
Rock Harbor, Isle Royale
Open: Daily, May 25–Sep. 7
Price: Inexpensive–Expensive
Cuisine: American, Continental
Serving: B, L, D
Credit Cards: Not accepted
Handicapped Access: Yes
Special Features: Lodge guests on the American plan have breakfast, lunch, and dinner included in their room rate.

The more formal dining room and the relaxed grill are the only dining options on Isle Royale that don't involve a campfire. Though the food is decent in the dining room—Continental classics with a few north-woods twists—frankly, it's overpriced ($30.50 a person for dinner), and it just seems weird to have cloth tablecloths and fine china on a wilderness island. The Greenstone Grill is much more like it, with a back patio, beer, and basics like burgers and club sandwiches. They do a mean veggie burger and tasty fries as well, and it's easy as pie to order a few things to go and take them to a picnic table.

KEWEENAW PENINSULA

The Ambassador

906-482-5054
126 Shelden Ave., Houghton, MI 49931
Open: Daily
Price: Inexpensive
Cuisine: Italian
Serving: L, D
Credit Cards: Not accepted
Handicapped Access: Limited—no handi-
   capped access in men's room
Special Features: Outdoor beer garden in
summer

Every college town needs its pizza joint, and the Ambassador is Houghton's. Except, this being the U.P., it's not just any old pizza place—this one is housed in a historic bar-room with century-old booths and stained glass, offset by German-inspired murals of drinking and carousing gnomes thought to have been painted during Prohibition. In the summertime an outdoor beer garden is a great place to sit and watch the boats go by on the Portage Canal. And the pizza is good too—thin crust with a variety of toppings, including all the usual suspects plus a very tasty assortment of specialty pies, among them the popular Garlic Chicken, Tostada Pizza, Chicken Broccoli, and Super Vegetarian.

The Gay Bar in Gay, Michigan

The only bar in this tiny town has taken advantage of the town's name and created a booming T-shirt business. Dozens of shirts in various designs sporting slogans like "I Went Straight to the Gay Bar" draw tourists well off the beaten path to Gay. Once they're here they take a photo next to the Gay Bar sign and head inside to grab lunch and another giggle: The Gay Bar's specialty is foot-long hot dogs and brats.

Tourists travel several miles out of their way for a photo and a T-shirt from The Gay Bar in Gay, Michigan.
Matt Girvan

★ Harbor Haus

906-289-4502
www.harborhaus.com
77 Brockway Ave., Copper Harbor
Open: Daily
Price: Moderate–Expensive
Cuisine: Continental
Serving: L, D (breakfast on Sat. and Sun.)
Credit Cards: AE, D, MC, V
Handicapped Access: Yes
Special Features: Boat dock for patrons;
bed-and-breakfast attached; full bar with
lots of German imports

Recommended highly by everyone in Copper
Harbor and known throughout the U.P., the
Harbor Haus is one of those spots capable of
delivering an absolutely perfect evening. The
setting is beautiful, from the large and heavy
copper door, to the picture windows looking
out on Lake Superior, to the light and cheery
dining room, with just enough German
kitsch in the exterior, the bar, and the uni-
forms to keep the place from feeling too formal. The food is varied, interesting, and
delicious, with an assortment of German,
Austrian, and Swedish imports, mixed with
local specialties. Though the menu changes
daily, certain items are almost always in rota-
tion, including a fantastic duck pâté with
crostini and lingonberries appetizer, and of
course fresh Lake Superior whitefish and
trout. The fish is cooked absolutely perfectly,
and German specialties like sauerbraten
(vinegar-marinated slow-roasted beef),
served with the traditional braised red cab-
bage and spaetzle (potato dumplings), are
delicious. Steaks are cooked exactly to order—
it's no easy task to cook a rare steak so that it's
good and bloody but not cold in the center. A
dinner companion who always orders steak
rare and almost never gets the steak he's after
was stunned to silence by the perfection
attained here. Homemade desserts also
change regularly, but the special raspberry
cobbler is always on the menu and well worth
ordering when you order your meal, as the

kitchen bakes each order fresh. Finally, of
course a restaurant called the Harbor Haus
has to have good beer on draft, and here they
continue to impress with imported German
Hefeweizen (wheat beer) and pilsner.

The Hut Inn

906-337-1133
www.hutinn.com
58542 Wolverine St., Calumet, MI 49913
Open: Tue.–Sat.
Price: Inexpensive
Cuisine: American
Serving: L, D
Credit Cards: MC, V
Handicapped Access: Yes
Special Features: Pasties to go

A classic U.P. joint, the Hut Inn has been in
business since 1952, and nothing much has
changed since then except for the fact that
it has officially become "Pasty Central."
Pasties are shipped all over the country
from this long motor lodge outpost near
Calumet. In addition to the pasties, the Hut
serves a full menu with burgers, pastas, and
even a handful of Mexican specialties "prepared for American tastes." Stick to local
favorites like pasties and fried whitefish
and the big juicy burgers and you can't go
wrong. If you've got any room left after a
piping hot pasty or a huge burger, the apple
dumplings are large and tasty here as well,
and the chocolate thimbleberry pie is
unique and delicious, as is the homemade
gingerbread with warm caramel.

Keweenaw Berry Farm Restaurant & Bakery

906-523-4271
39795 US 41, Chassell, MI 49916
Open: Daily, May–Oct.
Price: Inexpensive
Cuisine: American, Scandinavian
Serving: B, L, D
Credit Cards: Not accepted
Handicapped Access: Yes
Special Features: Gift shop and bakery sell-

ing homemade jams, cinnamon rolls, and Scandinavian baked goods; animal farm

The influence of the Keweenaw's Scandinavian immigrants is strongly felt here, both in the bakery, where classics like *nisu*—a sweet, cardamom-flavored braided bread—are sold alongside giant cinnamon rolls and fresh-baked breads, and in the restaurant, where the most popular menu item is the Finnish pancake (*pannukakku*). In addition to the bakery, the Berry Farm does sell a large variety of berry jams, although they all come from nearby farms. There is no more berry farm at the Berry Farm, just this cheery restaurant and a store that sells various berry-related goods. With large tasty breakfasts, homemade pasties for lunch, and rotating daily specials for dinner, plus the gift shop and a neighboring animal farm, the Berry Farm is not only a great place to stumble across on a road trip, but a destination not to be missed.

The Library Restaurant & Brewpub
906-487-5882
www.librarybrewpub.com
62 N. Isle Royale St., Houghton, MI 49931
Open: Daily
Price: Inexpensive—Moderate
Cuisine: American
Serving: L, D
Credit Cards: AE, D, MC, V
Handicapped Access: Yes
Special Features: Brewery; full bar

Tucked away in a lovely old redbrick building on a side street with a fantastic waterfront view, the Library, with its varied menu, French waitress, and large dining room, feels like it's in a much bigger town. The food is still mostly locally inspired, however, with fresh whitefish daily, as well as an assortment of other fish, including salmon, sea bass, and a Hawaiian fish special that changes daily. We're not quite sure why they feel the need to fly fish in from Hawaii when they're surrounded by fish-filled waters, but I suppose one does get tired of whitefish after a while. In addition to the seafood, the restaurant offers a dizzying assortment of pastas, sandwiches, burgers, steaks, chicken, salads, appetizers, and even sushi and Mexican food. Usually when you get that kind of variety, none of it's all that good. Here, though, they somehow manage to handle it all well. The Library also brews its own beer, which goes nicely with almost everything on the menu—particularly the light and refreshing Keweenaw Golden Ale. The restaurant also offers a beer sampler for those who want to try a few of the creations.

★ Michigan House Café and Brewpub
906-337-1910
www.michiganhousecafe.com
300 Sixth St., Calumet, MI 49913
Open: Daily except Wed.
Price: Inexpensive
Cuisine: American
Serving: L, D
Credit Cards: MC, V
Handicapped Access: Yes
Special Features: Housed in a historic building; beer brewed on-site

A real gem in every way, from the early-1900s mining vibe to the outstanding food, which includes pub classics like a Black Angus burger, with modern additions like a Kahlua Pig sandwich and a black-bean quinoa patty substitute for the burgers. The Michigan House's on-site brewery (the Red Jacket Brewing Company, in honor of Calumet's first name) completes the establishment's trip down memory lane—it occupies the site of a former hotel/saloon/restaurant/brewery, and with two vintage apartments for rent upstairs and a bar and restaurant downstairs, the brewery was all that was missing. The brewery is focusing on reviving the past as well, working with a recipe that's reminiscent of pre-Prohibition ales. The resulting Oatmeal

Espress Stout has a higher alcohol content than most beers and uses oatmeal and espresso to give it its flavor and some of its oomph. The beer is brewed one barrel at a time, on Wednesday when the restaurant is closed. When it's not being used for beer, the espresso here is delicious on its own—fresh-ground beans brewed in a vintage hand extraction process, of course. In addition to burgers, salads, and sandwiches, the restaurant serves an assortment of pastas, steaks, pork chops, shepherd's pie, and locally caught fish prepared a variety of ways, including fish-and-chips. Desserts are homemade. The cheesecake is delicious, and we're dying to try the beer-battered chocolate.

Pilgrim River Steakhouse

906-482-8595
47409 US 41, Houghton, MI 49931
Open: Daily
Price: Moderate
Cuisine: American
Serving: L, D
Credit Cards: MC, V
Handicapped Access: Yes
Special Features: Prime rib every day; full bar

A steak lover's steakhouse, the Pilgrim River does just about everything right, from the huge assortment of cuts to the homemade bread served with every meal to the fact that they serve prime rib every day and not just on Sunday. And, as with any great steakhouse, the sides are just as good as the meat, whether you choose homemade soup, their famous spinach salad with hot bacon dressing, or the homemade steak fries. Despite the word "steakhouse" in its name, the Pilgrim River does seafood exceedingly well, especially whitefish and trout and the Friday special seafood platter. Homemade desserts are worth saving room for, and this is a great lunch spot as well, with big juicy burgers and tasty entrée-size salads.

MARQUETTE AND THE MARQUETTE RANGE

Casa Calabria

906-228-5012
www.thecasa.us
1106 N. Third St., Marquette, MI 49855
Open: Daily
Price: Inexpensive—Moderate
Cuisine: Italian
Serving: D
Credit Cards: AE, D, MC, V
Handicapped Access: Yes
Special Features: Large parking lot; good for groups; takeout available

Perfect for family dinners out, Casa Calabria is one of those hearty, satisfying Italian places that heaps your plate high with warm and filling pasta, often loaded with cheese. Healthy? No, but one bite in and you won't care. From the giant chunks of homemade, toasty garlic bread dripping with olive oil, to the baked pastas bubbling with cheese, Casa Calabria is exactly what you're looking for on a cold Marquette day. Its large dining room is also a good place to head with big groups. In addition to the pastas, this *casa* is known for its steaks—certified Black Angus and USDA prime sirloin, served with garlic bread. Casa Calabria is a good place to try out the *cudighi*, a spicy Italian sausage sub that has been a Marquette staple since it was introduced in the early mining days.

★ Gemignani's Italian Restaurant

906-482-2902
512 Quincy St., Hancock, MI 49930
Open: Mon.–Sat.
Price: Inexpensive—Moderate
Cuisine: Italian
Serving: L, D
Credit Cards: MC, V
Handicapped Access: Yes
Special Features: Beer and wine only; no smoking; homemade pies; espresso drinks

Gemignani's in Hancock. Matt Girvan

Patrons at Marquette's popular Lagniappe can enter through Jackson Cut Alley or through the classic Delft Theater. Marjorie O'Brien

The Gemignanis have been making spaghetti for hungry Copper Country diners for 75 years and counting. Gino, the grandfather of the current owner, Tony, started back in the late 1920s and early 1930s with a restaurant in Hancock called Gino's. Gino's meat sauce became so famous the family began canning it and selling it in grocery stores in the 1960s and 1970s. In 1982 Gino's son Rudy opened Gemignani's in Hancock in the same bright red and green building it occupies now. By 1994 Rudy was ready to retire and sell the place, but his son Tony decided to buy it off him instead and keep it in the family. Now Tony is selling the Gemignani sauce, too, but not in cans—just spice packs so that people can make the famous sauce at home. In addition to the sauce, Tony and his wife, Rose, hand make most of the pastas, including delicious ravioli and cannelloni. The restaurant also serves a variety of traditional meat dishes, including chicken marsala and veal piccata, and an assortment of vegetarian options. At lunchtime, big sandwiches on crusty bread are a local favorite.

★ Lagniappe Cajun Creole Eatery

906-226-8200
145 Jackson St, Marquette, MI 49855
Open: Mon.–Sat.
Price: Expensive
Cuisine: Cajun
Serving: L., D
Credit Cards: AE, D, MC, V
Handicapped Access: No

A relatively recent arrival to the Marquette dining scene, Lagniappe (Creole for "gift") has quickly gained repeat customers, thanks both to its jazz-inspired setting—the brick-walled basement of a nightclub, with low lighting and oversize, private booths— and to its delicious menu featuring New Orleans classics such as seafood bisque, crab cakes, crawdad étouffée, gumbo, hot beignets, and bread pudding with Jack

Daniels sauce, as well as modern spins on the Big Easy, including crawfish nachos and seafood fondeaux (a Lagniappe creation: fondue made with two types of seafood). Service is very good, and the quality and inventiveness of the food makes it worth the slightly higher prices. The bar is also popular with locals looking to grab a martini after work.

New York Deli & Italian Place

906-226-3032
102 W. Washington St., Marquette, MI
    49855-4368
Open: Mon.–Sat.
Price: Inexpensive–Moderate
Cuisine: Kosher deli; Italian
Serving: L, D
Credit Cards: MC, V
Handicapped Access: Yes

Typical New York deli by day and sit-down Italian restaurant by night, this spot packs them in for both. Sandwiches are piled so high they're actually hard to eat. People have been known to remove some of the fillings to take home. This is also the best place to get real, New York–style bagels and lox in Marquette. Soups are homemade and change often, but the tomato basil is a standout. They also serve a variety of salads at lunch, although the dressing is always oil and vinegar. For dinner, pastas, pizzas, and lasagna are done consistently well, and the broasted chicken specials are always a hit.

★ Nordic Bay Restaurant & Bar

906-225-1896
www.nordicbay.com
1880 US 41 South, Marquette, MI 49855
Open: Daily
Price: Moderate
Cuisine: Continental
Serving: Dinner Mon.–Sat., breakfast
    served Sat. and Sun.
Credit Cards: MC, V
Handicapped Access: No

The Nordic Bay Restaurant serves inventive fish and meat dishes in a warm and intimate wine-cellar-like space. Fish preparations allow the freshness of the fish to shine, with simple additions like lime and garlic on Munising Bay trout, or a light blend of butter and lemon on Lake Superior whitefish. Meat is equally as fresh and locally sourced; the filet is a standout, wrapped in bacon and finished with smoked sea salt. All dinners come with dinner salad or soup and a starch of your choice—the baked sweet potato is fantastic, as is the French onion soup. For a lighter meal, the blackened salmon salad is light and delicious. The wine list is long and varied, and servers are well-versed enough to make spot-on recommendations for your meal. The bar also carries a wide selection of microbrews. Saturday or Sunday brunch is a treat—though the breakfast selections are solid, lunch options like lager-steeped mussels and the blackened whitefish sandwich are downright delicious.

★ Sweet Water Café

906-226-7009
517 N. Third St., Marquette, MI 49855
Open: Daily
Price: Inexpensive–Moderate
Cuisine: International
Serving: B, L, D
Credit Cards: MC, V
Handicapped Access: Yes
Special Features: Emphasis on organic, healthy food; on-site bakery; better-than-average coffee; local art displayed

A popular spot with the college crowd in Marquette, thanks to its focus on organic, locally sourced foods and tasty vegetarian options, the Sweet Water isn't a vegetarian restaurant at all—it just provides lots of options. Breakfast at Sweet Water is hands-down the best in town and possibly the best

Sweet Water Café, Marquette Amy Westervelt

in the U.P. It's really that good, from the almondine lattes to the fresh juices to farm-fresh eggs, French toast made from fresh-baked bread, and thick-cut bacon from a local butcher. Vegetarian and vegan scrambles are also available, as is a warm and hearty "winter cereal" composed of oatmeal, wheat berries, brown rice, millet, dried cranberries, and raisins boiled and topped with toasted almonds. Lunch and dinner are equally as inventive and delicious, with everything from a world-class cheeseburger to the café's Orbit Burger, a grain and lentil patty. While it sounds boring, when served with pesto, tomato slices, and Swiss cheese atop fresh-baked bread, it's absolutely delicious. Lunch sandwiches and salads are available any time of day, but the café does a special dinner menu Wednesday through Sunday as well, with a menu that changes weekly but always includes an option from every category: red meat, pasta, vegan, fish, and chicken or pork, each listed with a suggested beer or wine. Desserts are baked fresh daily and well worth saving room for.

The Vierling Brewpub & Restaurant

906-228-3533
www.thevierling.com
119 S. Front St., Marquette, MI 49855
Open: Mon.–Sat.
Price: Inexpensive–Moderate
Cuisine: Italian, British
Serving: L, D
Credit Cards: AE, D, MC, V
Handicapped Access: Yes
Special Features: On-site brewery; housed in historic 100-plus-year-old saloon

Though the owners have certainly pulled off their refurbishment of this historic saloon, it's far more of a proper restaurant these days than a wild and woolly drinking hall, with the possible exception of its popular Friday fish fry. Instead, guests nosh sedately on grilled sandwiches and large salads at lunch, and a variety of Italian specialties plus steaks and whitefish done a number of ways (grilled, Cajun, fried, you name it) at dinner. We don't really understand why they bother with the steaks or the Italian food—their specialty is clearly seafood, and they do it very well, but most everything else on the dinner menu is just OK. The lunch menu, on the other hand, is good across the board, with a really wide variety of tasty salads. The Vierling also brews its own beer, creating English-style ales with modern twists in the downstairs brewery, which is viewable from the street.

ONTONAGON AND THE PORKIES

Antonio's

906-885-5223
Mineral River Plaza, White Pine, MI 49971
Open: Daily
Price: Inexpensive
Cuisine: American, Italian
Serving: B, L, D
Credit Cards: Not accepted
Handicapped Access: Yes

Known for its 1/3-pound burgers and its thin-crust pizza, Antonio's is a western U.P. institution. The original Antonio's was opened in Iron River by the Italian father of the owner of this Antonio's. The son also owns another outpost in nearby Bergland. Both locations are local hangouts, with a 1950s diner feel, and both serve up a fairly tasty Italian menu in addition to the pizza and burger standbys, for unbelievably low prices. Pasties are also made fresh daily.

Henry's Never Inn

906-886-9910
74 National Ave., Rockland, MI 49960
Open: Daily
Price: Inexpensive
Cuisine: American
Serving: L, D
Credit Cards: Not accepted

Handicapped Access: No

An old miner's bar turned restaurant, Henry's specializes in the namesake's famous homemade soups and chili served with garlic toast, as well as big, juicy burgers and Reubens. Nightly dinners feature weekly, rotating specials, including build-your-own-pizza-night on Wednesday, smorgasbords on weekends, Italian night on Saturday, and of course the Friday fish fry.

FOOD PURVEYORS

Babycakes Muffin Company (906-226-7744; www.babycakesmuffincompany.com; 223 W. Washington St., Marquette) Delicious muffins, scones, croissants, cookies, and breads baked fresh daily.

Berry Patch (906-289-4602; 920 Gratiot Ave., Copper Harbor) Delicious fresh wild berry jams and sauces, as well as assorted gift items. Open in summer only.

Dead River Coffee (906-226-2112; 143 Washington St., Marquette) Sustainably sourced coffee roasted on-site in small batches has quickly made Dead River a local Marquette choice for best coffee. Pick up a half-pound to take home with you and your morning coffee is on them.

Doncker's Candy & Gifts (906-226-6110, 137 W. Washington St., Marquette) An institution dating back to 1896, Doncker's is known for its fudge and its pay-by-the-pound bulk candy. A good stop if you're fueling up for a road trip.

Four Seasons Tea Room (906-482-3233; www.fourseasonstearoom.com; 606 Shelden Ave., Houghton) A 1940s-inspired tearoom with a variety of tea services, sandwiches, and cakes, Four Seasons is a fantastic place to while away an afternoon. All the teas and some of the cakes are also sold in their shop, along with teapots, teacups, and various other tea accessories.

Gophers (906-226-0900; www.gophersnacks.com; 910 N. Third St.,

Marquette) Located in a cute older house in downtown Marquette, this popular lunch spot and bakery is famous for its desserts—especially double-lemon cream cake, cheesecake, and fruit tarts—as well as Belgian chocolates and pralines.

The Jampot (www.societystjohn.com; 6500 MI 26; 3 miles east of Eagle River and 5 miles west of Eagle Harbor, right next to Jacob's Creek Falls) The jam, fruit butters, and baked goods here are delicious, but people are equally motivated to visit this tiny store on the road between Eagle River and Eagle Harbor just for the story behind it. Started by three monks from the Society of St. John, the store is still run by the order, who have since grown in number and built an ornate church just up the road. The monks felt the area lent itself well to a monastic life, and they now also lead monastic retreats here for others. Although they are always very friendly and pleasant, don't expect the monks to be too chatty—they prefer to spend most of their time in quiet reflection. When they're not tending to their booming online jam business, that is.

Jean Kay's Pasties (two locations: 906-774-0430, 204 E. B St. in Iron Mountain, and 906-228-5310, 1639 Presque Isle Ave. in Marquette; www.jeankays.com) Well-known throughout the U.P., with a thriving mail-order business, Jean Kay's uses cubed flank steak plus potatoes, onions, and optional rutabagas for the traditional meat pasty, and offers a vegetarian version with broccoli, cauliflower, celery, onions, carrots, potatoes, peppers, mushrooms, and low-fat cream cheese in a whole-wheat crust.

Jilbert's Dairy (906-225-1363; www.jilbertdairy.com; 200 Meeske Ave., Marquette) The U.P.'s favorite ice cream maker is based here in Marquette. The dairy welcomes visitors to its retail store and ice cream parlor, where they can watch the whole operation, test out new Jilbert's sundae creations, and pick up a few pints.

Joe's Pasty Shop (906-932-4412; 116 W.

Aurora St., Ironwood) Some nominate this very popular shop as home of the best pasty. Options include traditional Cornish—ground sirloin with rutabagas, potatoes, and onions—a breakfast pasty, a vegetable version, and the occasional specialty pasty.

Sheldon's Pasties & Bakery (906-487-6166; www.sheldonsbakery.com; 901 W. Sharon Ave., Houghton) Winner of the 2007 Pasty Fest Copper County award in the commercial division and the nontraditional division. Sheldon's traditional pasty won't pass muster with pasty purists for its use of a blend of ground pork and beef and the addition of carrots, but for those without any hard-and-fast pasty rules, they are delicious. The breakfast pasty, which is what won the "nontraditional" award, is filled with pork sausage, potatoes, cheese, eggs, and seasoning. In addition to pasties, which Sheldon's ships anywhere in the country, the bakery also sells pies, muffins, pastries, and doughnuts.

Toni's Country Kitchen and Bakery (906-337-0611; 79 Third St., Laurium) Toni's wins many "best pasty" honors for its famous 1-pound pasty, made with ground chuck, potatoes, onion, and rutabagas.

RECREATION

In addition to one of the U.P.'s most popular outdoor attractions—Pictured Rocks National Lakeshore—and Lake Superior, the largest of the Great Lakes by far, this section of the U.P. is absolutely teeming with recreational opportunities. Snowmobilers tear around on hundreds of miles of trails in winter and still don't come close enough to bug cross-country skiers. Alpine skiers have access to several large mountains, a world-famous ski jump, and a new-kid-on-the-block resort that's intent on giving the Rockies a run for their money.

Hundreds of waterfalls draw hikers and families in the summer; rivers, streams, and inland lakes full of trout, perch, bass, walleye, and whitefish bring anglers from all over the country; and paddlers have hundreds of shoreline miles at their disposal.

The wilderness outpost of Isle Royale alone offers enough possible activities to fill weeks, from backcountry hiking to paddling to unparalleled wildlife viewing, including rare birds to moose to notoriously elusive gray wolves. In the fall, flaming red and glowing gold leaves light up Lake Superior's shore, providing some of the best fall color views in the country. Fall also brings Michigan's popular deer hunting season, followed by black bear hunts.

It's important to remember that, due to its large size, Lake Superior takes a very long time to warm up in the summer once the winter ice melts. August waters are generally warm, and pleasant swimming can be found earlier in the summer at some of the region's smaller, shallower inland lakes.

Beaches

Agate Beach (aka Santa Monica Beach). Take MI 26 to Toivola, about 15 miles southwest of Houghton, then head west on Misery Bay Rd. This sandy crescent beach is good for swimming, and there are plenty of colorful rocks to be found, including agates from time to time. Picnic facilities available.

Baraga State Park, off US 41 in Baraga. This long sandy beach overlooking Keweenaw Bay has sand tinged gray from iron ore. The park also allows camping. Playground, picnic facilities, and flush toilets available.

Great Sand Bay is an idyllic sandy beach and protected bay between Eagle River and Eagle Harbor. Matt Girvan

Great Sand Bay, off MI 26 between Eagle River and Eagle Harbor. A perfect sandy crescent and a calm bay for swimming, ringed by woods and backed by dunes.

Lake Gogebic, N 9995 MI 64 in Marenisco. This large inland lake is popular for swimming due to its large sandy beach and shallow water that warms up earlier in the summer than Lake Superior. Playground, picnic areas, grills, and flush toilets available.

Lake Manganese and Manganese Falls, Lake Manganese Rd., just south of Copper Harbor off US 41. The crystal-clear, fairly shallow waters here warm up early in the summer. The sandy beach is bordered by hemlock groves, and a boat launch is provided for those who want to take advantage of the lake's good fishing. A short hike to nearby Manganese Falls reveals a lovely 45-foot waterfall tumbling through a deep gorge covered in bright green moss.

McClain State Park, 18350 MI 203, Hancock. Wind surfing is popular on this 2-mile-long sand beach on Lake Superior, as is berry-picking from nearby fields.

South Beach, Lake St., Marquette. This long, wide sandy beach is a popular swimming beach on Lake Superior. Water is chilly until August.

Bicycling

Rentals
Cross-Country Sports (906-337-4520; 507 Oak St., Calumet)
Down Wind Sports (906-482-2500; 308 Shelden Ave., Houghton)
Keweenaw Adventure Company (906-289-4303; 155 Gratiot St., Copper Harbor)
Lakeshore Bike (906-228-7547; 505 Lakeshore Blvd., Marquette)
Trek & Trail (906-932-5858; 1310 E. Cloverland Dr., Ironwood)

Top Rides

Big Bay Trail. From Marquette, take CR 550 about 22 miles to Big Bay. Turn left (west) onto Dump Rd. Travel 3/4 of a mile; trailhead and parking are on the right. A popular part of the Noquemanon Trail Network loops around Big Bay, offering both woods and lake views.

Bruno's Run, Hiawatha National Forest, 6 miles south of Munising on MI 94. A section of the Valley Spur cross-country ski trails that crisscross through the Hiawatha Forest near Munising, Bruno's Run is a fairly challenging but fun ride through the woods with views of Pete's Lake and Indian River. Exposed roots and lots of up-and-downhill action.

Jack Stevens Hancock–Calumet Rail Trail. Trailhead is at Portage Lake lift bridge that connects Hancock to Houghton. This 14-mile trail follows a former railroad grade from Hancock to Calumet. The trail is rough, with ATVs on it regularly in summer and snowmobiles in winter, and only suitable for mountain bikes. For road cyclists, MI 203 has a paved bike shoulder from Hancock to Calumet.

Marquette Lakeside Path. Bicycle is the best way to get around Marquette, and this bike path is one of the reasons why. Looping around the lake from the harbor down to Presque Isle Park at the north end of town, the path provides a pleasant 5-mile (each way) lakeside bike ride, and an easy way to get from one side of town to the other without dealing with any of the hills.

Pomeroy/Henry Lake Mountain Bike Complex (1-800-659-3232). Part of the over 200 miles of trails that run through Iron County and down into Wisconsin to make up the Pines and Mines trails, this family-friendly 100-mile complex of loops provides a number of options, from shorter 7-mile rides to challenging longer rides. Trails lead through Ottawa National Forest and pass by various lakes, streams, and wetlands.

Porcupine Mountains State Park (906-885-5275; www.michigan.gov/dnr), 3 miles west of Silver City on MI 107. The state park offers dozens of trails, many of which provide access to parts of the park that are otherwise tough to get to. Park officials have prepared a detailed and comprehensive mountain biking map that guests can pick up at the park's visitor center or download and print from the Michigan DNR Web site.

Wolverine Mountain Bike Trail (906-932-5858), 1 mile east of Ironwood and 1 mile north of US 2 on Sunset Rd. Near Big Powderhorn ski resort, this popular cross-country ski complex becomes a network of mountain bike trails in the summer.

Bird-Watching

Au Train Songbird Trail, in the Hiawatha Forest, west of Munising, at Au Train. From Au Train head south on FR HO3 for about 4 miles, then go 1 mile east on FR 2276 and then 2 miles north on FR 2596. At the grocery store in Au Train, bird-watchers can check out binoculars and a taped bird guide that describes the markings and songs of 20 common songbirds found along the trail. It's a great way for amateur birders to get up to speed quickly, and the tape itself can sometimes serve as a bird call. The trail is about 2 miles long, passing through uplands and forest, along a stream, past a bog and a wooden platform overlooking Au Train Lake. May and June are particularly good for viewing, when visitors have a high chance of spotting various warblers, osprey, bald eagles, and sandpipers, among many others.

Black River Songbird Trail (906-667-0261) From Bessemer follow US 2 east about 1 mile to CR 513 (Black River Rd.); turn left (north) and follow the signs for the Black River Scenic Byway. Another songbird interpretive trail developed by the Department of Natural Resources, Black River also offers a tape and guide to songbirds commonly spotted on the

Brockway Mountain Drive is known for its views of Copper Harbor and for regular hawk sightings. Matt Girvan

trail. In addition, this is a prime spot to view migrating waterbirds during spring and fall migrations. Merlins have also been known to nest in the bluffs around the harbor.

Brockway Mountain Drive, Copper Harbor. Known for its spectacular views of Copper Harbor and the Keweenaw Peninsula, Brockway is also a great place to spot hawks.

Isle Royale. According to the National Park Service, there are more species of birds on Isle Royale than any other living thing. Interestingly, you won't always see the same birds here that you would on the mainland. Bring binoculars, as numerous trails provide great opportunities to spot birds.

Seney National Wildlife Refuge (906-586-9851; www.fws.gov/midwest/seney/), off MI 77, 5 miles south of Seney and 2 miles north of Germfask. Established in 1935 as a refuge and breeding ground for migratory birds and other wildlife, Seney today attracts birders from all over the world, hoping to see glimpses of rare breeds like the yellow rail and the bald eagle. Check in with the experts at the visitor center when you arrive for of-the-minute advice on where to see what, but as a general rule early morning or evening are the best times to view wildlife.

Canoeing and Kayaking

Rentals

Keweenaw Adventure Company and Harbor Kayak Paddle (906-289-4303145; www.keweenawadventure.com; Gratiot St. / US 41, Copper Harbor, MI 49918)

Big Bay Outfitters/Anatomy of a Canoe (906-345-9399; CR 550, P.O. Box 38, Big Bay, MI 49808)

Northern Waters Sea Kayaking (906-387-2323; 129 E. Munising St., Munising) For guided kayak tours of Pictured Rocks and Grand Island, among other spots.

Porcupine Mountain State Park Concessionaire (906-885-5612; 3 miles west of Silver City on MI 107)

Top Paddles

Au Train River, in the Hiawatha National Forest. West of Munising, at Au Train, travel south on FR HO3 for about 4 miles, then go 1 mile east on FR 2276 and then 2 miles north on FR 2596. A slow and meandering 10-mile canoe trip that starts at the Au Train Lake Campground and leads to a sandy beach on Lake Superior. Paddlers can either get out at the beach or continue on to brave the big lake.

Grand Island (906-387-3700). Experienced paddlers can head from the docks at Munising out to and around Grand Island. There are even beachfront campsites set up on the island, which put paddlers in perfect position for tackling Pictured Rocks National Lakeshore.

Hiawatha Water Trail (www.hiawathawatertrail.org; info@hiawathawatertrail.org), Lake Superior. A fantastic 120-mile stretch of Lake Superior paddling stretching east from Big Bay to Grand Marais, the Hiawatha Water Trail is what Pictured Rocks paddlers generally use. The Hiawatha Water Trail Association provides lots of information about the trail, including a map of the trail with various put-in and take-out points.

Indian River Canoe Trail (906-786-4062), in the Hiawatha National Forest. Indian River begins at Fish Lake, 15 miles south of Munising, and flows down to Indian Lake, 36 miles northwest of Manistique. This is a great trip for a group with varying skill levels. The Indian River is wide and gentle, but the trail is long (36 miles) if you want to add a little challenge to it, plus trout fishing is decent despite the popularity of the river, and the river flows through various woods and wetlands that are good for spotting birds and wildlife.

Isle Royale (www.nps.gov/isro/). One of the best ways to explore this wilderness isle is by kayak. The park's newsletter *The Greenstone* includes a detailed map highlighting trails. Kayakers are encouraged to use the inland lakes as much as possible as opposed to unreliable Superior. Park rangers also ask that kayakers wash off kayaks that have been in Lake Superior before entering one of the inland lakes on Isle Royale, in order to avoid the transfer of invasive species from one to the other. Very experienced and fit paddlers can make a 14-mile circle tour through the island. Those who attempt it will be rewarded with solitude and breathtaking natural beauty.

Ontonagon River, Middle, South, and East Branches (906-932-1330). The Ontonagon River has something for every level of paddler, from slow, scenic rides on the Middle Branch to a mix of easy paddles with decently challenging white water at the end of the South Branch to nonstop rapids on the East Branch.

Pictured Rocks National Lakeshore (906-387-3700). The only way to really view Pictured Rocks is by boat, and in a kayak you can land close enough to get a really close look at those vibrant colors. With Lake Superior's erratic weather, however, only experienced paddlers should take on this trip.

Presque Isle River (906-885-5612), Porcupine Mountain State Park. Considered some of the Midwest's most challenging white water, the last few miles of this river draw experienced paddlers from all over the state.

Isle Royale's crystal-clear waters are popular with kayakers. Matt Girvan

Superior Sunsets

There are numerous spots around Lake Superior known for incredible sunsets. Following are some favorites:

Brockway Mountain Drive, Copper Harbor. With panoramic views as far away as Isle Royale, sunsets here are breathtaking, particularly during the fall color season.

Pictured Rocks National Lakeshore. On a clear, sunny day, when the water is turquoise and the sun begins to set on the rocks, playing up their pinks, reds, oranges, and blacks, you'll feel like you've somehow stepped off a boat and into a surrealist painting.

Chicken Bone Lake, Isle Royale. This interior lake on Isle Royale is one of the best spots in the park to see moose, and they like sunset almost as much as they like sunrise. If you're quiet and still, you'll spot them cruising around the lake just about the time it starts to get that pretty evening glow.

Fishing

While fishing centers predominantly on the inland lakes in the southern U.P. near Lake Michigan, in the north, along Lake Superior's shores, anglers flock to the many rivers and streams rushing toward the Great Lake. Trout and salmon fishing are particularly good here.

Places to Fish

Carp River. The mouth of the river is at Marquette Lower Harbor. The river is known for its crystal-clear waters and an abundance of steelhead, king salmon, coho salmon, brown trout, and brook trout.

Chocolay River. Running through Marquette County and dumping into Lake Superior at Harvey, a few miles east of Marquette, the Chocolay is known for steelhead trout, but there are also brown trout, brook trout, and salmon in its waters. The river stays free of ice most of the year as well.

Craig Lake State Park (906-339-4461) From Michigamme take US 41 about a mile west of Michigamme and turn on Keewaydin Lake Rd. Follow signs 8 miles north to parking lot. A gigantic 6,000-plus-acre state park with several lakes, the largest of which is Craig Lake. All the lakes in the park are known for good fishing, but Craig is particularly good for muskellunge, bass, walleye, and northern pike, while Teddy Lake has perch and panfish. Motorized boats are not allowed except on Keewaydin Lake. Fishing is allowed by artificial lure only, and a catch-and-release policy is in place for northern pike, muskellunge, and bass.

Grand Island. Some of the U.P.'s best fishing is to be had in the waters surrounding Grand Island. Trout Bay is excellent for lake trout and coho salmon; Murray Bay has perch, pike, walleye, and rock bass; Echo Lake, in the interior of the island, is known for bass, pike, and panfish. Largely surrounded by woods and sheer sandstone cliffs, this is also one of the area's most picturesque fishing spots.

Licensing

Fishing is abundant in the U.P., but you must purchase a valid Michigan State fishing license before engaging in it, even if you plan to catch and release. Visit www.michigan.gov/dnr for details.

Gratiot River. Begins at No Name Pond east of MI 26 / US 41 about 5 miles northeast of Mohawk and runs 20 miles to empty into Lake Superior near Seven Mile Point. The upper portion, including No Name Pond, is good for brook trout, while the last mile downstream from Lower Falls hosts spring runs of steelhead. From Upper Falls to the river's mouth the river is home to rainbow trout, along with the occasional coho salmon.

Yellow Dog River. Easy access from Big Bay, CR 550, north of Marquette. The Yellow Dog runs from Bulldog Lake in the McCormick Wilderness on the border of Marquette and Baraga Counties to Lake Independence in Marquette County near Lake Superior. One of the best-known trout streams in the U.P., the Yellow Dog draws anglers from all over the country every year, fishing for brown, brook, and rainbow trout.

Golf

Gogebic Country Club (906-932-2515; 200 Country Club Rd., Ironwood) An older, public course, opened in the early 1920s, Gogebic offers plenty of hills and tree-lined fairways, and a very pleasant clubhouse. 18 holes, 5752 yards, par 71. Cart rental, putting green, restaurant, bar.

Greywalls at Marquette Golf Club (906-225-0721; www.marquettegolfclub.com; 1075 Grove St., Marquette) The U.P.'s only 36-hole club boasts two 18-hole courses, one of which—Greywalls—is nationally ranked and has been earning praise and plaudits since its opening in 2005. The club's other course, Heritage, is a good, solid course, but Greywalls is magnificent, with undulating fairways banked by hemlock groves that open up to give sudden and spectacular Lake Superior views every once in a while. In the fall the color of the trees provides an incredibly beautiful contrast to the green of the fairways, making the scenery all the more appealing. 36 holes, 6,828 yards, both par 71. Cart rental, restaurant, bar.

The Yellow Dog River is one of Michigan's best trout streams. Courtesy Save the Wild UP

Keweenaw Mountain Lodge Golf (906-289-4403; www.atthelodge.com; US 41, just south of Copper Harbor) A pleasant 9-hole, 36-par course, set on rolling, wooded hills that dates back to the government's Public Works program in the 1930s.

Hiking

Chapel Basin (906-387-3700; www.nps.gov/piro/) Located in Pictured Rocks National Lakeshore, this trail offers several choices, depending on the time you have available. A 3-mile hike leads to impressive Chapel Falls, plunging 60 feet over the cliffs. Just a mile and a half or so beyond the falls is Chapel Rock, and hikers can then continue on the same trail to Mosquito River.

Escarpment Trail (906-885-5275) From the Government Peak trailhead, Porcupine Mountains State Park, this popular loop trail follows a high ridge over the Big Carp River Basin, offering dramatic views of the valley and spectacular fall color. The slightly shorter Overlook Trail starts in the same place and provides similar views, and for those short on time, the Lake of the Clouds Overlook provides the terrific view without the hike.

Scoville Point Loop, Isle Royale (www.nps.gov/isro/) There are numerous backcountry hikes on Isle Royale, but this 4-mile loop near Rock Harbor is a great way for newcomers to acclimate themselves to the island and take in some fantastic views. The trail winds up and along the bluffs from Rock Harbor, through the trees, past old copper mines to lovely and isolated Scoville Point, and loops back past an inland lake to Rock Harbor.

View from Lake of the Clouds overlook. Matt Girvan

The Trap Hills (906-932-1330; E6248 US 2, Ironwood) A section of the North Country Trail runs through these bluffs in the Ottawa National Forest. Though it's a bit remote, the views from these hills are spectacular, incorporating Lake Superior, the Porcupine Mountains, and Lake Gogebic in one panoramic sweep.

Yellowdog River Falls. From CR 550 between Marquette and Big Bay, take CR 510, turn right on CR KAA, which becomes CR AAA, then CR IAA. Stay on this road for a little less than 2 miles and park at the trailhead. From here it's a fantastic, challenging hike between Big Bay and Marquette that follows the Yellow River as it dips and drops several times to create a network of waterfalls and pools. You have to climb and dip, so it's not an easy woodland walk, but it's still pretty straightforward, and the scenery is excellent.

Hunting

Game/Season
White-tailed deer—Bow: Oct. 1–Nov. 14 and Dec. 1–Jan. 2; regular firearm: Nov. 15–30; muzzle loaders: Dec. 2–18
Russian boar—Year-round (hunters can hunt boar with any valid hunting license)
Black bear—Sep. 10–Oct. 26

Elk—Aug. 25–29; Sep. 15–18; Dec. 11–18
Wild turkey—Oct. 8–Nov. 14
American woodcock—Sep. 22–Nov. 5
Pheasant—(Males only) Oct. 10–Nov. 14
Ruffed grouse—Sep. 15–Nov. 14; Dec. 1–Jan. 1
Ducks and mergansers—Sep. 29–Nov. 27
Canada geese—Sep. 18–Nov. 1

Guides and Lodges

The Timbers Resort–Lake Gogebic, north end of lake, MI 28, Bergland; 906-575-3542

Bear Mountain (906-475-9676; www.bearmountainquest.com; 91 N. Basin Dr., Negaunee) A private hunting ranch focused solely on Russian boar, which hunters are entitled to kill at will in the U.P. because they pose a nuisance to most crops as well as a safety hazard. Bear Mountain also leads fishing expeditions and provides lodging on-site.

Hunting Areas

Craig Lake State Park (906-339-4461, 851 County Road AKE, Champion) Much of this 6,000-acre park is ideal habitat for deer, bear, rabbit, and grouse, which you can hunt for here in season. The park also allows trapping of muskrat, beaver, and mink. Snow can come early and fall heavy here, so hunters are advised to be careful in the fall.

Porcupine Mountain State Park (906-885-5275; 3 miles west of Silver City on MI 107) Nearly all of the Porkies' 60,000 acres are open to hunters during the season. Deer and black bear are plentiful here, and the park's cabins and yurts are well-placed in the wilderness for hunters.

Cross-Country Skiing

ABR Ski Trails (906-932-3502; www.abrski.com; E5299 W. Pioneer Rd., Ironwood) A 600-acre cross-country ski resort with 42 spectacular kilometers of cross-country trails, groomed daily.

Lower Noquemanon Trail (From Marquette follow Wright St. north off US 41 for approximately 1 mile to Forestville Rd. Turn left and follow Forestville Rd. for 3 miles. Watch for railroad tracks to the right. Turn right and cross tracks. Immediately turn left for trailhead, restroom, and parking.) Groomed 25-kilometer trail includes several hills and is rated intermediate to difficult. The trail is part of the Noquemanon Trail System, a 75-kilometer system being developed in and around Marquette and Big Bay.

Munising Trails—Pictured Rocks National Lakeshore (906-387-3700; www.nps.gov/piro/) Beginning at Munising Falls, this network of loops spreads out to Miner's Castle, providing several options depending on your time and skill level. The trails weave through the trees and are dotted with informative interpretive stations.

Swedetown Cross-Country Ski Trails (906-337-1170; www.keweenawtrails.com; Agent St., Calumet) Popular Keweenaw cross-country complex with more than 30 kilometers of groomed cross-country ski and snowshoe trails in Calumet, including several loops with varying difficulty levels, from beginner loops with few if any hills to advanced, hilly loops. Swedetown keeps 4.5 kilometers of trails lit until 10 pm during the winter. Attached chalet includes a snack bar and a groomed sledding hill.

Valley Spur Cross-Country Ski Trail (6 miles south of Munising on MI 94) A 38-mile cross-country trail system in the Hiawatha National Forest that is rarely if ever crowded,

Valley Spur includes 11 loops of varying difficulty, each of which passes through different scenery, from hemlock groves to inland lakes.

Wolverine Ski Club Nordic Trails (906-932-5858; 1 mile east of Ironwood and 1 mile north of US 2 on Sunset Rd.) Open daily 8–8. Five different loops through rolling hills and woods that provide 18 kilometers of skiing for both striders and skaters of all levels, though the emphasis is on more experienced skiers. Wolverine also allows snowshoes on its tracks and provides a warming lodge for all. Some of the loops cross over onto Big Powderhorn ski resort and can also be accessed from the resort side.

Downhill Skiing and Snowboarding

Big Powderhorn (906-932-4838 or 1-800-501-7669; www.bigpowderhorn.net; N11375 Powderhorn Rd., Bessemer) 600-foot vertical drop, nine chairlifts, 29 runs, three terrain parks, lodging, restaurants, bar.

BlackJack (906-229-5115; www.skiblackjack.com; N11251 Blackjack Rd., Bessemer) 466-foot vertical drop, six chairlifts, 20 runs, two terrain parks, two half pipes, restaurant, lodging.

Indianhead (1-800-346-3426; www.indianheadmtn.com; 500 Indianhead Rd., Wakefield) 638-foot vertical drop, nine chairlifts, 28 runs, two terrain parks, lodging, restaurant, bar. Indianhead is the nicest all-around resort in Big Snow Country, with the most options for everyone in the family and the best-kept lodging and restaurants.

Mount Bohemia (902-360-7240; www.mtbohemia.com; 100 Lac La Belle Rd., Lac La Belle, about 35 miles north of Houghton) 900-foot vertical drop, two hoist lifts, 71 runs (including 17 backcountry runs). An X-Games style extreme winter sports haven, Mount Bohemia was hotly contested by locals when it was first built; people are never thrilled about development in these parts, and Mount Bohemia's developers weren't just talking about a ski resort but numerous lodges built out around the resort and Lac La Belle. Though it's still a sore point, the ski resort has gained fans fairly quickly for its steep and challenging runs and its hard-core backcountry. The mountain gets 270-plus inches of snow each season, and the average run is pitched at 31 degrees. The "Extreme Backcountry" runs include 40-foot cliff drops.

Porcupine Mountains State Park (231-420-5405; www.skitheporkies.com; Porcupine Mountain, 36606 MI 107, Ontonagon) Two lifts, 42 runs, 787-foot vertical, no lodge or restaurant. One of the few state parks in the country to offer prime downhill skiing, Porcupine Mountain with its 787-foot vertical drop makes for better skiing than the Big Snow Country resorts, especially with its 16 newly opened double-black-diamond Everest runs.

Snowmobiling

Rentals
Copper Country Rentals (906-337-9905; www.coppercountryrental.com; Mine Street Station, Calumet)

Grand Island Snowmobile Rentals (906-387-2132; 925 W. Munising Ave., Munising)

Midway Rentals (906-228-4200; www.midwayrentalsandsales.com; 43 Industrial Park Rd., Negaunee)

Timberline Sports (906-575-3397; www.timberlinesport.com; MI 28 1.5 miles west of Bergland)

Snowmobile Trails

Alligator Eye. MI 64, 2 miles south of Gogebic. Short, steep trail leads to the top of this bluff with panoramic views.

Bill Nicholls Trail. Very popular trail that follows an old railroad from Adventure Mountain in Ontonagon to Houghton in the Keweenaw Peninsula.

Brockway Mountain Trail. Follows popular Brockway Mountain Rd. scenic route to the top of Brockway Mountain for 360-degree views of the Keweenaw.

Grand Island. When Lake Superior is sufficiently frozen, snowmobilers head out to Grand Island to check out its frozen sea caves and icy cliffs.

Great Kingston Plains. The remnants of a clear-cut forest make for prime riding 29 miles east of Munising.

Greenland-Bruce Crossing Trail (Trail 3). Runs through the Ottawa National Forest near Ontonagon to connect to Bruce Crossing. From here, it connects with dozens of other trails in the forest. Riders can stay on Trail 3 to Watersmeet, or head west to Bergland, near Lake Gogebic, or east to Agate Falls.

L'Anse to Big Bay. The AAA Trail brings snowmobilers on a fantastic ride through the Huron Mountains and the Yellowdog Plains to the town of Big Bay. Once in Big Bay, riders can take advantage of the 148 miles of groomed snowmobile trails around the bay as well.

FAMILY FUN

Copper Peak International Ski Flying Hill (906-932-3500; www.copperpeak.org; Ironwood) The tallest man-made ski jump in the world, Copper Peak is open to visitors during the summer, when you can crawl up its 18 stories and marvel at both the view and how terrifying it would be to go hurtling down this monster on skis. Just to put the hill into perspective, in the Olympics, ski jumpers compete on two different-size hills, small (90 meters) and large (120 meters). Copper Peak is a 170-meter hill. There are five ski-flying hills in Europe, but Copper Peak is the only ski-flying facility in the Western Hemisphere. As of spring 2007 Copper Peak was in the process of finishing various improvements required by the FIS (Fédération Internationale de Ski) in order to host ski-flying competitions. When the hill hosts another competition, it will be an event not to be missed!

Ice Caves of Eben. 15 miles west of Munising. (Access is through private property; ask at the Hiawatha National Forest visitor center in Munising about current access and directions.) This is one of the coolest sights in the U.P. during the winter. Technically located on private property, the ice caves are reached through a fairly easy 1-mile trail (2 miles round-trip) through the generous landlord's birch woods. Trails approach from both the top and the bottom of the caves—it's obviously best to approach from the bottom. We found out the hard way one day how slippery those caves are when trying to scramble down from the top. Though they are referred to as the ice "caves," there's really only one big cave. Ice hangs over it and coats the interior in a layer so thick it turns various shades of blue during the day, similar to a glacier. It's a lot of fun to climb in and around the cave, but be very careful not to slip.

Keweenaw Berry Farm (906-523-4271; 39795 US 41, Chassell) You don't get a much better kiddie triumvirate than mini-golf, ice cream, and a petting zoo. The Keweenaw Berry Farm is a restaurant, store, and bakery, but behind those establishments the owners

Copper Peak is the only ski-flying hill in the United States. Jeremy Nelson

have set up a little petting zoo fairy-tale land with emus, llamas, fallow deer, pygmy goats, pheasants, even miniature donkeys and horses. There's also a little mini-golf course in the back, which is only $2 to play. And when you've petted and putted your fill, the restaurant serves Jilbert's ice cream.

Lake Superior Glass-Bottom Boat Shipwreck Tours (906-387-4477; www.shipwrecktours.com; 1204 Commercial St., Munising) This is really interesting for the whole family—kids will love the glass-bottom boat, with fish sweeping by and pirate-looking shipwrecks rising up below, while parents marvel at the hundreds of boats this seemingly calm lake has sunk.

Pictured Rocks Cruise (800-650-2379; www.picturedrocks.com; Munising Harbor) Although some kids do get bored on the three-hour boat tour from Munising out to the Pictured Rocks and back, most are thrilled by the boat and the unusual colors and formations of the rocks. Waving and hollering at the occasional backcountry hiker is another favorite part of this trip.

Presque Isle River Waterfalls (See "Waterfalls" below for complete description) Kids absolutely love the suspension bridge here, and the wooden boardwalk provides an easy, safe way for small children to do a waterfall hike.

Quincy Mine Tour (906-482-3101; www.quincymine.com; US 41, 1 mile north of Hancock; tours available Apr. to late Oct.) A fantastic underground mine tour in the landmark Quincy copper mine, overlooking Hancock. There are three tour options—we recommend going for the full tour, which includes a cog-rail tram car ride down the hill to the mine entrance and a tractor-pulled wagon ride into the mine, seven levels underground. The underground tour includes a look at a large stope—a hole through which copper was excavated. All tours also include a video tour of one of the mine shafts, a guided tour through the mine's museum, and a tour of the 1918 Nordberg Steam Hoist, the world's largest steam-powered hoist engine. It's a lot of fun, and a great history and science lesson at the same time.

Summit Peak Observation Tower (Porcupine Mountains State Park, middle of S. Boundary Rd.) A wooden boardwalk leads through hemlock and maple groves to this 40-foot tower at the park's highest point. The climb up is fun, and it feels like you can view the whole county and then some from up here, with views of Wisconsin's Apostle Islands in the distance. In the fall the tower looks out over a sea of brilliant colors.

Waterfalls

Agate Falls. From Bruce Crossing follow signs 6 miles east on MI 28 to these popular large, tiered, multilevel falls created by the Ontonagon River.

Black River Harbor and Falls (906-667-0261) From Bessemer drive east on US 2 about 1 mile to CR 513 (Black River Rd.); turn left (north) and follow the signs for the Black River Scenic Byway. Five different waterfalls are viewable along the Black River via either Black River Road by car or the North Country Scenic Trail on foot—Great Conglomerate, Potawatomi, Gorge, Sandstone, and Rainbow. At the end of the river, Black River Harbor provides a pleasant beach and picnic area known for bird-watching.

Canyon Falls—Sturgeon River. North of the US 41 and MI 141 junction, south of Alberta, large, wide falls stretch across a pretty canyon on the upper Sturgeon River.

Munising Falls. From Munising take MI 28 north toward Grand Marais; at the "Y" turn left on Washington Rd. and follow the signs to Munising Falls, about two blocks. Set back at the end of a lovely boardwalk through the woods, Munising Falls is fairly large and framed

Summit Peak Overlook in Porcupine Mountains State Park. Matt Girvan

Agate Falls are among the U.P.'s most popular waterfalls. Matt Girvan

perfectly by the woods and boulders on either side, making it an ideal photographic sub-ject. Popular even in the off-season, when it's lovely to see the occasional rivulet breaking through the frozen falls, this spot can get positively jammed in summer. Head out early to avoid the largest crowds.

Presque Isle River Waterfalls. Porcupine Mountains State Park, S. Boundary Rd., approximately 30 miles south of the visitor center. A pleasant and easily traversed shaded woodland boardwalk follows the river, revealing various falls along the way. On one end of the trail a suspension bridge over the river provides a fantastic view of the falls and a great photo op; at the other end the boardwalk stops, but the trail continues a quarter mile to a final set of falls.

Superior Falls. US 2, 11 miles west of Hurley, WI (Hurley straddles the border with Ironwood), go north on WI 122, cross back into Michigan, turn left into Wisconsin Electric Power Station. These dramatic falls are created as the Montreal River flows through a steep and narrow gorge on its way to Lake Superior near the Wisconsin-Michigan border. The Wisconsin Electric Power Station harnesses the power of the water to generate electricity and has built a viewing platform for the falls. The river first thunders 40 feet over a sheer cliff, pools, then flows on through the tree-lined walls of the gorge.

Shopping

Due largely to its two state universities, this area of the U.P. boasts a collection of varied and interesting shops, as well as a wide selection of independent bookstores. Antiques are plentiful, many of them dating to the wealthy mining days, and of course various copper items are for sale throughout the Keweenaw Peninsula, from jewelry to cookware.

Antiques

Butler Theater Antique Mall (906-486-8680; 119 S. Main St., Ishpeming) Housed in a 1915 movie theater and an adjacent store, the antiques mall is divided into stalls for 18 different dealers, all of whom sell very well-priced collectibles ranging from costume jewelry and pottery to furniture. The theater itself is a good reason to pop in, even if you're not in the market for antiques. The art deco elements of a 1950 renovation are still intact, and the theater hosted the premiere of *Anatomy of a Murder* back in 1959, making it something of a local landmark. Several of the movie's stars actually came to the premiere in Ishpeming, out of respect for John Voelker, who wrote the novel that the film was based on (under the pen name Robert Traver) and grew up in Ishpeming.

Keweenaw Keepsakes (906-337-4326; 305 Hecla St., Laurium) Housed in the historic First National Bank building in downtown Laurium, this place is worth a visit just to check out the original tin ceiling, tile floors, and display windows. The antiques collection is decent as well, with furniture, jewelry, and knickknacks culled from throughout the peninsula. The vintage clothes racks occasionally provide a good find, and the store also sells an assortment of new items, including toys and local crafts.

Last Place on Earth (906-337-1014; 59621 US 41, Phillipsville) A bright redbrick building just outside Kearsarge announces in block white letters Last Place on Earth. It's a familiar landmark in these parts that doubles as a unique and popular store selling antiques and collectibles, landscape paintings from one of the owners, and of course the bird's-eye spoons the store is locally famous for. After all, as their sign clearly states, this is "the home of the spoon maker."

North Depot Antiques & Gifts (906-932-0900; 318 N. Lake St., Ironwood) In a renovated former railroad freight warehouse, North Depot consists of a series of nicely laid-out rooms full of vintage collectibles and a handful of new gift items, including stationery, soaps, candy, books, and gourmet foods. Antique furniture, pottery, lamps, vintage jewelry and vintage toys, and stacks of old magazines are all on offer. The furniture and home accessories tend to lean toward a country, homestead aesthetic.

Art

Copper Country Community Arts Center (906-482-2333, www.coppercountryarts.com; 126 Quincy St., Hancock) An active and popular arts center and gallery housed in a large historic art deco brick building on Quincy Street, the CCCAC is one of Hancock's gems. In addition to its exhibition gallery and education programs, the art center's Artists' Market sells the work of over 200 local artists and craftspeople. If it feels like a curated collection, that's because it essentially is. Each artist's work is evaluated by a panel of artists before it is allowed to be sold in the store. The center also hosts a couple of large fund-raiser sales every year, including the Poor Artists' Sale, a popular holiday shopping event.

The Northwoods Niche (906-932-3316; 210 S. Suffolk St., Ironwood) Part coffee shop, part gift store, and part gallery, the Northwoods Niche has a primary goal of providing a

Marquette's classic Butler Theater has been restored and converted into an antiques mall full of great deals.

Marjorie O'Brien

marketplace for local artists. Currently the shop sells the work of 70 local artists, including everything from hand-carved wood bowls to photography. The artists also help to staff the store, which sometimes creates the rare situation of a customer buying directly from the artist. The store also saves a room in the back for "Northwoods Treasures," a collection of local antiques and collectibles, also for sale.

Omphale Gallery (906-337-2036; 431 Fifth St., Calumet) Charged with creative energy and artistic experimentation, Omphale seems more like it's in Brooklyn than Calumet. The gallery is a co-op of artists, each of whom acts as curator for various shows throughout the year. The gallery is supported by donations and commissions from art sales, and it also functions as a group work studio, with various local artists meeting here occasionally to work together. Focused on contemporary art, the gallery showcases the work of local artists, as well as that of some out-of-towners and even out-of-staters. Omphale is also something of a social center in Calumet—the gallery hosts a free reception at the start of every show and invites the whole town.

Studio Gallery (906-228-2466; 2905 Lake Shore Blvd., Marquette) Located in a small blue A-frame house with neat white trim near Presque Isle Park, the Studio Gallery displays and sells the artwork of four local female artists. Three of the women are nationally known: watercolorists Kathleen Conover and Maggie Linn, and sculptor and jeweler Vicki Allison Phillips. The newest addition to the group is Yvonne Lemire, a sculptor, jeweler, and professional welder whose jewelry and home accents are big sellers. The women maintain a working studio in the back, and at least one of them is always on hand to answer questions or greet patrons.

A department store in the early 1900s, the Vertin is now a popular art gallery filled with wonderful pieces from dozens of local artists. Matt Girvan

Vertin Gallery (906-337-2200; 220 Sixth St., Calumet) Housed in a huge historic building that has been carefully and faithfully restored, the Vertin is an extremely impressive place. First, the gallery itself, on the first floor of what was once a department store, is large and beautiful, with big display windows that let in a lot of light, hardwood floors, and freestanding white walls thrown up here and there for hanging artwork and dividing up the space. The layout pulls you in right off the bat, and then you slowly notice that absolutely every piece in this gallery is of very high quality. People from cities tend to assume that only city people can be artists. Not so, and the Vertin proves it emphatically. Displaying the work of the 50-odd artists that work in the studios above the gallery, the store sells beautiful handcrafted pottery, sculptural wood bowls, stunning jewelry, gasp-worthy paintings, photographs, and sculptures. It would be easy to spend a few hours in this place, carefully examining each beautiful thing. And the prices make it easy to actually purchase some of this original work.

Bookstores

Artis Books & Antiques (906-337-1534; 425 Fifth St., Calumet) One of those rare bookshops that makes readers want to move in, Artis is one of the top five reasons to stop in Calumet. The store specializes in used and rare books, which makes it an excellent place to spend an afternoon ogling beautifully kept classics. The store also sells a small selection of antiques, all carefully selected by the owners. A fantastic old-book smell, combined with the antiques and the shop's historic building, create a lovely time-warp experience here.

Falling Rock Café & Bookstore (906-387-3008; www.fallingrockcafe.com, 104 E. Munising Ave., Munising) Falling Rock is a magical little place with vintage chairs and couches spaced throughout the store in just the right places to encourage people to sit down and stay awhile. Comprising two large, rambling rooms full of books plus a popular café, Falling Rock almost feels more like a community center or a library than a retail shop. The books are, in fact, for sale, and there are a number of good ones to choose from, whether you're looking for a hardbound classic, a cookbook, or a brand-new novel.

Grandpa's Barn (906-289-4377; 371 Fourth St., Copper Harbor) Housed in an old hay barn looking out over a meadow, and full of little pieces of Keweenaw's history, Grandpa's sells a good selection of fiction and nonfiction, including regional guides, nature guides, and children's books.

North Winds Books (906-487-7217; 437 Quincy St., Hancock) Owned by Finlandia University and located next door to the Finnish-American Heritage Center, North Winds sells the Finnish and Finnish-American books one would expect, as well as a number of books focused on local history or written by local authors. North Winds also sells music, clothing, and a number of Finnish design items, including simple, modern, hand-woven table linens, and home accessories.

Snowbound Books (906-228-4448; 118 N. Third St., Marquette) A popular bookshop with an assortment of new, used, and rare books, Snowbound is known for carrying the biggest variety of regional and U.P.-specific books anywhere, as well as an assortment of books by local authors. Which is not to say that they sell only U.P. or Michigan-related books—various categories are well represented in this larger-than-average bookstore.

Gift and Specialty Shops

Copper World (906-337-4016; www.copperworld.com; 101 Fifth St., Calumet) The name says it all—this is your one-stop Copper Country shop for all things copper. Housed in a darling historic building painted red with white trim in downtown Calumet, Copper World is a good place to stop if you need to bring gifts back home, or if you want to be sure to pick up something copper while you're in the area.

Julie's Ballroom Giftshop (906-337-2549; 320 Tamarack St., Laurium) Located in the Laurium Manor B&B, this charming little shop is run by Julie Sprenger, one part of the couple responsible for the amazing restoration of the manor. Julie's good taste is in evidence throughout the manor, but it really shines through in her store, where she has gathered an outstanding assortment of jewelry, apparel, gifts, and home furnishings. The added bonus, of course, is that the shop is located in the grand third-floor ballroom of the manor.

Keweenaw Gem & Jewelry (906-482-8447; www.copperconnection2.com; 1007 W. Memorial Dr., Houghton) A gemologist and geologist couple own this large red, wood-sided store filled with gifts and jewelry all made from locally found rocks and gems. A great place to find something truly unique to the area.

CULTURE

There is more going on culturally in this area than anywhere else in the U.P. Some eastern Yoopers might argue that point, but we'll stick by it for a number of reasons. First, as with the rest of the U.P., there's an incredible mix of cultural ancestry here, thanks to the various immigrant groups brought to the area by the mining industry. This holds true more so in this area than the rest of the U.P., because both iron and copper mining were active here. At one point this region was the world's largest copper producer and the country's largest iron producer; just think about how many miners were needed to keep up with that sort of production. Skilled miners and unskilled laborers from England, Finland, Germany, the Balkans, and Italy flocked here to take the numerous mining jobs available. Their influence

Marquette's mining history brought big money and beautiful buildings to Lake Superior's shores, such as the County Courthouse. Marjorie O'Brien

is still felt throughout the region today. Hancock, for example, is considered "the most Finnish town in America." Just under half of Hancock's population is of Finnish descent, a fact that is evident in many of the town's business names and annual events, like Heikinpaiva, the annual midwinter celebration (the word means "when the bear rolls over"), during which various town residents take a frigid plunge in Lake Superior.

A second, and related, component of the area's cultural history is the wealth that was amassed and kept here for several decades. While the rest of the U.P. mining areas suffered continuous boom-and-bust cycles, the Keweenaw Copper Country and the Marquette iron range held on to money for longer, building fancy homes, schools, libraries, museums, theaters, and even opera houses that are still around to be appreciated today. The Keweenaw did eventually suffer the same fate as the other mining boom areas, resulting in the abandonment of several beautiful buildings throughout the peninsula and particularly in Calumet. Ironwood and the Gogebic Range never held on to the iron money long enough to invest much in the area's buildings, and after the mines closed the area languished for years in economic depression that some would argue is still going on.

The region's two distinct college towns have also inspired more cultural goings-on in this region than in the rest of the U.P., from art galleries and theater productions to lively music scenes to the usual assortment of independent bookstores and cafés that sprout up in any college town. Finally, as with the rest of the peninsula, this area was heavily populated by Native American tribes long before any miners made their way here from Europe. Their ancestors are still active in the community, and the Ojibwa culture is an integral part of the hybrid culture of the region.

Historic Buildings and Sites

CALUMET

Calumet was more directly created with money from the mines than most towns. Initially called Red Jacket, the town was literally taken over, planned, and paid for by the Calumet & Hecla mining company. The town has since been designated a historic preservation area by the National Park System, through legislation describing Calumet as an unprecedented example of American corporate paternalism. Its Main Street and North End (intersection of Fifth and Sixth with Pine) were built out to include the mansions of wealthy copper barons, ornate office buildings for successful businessmen, an opera house, a theater, and fanciful stores and saloons. Although it suffered a period of depression after the mines closed that is still evident in an assortment of derelict houses around town, recently Calumet has been on an upswing. In addition to the National Park Service's commitment to preserving several historic landmarks downtown, in 2003 Calumet began receiving grant money from the National Trust for Historic Preservation to aid in the restoration of its downtown. Far from a depressed mining town, Calumet has become somewhat of a magnet for artistic types, many of whom are working hard to restore its historical buildings. Their work has been rewarded with an increase in both visitor interest and transplants moving to Calumet, mostly from elsewhere in Michigan or the U.P.

Calumet Preservation

The legislation designating Calumet as a historic preservation site provides a good summary of the history lesson this town continues to tell: "The corporate-sponsored community planning in Calumet, Michigan, as evidenced in the architecture, municipal design, surnames, foods, and traditions, and the large scale corporate paternalism was unprecedented in American industry and continues to express the heritage of the district. The . . . picture of copper mining on Michigan's Keweenaw Peninsula is best represented by . . . the Village of Calumet, [and] the former Calumet & Hecla Mining Company properties."

Italian Memorial Park (401 Seventh St., Calumet) A large, freestanding sandstone and brick archway leads to a small park on the site of the former Italian Hall, commemorating a bleak point in Calumet history. The story goes that five months into a bitter copper mine strike, at a Christmas Party at Calumet's Italian Hall, someone yelled "Fire!" though there was, in fact, no fire, and the resulting stampede of people rushing out of the building killed 73 people, mostly children, who were trapped in a stairwell with doors that opened inward and were said to have been locked shut. Some speculated that the mine bosses staged the

This arch and plaque are all that's left of the Italian Hall, where 73 people were killed in a 1913 tragedy.
Matt Girvan

The former Ste. Anne's Catholic Church is now Calumet's cultural center. Matt Girvan

whole thing, which is entirely possible, but no evidence was ever found to prove it. Lack of evidence didn't keep Woody Guthrie from composing a song about it, "1913 Massacre," that blamed the bosses, and it hasn't kept people from blaming them ever since.

Calumet Theatre (906-337-2610; www.calumettheatre.com; 340 Sixth St., Calumet) See "Theaters" for description.

Keweenaw Heritage Center at St. Anne's Church (25880 Red Jacket Rd., Calumet) This fantastic Gothic-style church sits at the head of downtown Calumet, reclaiming its place as a central structure in the town. As with many of the buildings in the area, St. Anne's is made of red sandstone from the Jacobsville quarry, cut into large rectangles like bricks. The facade's three entries feature ornate doorways typical of late French Gothic buildings, and the interior features the vaulted ceilings and ornate moldings and eves also typical within the aesthetic. Historians believe the church was built with various French design touches to please what was at the time predominantly French-Canadian parishioners. Deconsecrated by the Catholic Church in the late 1960s, the building hosted a flea market for a time in the 1980s before lying vacant and neglected for decades. Now a designated Keweenaw Heritage Site, the church serves as the heritage center for the town and has been almost completely restored to its former glory.

The Michigan House Café and Brew Pub (906-337-1910; www.michiganhousecafe .com, 300 Sixth St., Calumet) The site of an 1896 railroad hotel, restaurant, and saloon by the same name that was torn down and rebuilt in 1905 by the Bosch Brewing Company, Michigan House still boasts its early 20th-century interiors, including ornately tiled floors and murals of jolly Germans drinking Bosch beer. The mammoth bar and fireplace complete the historical feel of the place, and the new owners have really brought the building back to its roots, starting a restaurant, a brewery, and a couple of hotel suites upstairs. The Milwaukee artists group that painted the mural here may well be the folks behind the mural at the Ambassador in Houghton (see "Restaurants"), but the link has never been proven.

Upper Peninsula Firefighters' Memorial Museum (906-337-4579; 327 Sixth St., Calumet) The former Red Jacket fire station is a very handsome building, made of Jacobsville sandstone that seems to be of a brighter red than average, highlighted by bright red painted doors over the old fire truck garages. The arched windows, bell tower, and elaborate eaves make it an interesting building to check out, even if the museum it encloses isn't all that fascinating.

Vertin Building (906-337-2200; www.vertingallery.com; 220 Sixth St., Calumet) Vertin Bros. and Company built a two-story sandstone building, originally a department store, with lots of windows in 1885 and in 1900 added the two floors and atrium that make the building seem so gigantic today. Vertin Bros. sold not only groceries and appliances, but the latest fashions, products, and home furnishings to supply the local copper millionaires. After sitting empty for a number of years, the building was taken over in 2004 by an art gallery that made the entire downstairs a gallery for local artists and turned several of the upstairs rooms into artists' studios. In honor of its historic home, the gallery is called the Vertin.

HANCOCK

Founded in 1859 by the Quincy Mining Company, the bulk of downtown Hancock, including the main drag—Quincy Street, of course—was made of wood buildings, most of which burned in an 1869 fire. The mining company rebuilt the town, primarily using Jacobsville sandstone, and Downtown Quincy Street is now listed on the National Register of Historic Places.

100 Block of Quincy Street. This row of storefronts was built from 1870 to 1900 and contained the bulk of the town's commerce. That is still the case today, and though some of the front windows have been modernized, the buildings have remained essentially the same.

City Hall (399 Quincy St., Hancock) Designed by Charlton, Gilbert, and Demar, the same firm responsible for St. Anne's (now the Keweenaw Heritage Center) in Calumet, along with numerous other classic Copper Country buildings, Hancock City Hall is reminiscent of the firm's other designs, with a large clock tower, gable-framed large arching windows, and a sprinkling of Gothic details. When it was built, in 1898–99, the original clock tower was 90 feet tall. The building was used for a while as a jail but has reverted to its original use as a combination city hall, police, and fire station.

Finnish-American Heritage Center (601 Quincy St., Hancock) In 1990 a rundown former Catholic church was renovated with an eye toward Finnish design and became the Finnish-American Heritage Center. With its clipped gable blue roof and white walls with white-trimmed windows, the building sticks out in the mostly red sandstone downtown as being different and decidedly Finnish. The center also regularly hosts interesting Finnish art and history exhibits that tend to be very well curated and displayed.

First National Bank Building (240 Quincy St., Hancock) A giant neoclassical beauty, built in 1905 and updated in 1913, with limestone balustrade and imposing columns, looks grandly over Quincy Street. It's easy to imagine the early copper millionaires swaggering into the bank in the glory days of mining.

Suomi Old Main (Quincy St., Hancock) A Finnish high school opened in 1896 by the Finnish Lutheran Church of the Suomi Synod ("Suomi" means homeland in Finnish;

Hancock's First National Bank is one of the area's first banks, built in 1905. Marjorie O'Brien

synod refers to a religious council), this academy eventually became Suomi College in 1924, eventually changing its name to Finlandia University. The Jacobsville sandstone edifice is built in a Richardsonian Romanesque style, with an arched entryway and large, somewhat intimidating tower. The complex holds various classrooms, a chapel, offices, and dorm rooms and is listed on the National Register of Historic Places.

HOUGHTON

Adventure Copper Mine (906-883-3371; 12 miles east of Ontonagon off MI 38 in Greenland) A well-respected, authentic copper mine tour gives visitors a firsthand look at what life was like in the mines. A few copper deposits were actually left behind in this mine, which makes for great viewing now. Guests are provided with hard hats and headlamps, but sturdy shoes and lightweight jackets are recommended. Certain areas of the mine are popular bat hibernation spots as well—the tour operators keep those sections closed off to protect the bats, but are happy to get into some bat talk if you're interested. For adventurous families with older kids, a rappelling and spelunking "Prospectors" tour is also available.

Douglass House Saloon (906-482-2003; 517 Shelden Ave., Houghton) A hotel and saloon dating back to 1902, when it was built by local businessmen who wanted Houghton to have a first-class hotel, Douglass House is now a popular bar, with all its original fixtures, from the large wooden bar to the Tiffany lamps hanging from the ceiling. The building itself remains a Houghton landmark, with its large redbrick facade and ornate white turret watching over downtown. Those early businessmen would be rolling over in their graves to hear that despite all its finery, Douglass House is generally considered a fun and funky dive bar, whose name is shortened by the local college kids to Doghouse.

Houghton, a Keweenaw mining town turned college town, is one of the cultural centers of this part of the U.P.
Matt Girvan

IRONWOOD

Ironwood Memorial Building (906-932-5050; 213 S. Marquette St., Ironwood) Built in the 1920s to commemorate local men who died in World War I, the ornate Ironwood Memorial Building now plays triple duty as a city hall with civic offices and a community center. Its auditorium is used for various community gatherings. The memorial is still intact, with various statues and plaques commemorating the nearly 1,600 Gogebic-area soldiers killed in the war. Built in the Beaux Arts style, the building's central rotunda, surrounded by stained glass, is not to be missed. The main lobby boasts the strangest stained glass we've ever seen, depicting the Battle of the Argonne, complete with flying shrapnel. The memorial building also includes various displays of Ironwood's history, and it still houses the Women's Club that helped raise money for the building.

World's Tallest Indian (Burma St., Ironwood) A 53-foot-tall fiberglass Indian on the outskirts of Ironwood is not an Ojibwa artwork or a tribute to the local tribes. It was part of a push by local business bureaus to promote tourism as the iron mines were closing. Not that the huge kitschy statue could be mistaken for authentic Native American art, with its red skin and giant headdress. Still, the idea wasn't wholly off the mark. Hundreds of U.P. visitors have had their picture taken with the Hiawatha since it was raised, despite the fact that it's in a residential Gogebic Range location that's not near much except a shut-down mine and Manny's, a local favorite Italian restaurant (see "Restaurants").

LAURIUM

Laurium Manor (906-337-2549; www.lauriummanorinn.com; 320 Tamarack St., Laurium) A huge, opulent, 45-room mansion built in 1908 by a copper baron. No expense was spared in the building or furnishing of this house, and current owners Dave and Julie Sprenger have put their all into researching its past and restoring it faithfully. The imposing, white-columned manor is now a bed-and-breakfast (see "Lodging"), but history buffs not staying there are welcome to pop in for a self-guided tour between 11 am and 5 pm (call if you want to stop by in the off-season).

MARQUETTE

Brewmaster's Castle Home (Washington St., Marquette) The brewmaster's house is all that's left of the former U.P. Brewery. Opened under the name Franklin Brewery in 1873, the business changed its name to the U.P. Brewery in 1886. When the brewery released its popular "Castle Brew," it changed the design theme to "Castle" and built a handful of new buildings to meet demand for the beer. In its heyday the brewery was producing 40,000 barrels a year, but when Prohibition was enacted in 1919 the brewery was forced to close. The German brewmaster who lived in this little sandstone castle eventually left town, and the house is now used as a business office, but the owner has no problem with visitors checking the place out from time to time during normal business hours.

Peter White Public Library (906-226-3571; 213 N. Front St., Marquette. In a lovely white Beaux Arts building dating to the early 1900s, the Peter White Public Library underwent a very tasteful renovation that added to its space without detracting from its style. The library is a great place to escape the cold for a minute if you're walking up Front Street and get hit by a Lake Superior breeze. In addition to plush chairs and a huge collection, the first level of the library includes a community arts center and gallery, as well as a café.

Ridge and Arch Historic District. This tony old Marquette neighborhood is where all the local barons lived at one point. Their beautiful and enormous old homes are evidence of a time when there was an awful lot of money flowing through this region. The Marquette

The Peter White Public Library is one of the best spots in Marquette to spend a wintry day. Marjorie O'Brien

County Historical Museum sells maps of the historical homes in the neighborhood, but the highlights include the sprawling Merritt Mansion at 410 E. Ridge St., two Gothic-revival homes at 430 E. Arch St. and 450 E. Ridge, and two stunning churches, a Methodist Romanesque revival and St. Paul's Episcopal, a truly amazing Gothic revival on which no expense was spared. A pleasant stroll around the neighborhood will reveal various treasures from the past, as well as a few new beauties that manage to fit in well to the neighborhood.

Henry Ford and Big Bay

When an 80-year-old Henry Ford bought the mill in Big Bay in 1943, it had been shut down for several years and not much was happening in the town. Ford dropped a lot of money into refurbishing the hotel and the area around it, but Big Bay never turned into the model company town he had hoped it would be. A week at the hotel was a perk for Ford execs that were doing well, while Ford himself kept a summer retreat at the Huron Mountain Club, a super-private fenced-off club for the very wealthy just outside of Big Bay where old-money billionaires like the Fords maintain summer wilderness retreats on 21,000 acres of lakes, forest, waterfalls, and mountains.

Overlooking the old sawmill that once produced wood panels for Henry Ford's early station wagons was a building that is now the **Thunder Bay Inn** (400 Bensinger St., Big Bay). The inn, built in 1910, was originally a warehouse and later a lumber company hotel but was purchased and renovated by Ford in 1940 as a vacation retreat for himself and his executives. In 1959 the hotel was the setting for the film *Anatomy of a Murder*, which was based on a novel about a real Big Bay case written by Marquette-area native John Voelker under the pen name Robert Traver. The Thunder Bay's pub was added on to the hotel specifically for the film. The hotel changed its name to the Thunder Bay Inn in 1986 when the present-day owners bought it, turned it into a B&B, and named it after the hotel in the movie. The hotel is full of history, from Ford and his ideas about company towns to the film, which was such a big deal to the area that it is still constantly referenced.

Wells Fargo (101 W. Washington St., Marquette) What better way to show that your town has money than to build a really over-the-top bank? This seems to have been the thinking throughout the U.P. during the mining boom, with ornate banks popping up throughout the Keweenaw Peninsula and the Marquette Range. This Wells Fargo was built in 1927, when Marquette needed to show that it wasn't going broke. It was designed in the Beaux Arts style, with massive columns, a 25-foot ceiling, and details inside like bronze doors and chandeliers.

Lighthouses

Big Bay Point Lighthouse (906-345-9957; www.bigbaylighthouse.com; 3 Lighthouse Rd., Big Bay) From Marquette take CR 550 to its end in Big Bay, turn onto Dam Rd. east around the bay, and take Lighthouse Rd. to the point. A big brick lighthouse-turned-bed-and-breakfast on a remote and picturesque piece of Lake Superior shoreline (see "Lodging" for details), Big Bay Lighthouse is open for tours June through September for $2 a person. The view from the tower is spectacular, and the grounds can be toured anytime for free.

Copper Harbor Lighthouse. A small white brick lighthouse with red roof, located at the point of the peninsula that forms Copper Harbor. The site includes an interpretive trail in the woods, with information about the discovery of copper here and the various ships that have wrecked on the rocky peninsula, as well as a handful of exhibits in the lighthouse and the small adjacent keeper's quarters. Visitors are taken by boat over to the lighthouse for tours. The lighthouse can also be reached by kayak or private boat.

Eagle Harbor Lighthouse & Museums (906-289-4990; follow signs from MI 26 in Eagle Harbor) The picturesque redbrick lighthouse with bright white turret is now joined by a maritime museum, commercial fishing museum, mining museum, and automotive museum, as well as the preserved keeper's quarters in the lighthouse, where visitors can marvel at the 14-

The tower at Eagle Harbor Lighthouse. Matt Girvan

inch-thick brick walls, built to keep keepers safe during harsh Lake Superior winters. The museums are delightful and well worth the $4 donation entry fee. Showcasing everything from examples of copper jewelry made by very early Native American miners to a handful of early automobiles that were rescued from a shipwreck on Lake Superior, and providing an in-depth look at how and why the lake has claimed so many ships (and lives), this spot gives a pretty comprehensive overview of the history of the Keweenaw.

Grand Island East Channel Lighthouse. One of the most picturesque and photographed lighthouses in the state, Grand Island's East Channel Lighthouse is unique in its use of wood, and not just brick, for structure. The lighthouse was recently restored, making it lovely for photographs, but its interior is not accessible to visitors.

Marquette Harbor Lighthouse (906-226-2006; 300 Lakeshore Blvd.) A standout in a sea of picturesque lighthouses, Marquette Harbor's bright red lighthouse, perched on a bluff overlooking the harbor, looks like it was just made to appear on postcards. Used as a Coast Guard residence up until the late 1990s, the lighthouse is now toured by the public as part of the adjacent Marquette Maritime Museum.

Isle Royale's Rock Harbor Lighthouse. Matt Girvan

Rock Harbor Lighthouse, Isle Royale (www.nps.gov/isro/; Isle Royale National Park) Set on its own little island all but connected to Isle Royale's shore, the Rock Harbor Lighthouse elicits squeals from visitors passing it on their way to Isle Royale. It's the first indication that they will soon reach their destination. Small and white and nestled between interesting rock formations, the lighthouse is a favorite photo subject. Tours to the lighthouse are available from the island during the summer and include a look at the connected commercial fishery—once truly commercial, and now focused on providing the island's diners and scientists with fish.

Museums and Galleries

HOUGHTON

A. E. Seaman Mineral Museum
906-487-2572
www.museum.mtu.edu
Email: sjdyl@mtu.edu

1400 Townsend Dr., Houghton, MI 49931
Open: Mon.–Fri. 9–4:30, Sat. and Sun. 12–5, July–Sep.; closed Sat. and Sun. Oct.–June
Admission: Free for MTU faculty and staff, children under 12; donations requested from others

Displaying around 8,000 specimens from its 30,000-piece collection of rare rocks and minerals from the Lake Superior region and the rest of the world, this hidden museum on the fifth floor of the Michigan Technological University's Electrical Resources Center is, well, a diamond in the rough. One day the school will raise enough money to build a proper home for all these treasures, but until then it's well worth a trip to the fifth floor. MTU's campus is actually very pretty, and the walk there from downtown is pleasant. Despite the small, obscure space, the museum is very well laid out, and the collection is impressive, even if you're not a hard-core geologist.

MARQUETTE

Da Yooper's Tourist Trap & Museum
906-485-5595
www.dayoopers.com
US 41, 1 mile west of Ishpeming; look for huge red billboard
Open: Mon.–Thu. 9–7; Fri. 9–8, Sat. 9–7, Sun. 10–6. Closes earlier in winter; call ahead
    for times.
Admission: Free

This is a really fun stop on your way into Marquette, where Da Yoopers musical comedy troupe has set up a museum devoted to various aspects of Yooper life. Equal parts comedy and history museum, the Tourist Trap features murals and models of Yooper life, including a deer camp diorama and a model of an iron mining drift, as well as various gag items, from recordings of the comedy troupe's skits—heavy on da Northwoods accent and toilet humor—to oversize models of Yooper tools (Big Gus is the world's largest chainsaw, Big Ernie is the world's largest rifle, etc.) and various Yooper innovations, like a Model A with a bucket on the front for snow removal. The head Yooper also happens to be into rock collecting, so there's a neat little rock shop attached as well, and visitors can buy all sorts of gag gift items in the Tourist Trap store, including the popular *Yooper Glossary,* which purports to unlock the mystery of "Yoopanese." Some of the exhibits and gags may not be suitable for children.

DeVos Art Museum
906-227-1481
www.art.nmu.edu
Northern Michigan University, 1401 Presque Isle Ave., Marquette, MI 49855
Open: Mon.–Fri. 10–5; Sat. and Sun. 1–4
Admission: Free

Marquette's first major art museum, the DeVos opened on Northern Michigan University's campus in 2005 in a brand-new, beautiful modern building designed by well-known HGA Architects. With a $1 million programming endowment from the DeVos Foundation in Grand Rapids, the museum has been able to expand the mission of the previous university art museum, bringing in not only local and regional exhibits but artists from elsewhere in the U.S. and the world, and building up a solid permanent collection as well. The DeVos focuses on contemporary art of various media, exhibited in two large open-plan galleries with hardwood floors, crisp white walls, and lots of natural light. An outdoor concert area and a sculpture garden are also part of the museum, which was designed to flow seamlessly from the rest of the university's Art and Design buildings. Irrespective of the exhibit, the museum is worth a visit for the building alone—the architects did a really impressive job of integrating the 20th-century-modern style of the museum and its Rhine zinc exterior with the 19th-century brick and sandstone of the building it connects to, without making the whole thing seem totally incongruous.

Marquette County History Museum
906-226-3571
www.marquettecohistory.org
213 N. Front St., Marquette, MI 49855
Open: Mon.–Fri. 10–5, Sat.–Sun. 11–4, July–Sep.; closed Sat. and Sun. Oct.–June
Admission: $3 for adults, $1 for students over 12, no charge for children or school groups
This private museum does a good job of telling the continuing history of the region, including a look at Native American culture and how it has affected and been affected by Anglo culture, plus the social and economic impacts of the various industries that have come and gone in the U.P., including mining, lumber, fishing, and shipping. The museum currently houses three small galleries, at least one of which is devoted to a revolving exhibit that looks at a different aspect of life in the U.P. Past examples include "Anatomy of a Yooper," which delved into the reasons behind various regional foods, slang, and cus-

The DeVos Art Museum seamlessly blends modern and old-fashioned architectural design. Marjorie O'Brien

toms, and "Person to Person," about the ways people have communicated in the U.P. over time. Early in 2007 the museum purchased a former bus shelter in downtown Marquette, with the intention of renovating it and eventually moving the museum into the much larger space. Currently only half the museum's collection is on display due to space constraints.

Oasis Gallery
906-225-1377
www.oasisgallery.com
130 W. Washington St., Marquette, MI 49855
Open: Tue.–Sat. 12–3
Admission: Free

Founded in 1987, the Oasis Gallery is an ongoing project by the Marquette Arts Council bringing together 11 artists, each of whom is responsible for curating one exhibit for the gallery per year. Exhibits can center on anything the artist/curator chooses—a particular theme, subject, style—and include the work of both local and international artists. Thanks to the near-total lack of restrictions placed on them, the artists always manage to put together a unique and interesting show, full of surprises. In a recent show entitled "Art for Artists: A Show of Artwork from Artists' Collections," artists got to introduce patrons to their favorite artists and share a little something about themselves at the same time. The gallery stays afloat by throwing two popular fund-raisers every year, the annual "Dinner by Artists" event at which the artist/curators cook for local patrons and host a silent auction for various artworks and door prizes, and the Holiday Sale, from Thanksgiving to Christmas, when the gallery invites all local artists to sell their work through the gallery. The gallery takes a 30 percent commission as a donation. The gallery also sells memberships on a sliding scale. In general it's one of those great art projects that is wholly embraced and supported by the community.

ONTONAGON

Ontonagon County Historical Society Museum
906-884-6165
www.ontonagonmuseum.org
422 River St., Ontonagon, MI 49953
Open: Mon.–Fri. 10–5, Sat. 10–4
Admission: $3

Housed in a former grocery store, the museum's treasures are collected in one large room. And there's a whole lot of artifacts packed in there, from the various phases of Ontonagon's history—as a harbor town, a mining town, and a Scandinavian village. Trinkets from early settlers, before-and-after pictures of an 1899 fire, and an exhibit of minerals and rocks pulled from the mines all combine to make this a charming and interesting small-town museum, well worth a stop if you're in Ontonagon. You can't miss the museum if you're driving through town—its building is painted baby blue with royal blue trim, and it's got the brightest pink door you've ever seen.

NIGHTLIFE

HOUGHTON

Three main bars cater to the Michigan Tech students and provide most of Houghton's nightlife:

Douglass House (906-482-2003; 517 Shelden Ave., Houghton) Known as the Doghouse, this old-time saloon has a pool table, a great long wooden bar, and a quieter, older feel than the other spots. Added bonus: free popcorn from a vintage popcorn maker.

The Downtowner Lounge (906-482-7305; 100 Shelden Ave., Houghton) Nicknamed the DT, the Downtowner is popular for its large outdoor patio.

The Ambassador (906-482-5054; 126 Shelden Ave., Houghton) Popular for its pizza, the Ambassador is also a favorite watering hole. Most nights you'll see MTU students huddled over the spot's famous fishbowls—giant cocktails served in bowls.

MARQUETTE

The Matrix Nightclub (145 Jackson St., Marquette) The only real nightclub in the county, the Matrix has a DJ on every night, playing a mix of 1980s favorites and current dance tracks. Downstairs is Lagniappe (see "Restaurants"), a Cajun/Creole restaurant and bar, which is a great spot to grab a drink and/or a meal before dancing.

Northland Pub in the Landmark Inn (906-228-2580; 230 N. Front St., Marquette) A fun and lively pub that really gets hopping on the occasional live music night or when there's a big sports event on. They serve food fairly late as well, in case you suddenly have a craving for nachos.

The Portside Inn (906-228-2041; 239 W. Washington St., Marquette) This popular pizza joint attracts a lively crowd of students, other residents, and visitors at night. People like the Portside for its selection of beers on tap, its pizza, live music on Thursday, and its patio.

Remie's Bar (906-226-9133; 111 Third St., Marquette) A Marquette institution since the early 1900s.

Shamrock Irish Bar (906-226-6734; 113 S. Front St., Marquette) A typical Irish pub, but the Shamrock is very large, which is good for groups, and they have a small dance floor area where they usually have either a DJ or a band.

UpFront and Co. (906-228-5200; 102 E. Main St., Marquette) Although people have differing opinions about the food, no one disputes the fact that UpFront is a much-loved part of Marquette's nightlife. Located in a restored historic building close to the water, the bar has live music most nights, featuring groups from across the musical spectrum.

One of the oldest municipally-built theaters in the country, the Calumet still hosts concerts, plays, and a monthly film series. Marjorie O'Brien

Vango's (906-228-7707; 927 N. Third St., Marquette) Local music on Thursday nights and a good crusty dive vibe keep Marquette locals loyal to Vango's.

Theaters

Calumet Theatre (906-337-2610; www.calumettheatre.com; 340 Sixth St., Calumet) Originally known as the Red Jacket Opera House, the renamed Calumet Theatre is one of the oldest municipally built theaters in the country, predating those built in Detroit, as locals are fond of pointing out. The 1,200-seat theater is a Keweenaw Heritage Site, protected by the National Park System, and it still hosts plays, concerts, and a monthly film series. Built with a mix of light sand-colored brick and deep red Jacobsville sandstone, alternating in patterns around the windows and the theater's main clock tower, the Calumet is clearly a landmark, but it's the interior that really shines, with richly colored murals, arches flecked with gold, carved wood balconies, and antique chandeliers. Tours are conducted regularly, but the best way to really appreciate the theater is to see a production there.

Ironwood Theatre (906-932-0618; www.ironwoodtheatre.net; 109 E. Aurora St., Ironwood) Built as a vaudeville and silent movie palace in 1928, the Ironwood Theatre has got a great Old Hollywood vibe. In addition to its organ—the original, installed to provide a soundtrack to silent movies, and still playable—the theater's domed ceiling features an elaborate proscenium mural that was discovered in the process of restoring the theater in the mid-1990s. It had been covered by a coat of dark blue paint in the 1970s, but a local artist helped the theater to bring back what could be salvaged—the outline of the mural— and restore it to its original glory. Though it no longer screens films, the theater is now used for Ironwood's musical concerts, for community theater productions, and for a community children's theater program.

SEASONAL EVENTS

JANUARY
Copper Island Classic (Cross-Country Ski Race), Chassell; 906-337-4579
Heikinpaiva Mid-Winter Festival, Hancock; 906-482-2720
Ice Fishing Derby, Chassell; 906-523-4417
Heikinpaiva Talvitohinat (Winter Scramble), Houghton; 906-482-0820

FEBRUARY
Suicide Bowl Ski Jumps, Marquette; 906-228-7749
Winter Carnival, Houghton; 906-487-2818

MARCH
River Valley Bank Great Bear Chase (Cross-Country Ski Race), Calumet; 906-337-4520
Snow-Go-Bye Festival, Ontonagon; 906-884-9101
Snowmobile Drag Races, Ontonagon; 906-884-9101
Yooper-Beiner Ski Race, Ironwood; 906-932-2604

APRIL
Hogathon Perch Fishing Tournament, Ontonagon; 906-575-3545
Spring Concert, Houghton; 906-487-3200

May
Country & Western Show, Chassell; 906-487-3200
Migratory Bird Day Festival, Copper Harbor; 906-289-4813
Ontonagon Lake Trout Classic, Ontonagon; 906-884-2770

June
Annual Walleye/Pike Fishing Tournament, Lac La Belle; 906-289-4293
Bridge Fest (for Portage Lift Bridge), Houghton; 906-482-5240
Michigan Free Fishing Weekend, U.P.-wide, all lakes, fishing license fees waived
Ontonagon River Fest, Ontonagon; 906-884-4735
Pasty Fest, Calumet; 906-337-6246
Seafood Feast, Houghton; 906-482-5240

July
Fourth of July Fireworks (906-482-0884), Lake Linden, South Range, Copper Harbor
Ironwood Festival, Ironwood; 906-932-1122

August
Annual Gun & Sports Show, Calumet; 906-337-2799
Art in the Park, Copper Harbor; 906-289-4363
Copperman Triathlon, Copper Harbor; 906-482-8201
Heritage Celebration, Calumet; 906-337-6246
Labor Day Festival, Ontonagon; 906-884-4196
Porcupine Mountains Music Festival, Porcupine Mountains State Park; 1-800-344-5355

September
Annual Lake Gogebic Walleye Tournament, Bergland; 1-888-464-3242
Blues Fest, Marquette; 906-226-5451
Copper Country Color Tour (bike), Keweenaw Peninsula; 262-442-5175
Fat Tire Festival, Copper Harbor; 906-289-4303
Hunters Harvest Festival, Porcupine Mountains State Park; 906-885-5275
Log Jamboree, Ewen; 906-988-2424
Multicultural Festival, Houghton; 906-487-2920

October
Marquette Art Stroll, Marquette; 906-228-0472
Pumpkin Fest, Bessemer; 906-667-0802

November
Holiday Art Sale, Marquette; 906-228-0472
Hometown Christmas, Ontonagon; 906-884-4837

December
Christmas in Calumet, Calumet; 906-337-6246
New Year's Eve Ball Drop, Marquette; 906-228-6213
USSA Senior National Cross Country Ski Races, Houghton; 906-487-2375

Tahquamenon's Upper Falls gets more than 200,000 visitors every year. Matt Girvan

5

EASTERN LAKE SUPERIOR AND WHITEFISH BAY

Water, Water Everywhere—Waterfalls, World-Class Trout Fishing, Shipwrecks, and the Soo Locks

Life in much of the U.P. revolves around water, but nowhere in the peninsula is water quite so important—and prevalent—as here. In addition to the most celebrated waterfall in a region full of falls (Tahquamenon), this area is home to some of the state's best trout streams, and its cold, deep lake waters mask the most shipwrecks in a lake known for sending ships to its floor. This is also where the U.P.'s most important river—the St. Mary's—serves as both a watery border between the U.S. and Canada and a migratory route for people, ships, and wildlife. Even the majority of the land is waterlogged, doomed to sterility by its flatness. Meanwhile, in the farthest east section of the region, Sault Ste. Marie is a city whose economic survival revolves around water, between the massive freighters moving through its Soo Locks and the groups of tourists coming to take a look at them. The regions around eastern Lake Superior and Whitefish Bay include Grand Marais, Whitefish Point, Tahquamenon Falls, and Sault Ste. Marie.

Grand Marais

With the exception of Sault Ste. Marie—the U.P.'s second-largest town, with a population of 16,500—this is one of the lesser populated and least developed regions of the U.P., its coastlines and riverbanks dotted with small, simple villages, despite the popularity of its attractions and recent efforts to turn portions of it into a summer destination for the wealthy. Grand Marais is an idyllic stereotype of a small American seaside village, flanked by great dunes, falls, and Pictured Rocks to the west, and long stretches of undeveloped Lake Superior wilderness to the east. It fills to capacity during the summer months, then returns to small-town life after the fall color season.

Whitefish Point

Down the coast to the east, tiny Paradise, a resort village built around Whitefish Bay in the 1920s, is similarly packed to the gills in summer, its proximity to the Whitefish Point Lighthouse and Tahquamenon Falls and relatively short distance from the Mackinac Bridge making it attractive to summer visitors. The white New England–style lighthouse at Whitefish Point is a favorite with photographers, its prim appearance belying the fact that

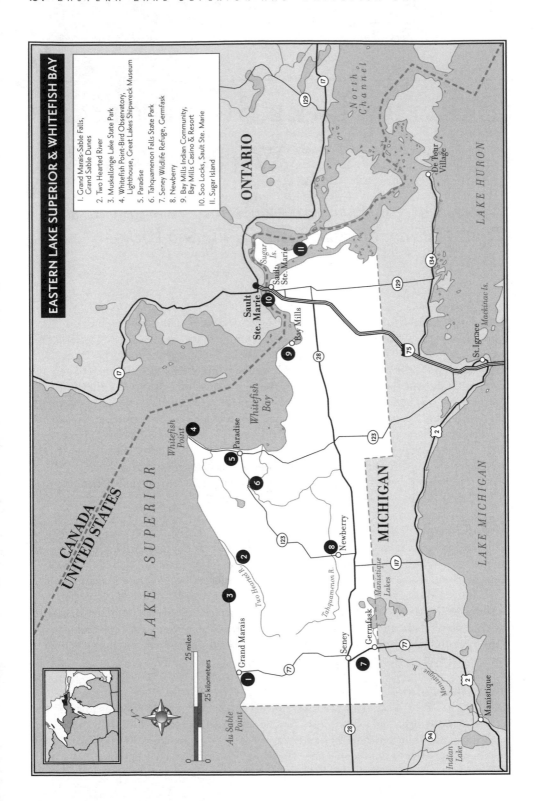

EASTERN LAKE SUPERIOR & WHITEFISH BAY

1. Grand Marais-Sable Falls, Grand Sable Dunes
2. Two Hearted River
3. Muskallonge Lake State Park
4. Whitefish Point-Bird Observatory, Lighthouse, Great Lakes Shipwreck Museum
5. Paradise
6. Tahquamenon Falls State Park
7. Seney Wildlife Refuge, Germfask
8. Newberry
9. Bay Mills Indian Community, Bay Mills Casino & Resort
10. Soo Locks, Sault Ste. Marie
11. Sugar Island

the waters it watches over are known as the "Graveyard of the Great Lakes." A popular shipwreck museum here tells the tales of the countless ships sitting on Superior's floor near Whitefish Bay, and scuba divers love the area for its amazing shipwreck dives.

Tahquamenon Falls

By far the most visited falls in the U.P., with around 750,000 visitors a year and growing, Tahquamenon Falls State Park does actually live up to the hype. And those who take the time to explore beyond the centerpiece Upper and Lower Falls will be rewarded with beautiful hikes and little to no crowds. On the southern side of the falls, Newberry is the only town in the area large enough to support grocery stores year-round, thanks to its lumber industry, its prison, and its popularity with snowmobilers. Newberry also offers more lodging options than any other town near the falls and thus draws the bulk of the park's overnight visitors.

Sault Ste. Marie

Nearly 70 miles long, the St. Mary's River provides a migratory route for dozens of bird species and has been providing transportation to humans for centuries—the Native Americans paddled canoes on the river to get between regions, French fur trappers used it to transport their wares from Michigan to Montreal, bootleggers used it to transport whiskey from Canada to the U.S. during Prohibition, and today it is a busy shipping thoroughfare. The various uses of the river make its shores an excellent place to sit and watch the world go by.

Sault Ste. Marie's lively waterfront, downtown businesses, popular locks, and huge casino have made it the hub of the eastern U.P. In addition to the locks, the coastal area

The coastline near Grand Marais is some of Lake Superior's most beautiful.
Courtesy U.S. Environmental Protection Agency

west of Sault Ste. Marie is known for its beaches, inland lakes, beautiful stretches of the Hiawatha National Forest, and the historic Iroquois Point Lighthouse. The town is also a gateway to Canada, with its more industrial sister city of Sault Ste. Marie, Ontario, just over the International Bridge. Many visitors travel over the bridge between the two cities every year—the Lake Superior coastline past the city is worth a drive over, but don't forget that you're crossing an international border. A law requiring a passport for land travel to and from Canada is currently in the works, with a deadline of June 1, 2009, for approval. Until then, visitors from the U.S. are usually OK with a driver's license and proof of citizenship, such as a birth certificate. The Canada Border Services Web site states, "If you are a citizen of the United States, you do not need a passport to enter Canada; however, you should carry proof of your citizenship such as a birth certificate, certificate of citizenship or naturalization or a Certificate of Indian Status, as well as a photo ID." In practice, the border agents rarely ask for more than a driver's license, but if you have a passport it's worth bringing with you, just in case. (For updated Canadian entry requirements see Citizenship and Immigration Canada at www.cic.gc.ca; for updated requirements for reentering the U.S. see the U.S. Department of State at www.travel.state.gov.)

Of course, Sault Ste. Marie has been a hub of life in the U.P. since long before the locks or the International Bridge were built. Known as Michigan's first city, Sault Ste. Marie, sometimes referred to as just "the Soo," has been a developed town since the mid 1600s, when it was a central fur trading post. For many centuries before that, the majority of Ojibwa lived in and around the area; today, the Sault tribe of Ojibwa remain an important part of the city and are the largest and most vocal of the U.P.'s tribes.

Ojibwa, Chippewa, and Anishinaabeg

It can get very confusing for non-Native Americans to understand the various tribal names and distinctions in the U.P. Here is a quick and easy breakdown: The Ojibwa, who are the most prevalent tribe in the U.P., are the largest of a group of tribes that share a similar group of languages (Algonquian), referred to collectively as the Anishinaabeg. "Chippewa" is an Anglicization of "Ojibwa" that has been widely accepted by the Ojibwa. The two are now used interchangeably.

LODGING

A number of hotels have been built up around Newberry over the years, making it the number-one lodging destination for Tahquamenon Falls' hundreds of thousands of yearly visitors. Lodging options are also available in Paradise, which is the closest town to the falls. Rooms tend to fill up quickly in Paradise, but nowhere near as quickly as they do in Grand Marais, where there are always more people than there are rooms—it's unclear why, with its idyllic setting and proximity to so many of the U.P.'s most popular sights, but there are also no bed-and-breakfasts around Grand Marais.

Rooms are almost always available in Sault Ste. Marie, but there is an unfortunate shortage of independent or charming lodging options in the town, as opposed to chain hotels. Every lodging option listed here is recommended, but we've noted standout locations with a star. Lodging options are listed by region, in alphabetical order. Camping options are listed in a separate "Camping" section after the regular lodging options and similarly divided up alphabetically by region.

Lodging Prices

Prices listed are based on a per-room, double-occupancy rate. Price ranges run from low off-season rates to higher summer rates.

Credit Cards

AE: American Express
D: Discover
MC: MasterCard
V: Visa

Grand Marais

★ Hilltop Cabins

Owners: John and Jeanette Bauknecht
906-494-2331
www.hilltopcabins.net
johnandjeanette@hilltopcabins.net
N14176 Ellen St., Grand Marais, MI 49839
MI 77 to Grand Marais, right on H58 East,
    right on Ellen St.
Price: $85–$175
Credit Cards: MC, V
Handicapped Access: Yes

A small log cabin motel and several stand-alone one-, two-, and three-bedroom log cabins look out over Lake Superior from a small bluff above Grand Marais. The cabins and motel have been recently renovated and furnished with custom-made wood furniture. Each cabin has a full kitchen, private bathroom, and living room, with towels and linens provided. All guests have access to a large deck with incredible views of the lake and a handful of barbecue grills. The recently added three-bedroom cabins all have Lake Superior views, whirlpool tubs, and fireplaces. Popular both with summer tourists and with snowmobilers in the winter, these cabins book up fast, so call ahead. The owners have four school-age kids, but that doesn't stop them from constantly trying to improve their resort and add new services. In addition to keeping up the cabins and the common areas, they rent ATVs in the summer and snowmobiles in the winter for those guests who haven't brought their own toys. Though the cabins are a bit removed from Grand Marais, set as they are up on the hill, they are still walking distance to the town and to a small nearby beach.

North Shore Lodge

906-494-2361
www.northshorelodgemi.com
22020 Coast Guard Point, Grand Marais,
    MI 49839
Price: $70–$90
Credit Cards: MC, V
Handicapped Access: Yes

The only Grand Marais hotel on the beach, this cute green A-frame on Coast Guard Point isn't fancy, but it makes up for anything lacking in the looks department with a good deal of comfort and convenience. Guests have access to a sandy private beach right out their front doors, rooms are large and clean with cable TV and in-room phones, there's an indoor pool, and the hotel operates a decent restaurant as well. Pets are allowed in all rooms, and kids stay free, making the North Shore very popular with families, who dominate both the motel and the lodge's eight housekeeping cabins. In the winter North Shore is a favorite with snowmobilers for its proximity to the trail—it's right smack on top of it—its snowmobile rental packages, and its restaurant, which also includes a full bar. Important to note: The North Shore Lodge usually closes for at least two weeks during either March or April.

★ Sunset Cabins

906-494-2693
E22424 H58, Grand Marais, MI 49839
sunset3@jamadots.com
Price: $85–$125
Credit Cards: Not accepted
Handicapped Access: Yes

These recently renovated cabins enjoy one of the most picturesque settings in the area, along the banks of what was once the unfortunately named Sucker River (it has since dried up), overlooking Lake Superior. Five stand-alone cabins are available—two one-bedrooms, two two-bedrooms, and one three-bedroom. Cabin 5 is more on the scale of a house than a cabin, with two bedrooms, a fireplace, and a washer and dryer. The cabins are walking distance to a sandy Lake Superior beach, and each has cable TV, plus its own deck, fire pit, and charcoal grill.

SAULT STE. MARIE

Askwith Lockview Motel

906-632-2491 or 1-800-854-0745
www.lockview.com
lockview@sbcglobal.net
327 W. Portage Ave., Sault Ste. Marie, MI 49783
From I-75 take exit 394, turn left on Easterday Ave., go over overpass to four-way stop, turn right on W. Portage Ave., stay in center lane and cross over bridge. Motel is just under 3 miles down on the right.
Price: $55–$76 (senior discount for guests 62 and older)
Credit Cards: MC, V
Handicapped Access: Yes

Next to the popular Lockview Restaurant and across from the locks' visitor center, the 47-room motel couldn't really be any better located. The motel looks as though it has been haphazardly added on to at various points, with a main building and then several cottage units, but there is still plenty of parking for all guests, and the rooms themselves are more pleasant than the drive-up motel layout would suggest. Most have antique beds, many have refrigerators, and all have cable TV. Hanging flower pots around the exterior give the place some charm. A free continental breakfast is served every morning in the lobby, and the motel provides a free shuttle to the Kewadin Casino.

Bay Mills Resort & Casino

1-888-422-9645
www.4baymills.com
1386 W. Lakeshore Dr., Brimley, MI 49715
Price: $89–$119
Credit Cards: MC, V
Handicapped Access: Yes

The waterfront location of the 142-room Bay Mills Resort puts it automatically ahead of its main competition—Kewadin Casino—as an overnight lodging option. The resort's waterfront, 6,988-yard, 18-hole, par-72 golf course helps strengthen that lead, as does its popular restaurant. Though it might feel a bit removed, Bay Mills is within a short drive to both Sault Ste. Marie and Tahquamenon Falls, and its proximity to a beautiful, largely undeveloped stretch of Lake Superior's shoreline makes it very desirable. The hotel is still relatively new, so the rooms are in good shape. The suites all have Jacuzzi tubs—although the tubs are oddly placed in the bedroom instead of the bathroom. The 15,000-square-foot casino is Michigan's only waterfront casino.

Kewadin Casino

1-800-539-2346
www.kewadin.com
2186 Shunk Rd., Sault Ste. Marie, MI 49783

Take I-75 N to exit 392. Turn right off the exit, and turn right at Mackinaw Trail (second light), then take an immediate left onto Three Mile Rd. Take another left onto Shunk Rd. and drive 1/2 mile; the casino will be on your left.
Price: $87–$136
Credit Cards: AE, D, MC, V
Handicapped Access: Yes

A huge, 320-room hotel is connected to the flagship casino of the Sault Ste. Marie tribe of Chippewa's empire. Rooms are similar to what you'd find at most Holiday Inn franchises—large, clean, comfortable, and reasonably priced. For about $20 extra a night you can upgrade to a whirlpool room, with an in-room Jacuzzi. In addition to the large casino downstairs, which is a popular destination throughout the U.P., guests have access to an indoor pool, hot tub, and weight room. The casino also often hosts live entertainment.

Longships Motel
906-632-2422
www.longshipsmotel.net
427 W. Portage Ave., Sault Ste. Marie, MI 49783
Price: $60–$75
Credit Cards: Not accepted
Handicapped Access: Yes

As one might suspect from the name, Longships is a nautically themed motel, which fits right in with its surroundings on pleasantly kitschy Portage Avenue, across the street from the Soo Locks. Its location is ideal, and rooms are basic but clean and well kept, with big windows and cable TV.

Plaza Motor Motel
906-635-1881
www.plazamotormotel.com
3901 I-75 Business Spur, Sault Ste. Marie, MI 49783
Price: $49–$81

The 1950s nautical theme of Longships Motel starts with its groovy neon sign. Marjorie O'Brien

Credit Cards: MC, V
Handicapped Access: Yes
Take exit 392 off I-75; the Plaza Motor Motel is just north of Three Mile Rd.

The convenience and low rates of a motor motel with the ambience and amenities of a B&B are what the Plaza Motor Motel promises, and it delivers. Rooms have a bit of unique style—a custom-made quilt here and a four-poster bed there put them a notch above the inexpensive chain motels in the area. All rooms are equipped with microwaves, mini-fridges, coffeemakers with Godiva or Wolfgang Puck gourmet coffee, cable TV, and high-speed Internet access. In addition to the comfort of the rooms, the Plaza far surpasses any standard motor motel with its award-winning garden. Complete with English roses, tulips, and a beautiful gazebo, it's a great place to sit and rest on a summer day, even if there is a Wal-Mart lurking just beyond the landscaped garden.

TAHQUAMENON FALLS

The Falls Hotel
906-293-8621
www.thefallshotel.com
301 Newberry Ave., Newberry, MI 49868
Price: $60–$100
Credit Cards: MC, V
Handicapped Access: Limited

A Newberry landmark, the brick facade of the Falls Hotel has watched over downtown since 1915. Rooms are outdated, but in an entertaining "I can't believe they ever made wallpaper with this pattern on it" sort of way. Still, the rooms are large, clean, and comfortable, with 12-foot ceilings and plenty of windows. The couple that owns Gordon's Resort in Curtis recently bought the Falls Hotel, renovated the lobby, and built out the restaurant, so the rooms may very well be their next project. The lobby looks fantastic—like something out of a John Wayne movie—and the relatively new restaurant has quickly become a local favorite, as has the adjacent lounge with its full bar and occasional live music.

Hulbert Lake Lodge
Owner: Marge Curtis
906-876-2324
Hulbert Lake, 5 1/2 miles from the junction of MI 28 and MI 123
Price: $95–$175
Credit Cards: Not accepted
Handicapped Access: Limited

Five adorable red and white cabins, plus a lodge, overlook Hulbert Lake, less than an hour's drive from Tahquamenon Falls and Whitefish Point. There are no phones or TV in the cabins, in order to keep the resort focused on the outdoors, but guests can use the phone in the lodge. The lake is literally at the front door of these cabins and is known for great trout, pike, and bass fishing, or you can hike on any of a number of trails crisscrossing the 1,000 acres surrounding the lodge. The lodge rents motorboats and rowboats for those interested in boating on the lake. The restaurant serves home-cooked breakfast and lunch specials every day but Tuesday during the winter, and just breakfast Wednesday through Sunday during the winter, when only two of the five cabins are available.

★ MacLeod House
Owners: Frank and Cheryl Cicala
906-293-3841
6211 CR 441, Newberry, MI 49868
Price: $75–$105
Credit Cards: MC, V
Handicapped Access: No

This Queen Anne—style home built by a local lumber tycoon in 1898 was faithfully restored and converted to a bed-and-breakfast in 1988. In addition to the charming exterior, the parlor is large and pleasant, with a copper fireplace, inlaid parquet floors, and a large red-oak staircase. The three guest rooms are beautiful, with large four-poster beds, hardwood floors, and Victorian-style striped wallpaper. Each room is equipped with a private bath, and the suite includes a whirlpool tub for two. The grounds are lovely, with unusual gardens and a large Chinese gazebo in the back. Tahquamenon Falls is 30 miles away.

★ Sandtown Farmhouse B&B

Owners: Tom and Carroll Harper
906-477-6163
www.sandtownfarmhouse.com
W 14142 Sandtown Rd., Engadine, MI 49827
From US 2 take MI 117 north at Engadine, drive straight for 7 miles, turn left on Sandtown Rd.
Price: $70–$80
Credit Cards: Not accepted
Handicapped Access: No

Located on an 80-acre farm in the middle of nowhere but close to everything, the Sandtown Farmhouse is a comfortable, homey place capable of making guests feel right at home and like they're at a really nice hotel both at the same time. Each room is truly unique—the Northwoods Room features a locally made cedar log bed, while the Rose Room is all antiques and frills, and the Stars & Stripes Room is pure Americana. All three rooms have private bathrooms. In the morning Carroll makes a warm, hearty north-woods breakfast on her woodburning stove. Guests have free range of Sandtown's acreage, which boasts great hunting, hiking trails, wildflowers in the spring, the Harpers' small herd of Tunis sheep, and snowmobiling, cross-country skiing, and snowshoeing in the winter. Tahquamenon Falls is 45 miles away, and the Seney National Wildlife Refuge is 14 miles away.

WHITEFISH POINT

★ Whitefish Point Light Station

1-800-635-1742
www.shipwreckmuseum.com
MI 123 north to the end of Whitefish Rd., 11 miles beyond Paradise
Price: $125–$150
Credit Cards: AE, D, MC, V
Handicapped Access: Limited

What a fantastic place to stay! There are other lighthouse inns in the U.P., but this is the only one operated by the same historical society that renovated the lighthouse. Room fees go toward keeping the station in shape and buy you entry to the adjacent Shipwreck Museum, a discount at the gift store, and a year's membership to the Great Lakes Shipwreck Historical Society, which includes quarterly installments of the *Shipwreck Journal*. On remote Whitefish Point, with nothing around but the Shipwreck Museum, it's absolutely delightful to burrow under a blanket and read in the lighthouse, particularly if you're there during a storm. Rooms, located in the 1923 Coast Guard Lifeboat Station crews' quarters, are small but cozy and nicely decorated with wooden beds and homemade quilts. All rooms have private baths and TV/VCR, and guests are given a complimentary deluxe continental breakfast every morning.

CAMPING

GRAND MARAIS

East Branch of Fox River

8 miles north of Seney toward Grand Marais via MI 77
Amenities: vault toilet, water hand pump, good trout stream
Fee: $15
Reservations: Not accepted
Sites: 19

In addition to being a popular tourist attraction, the Whitefish Point Light Station is a cozy and unique B&B.

Matt Girvan

Though pretty enough, this campground is popular for one thing and one thing only: trout fishing. The Fox River is a widely renowned trout stream.

Kingston Lake State Park

16 miles NE of Melstrand via H58, Au Sable Point Rd.

Amenities: Vault toilet, water hand pump, boat launch

Fee: $15

Reservations: Not accepted

Sites: 16

Open: May–Oct.

Located on a pretty inland lake just 5 miles from Pictured Rocks's popular Twelvemile Beach, Kingston provides an ideal home base for exploring the area. Fishing is good in the lake as well, particularly for walleye, and kayakers like to paddle here.

SAULT STE. MARIE

Monocle Lake

In Hiawatha National Forest, 1/2 mile west of Bay Mills Indian community off Lake Shore Drive, on FR 3699, 1 mile east of Point Iroquois.

Amenities: vault toilets, water hand pump, boat launch

Fee: $12

Reservations: Not accepted

Open: May–Oct.

Set in a hardwood forest around beautiful Monocle Lake and within walking distance of the Point Iroquois Lighthouse, the campground is well placed for exploring this section of Lake Superior's coast as well as the nearby Bay Mills Indian community. Hiking is great here, particularly to the lighthouse or the Monocle Lake overlook.

TAHQUAMENON

Muskallonge Lake State Park

Take MI 123 north through Newberry to CR 407 west. Park is 30 miles northwest of Newberry on CR 407.

Amenities: Flushable toilets, hot showers, electric plug-ins (20 and 30 amp)

Fee: $16 a night RV, $14 a night tent

Reservations: www.midnrreservations.com

Sites: 159

Open: May–Oct.

It's hard to believe that Muskallonge was once the site of the Deer Park lumber town. Now it is a peaceful lake, surrounded by deep, quiet forests full of deer, numerous rivers and other inland lakes, sand dunes, and the nearby Lake Superior shore. The North Country Trail passes through this park, and there are various short loop trails that lead hikers to it, as well as to a particularly beautiful stretch of Lake Superior's coastline. Despite the large number of sites, Muskallonge fills up fast, so be sure to reserve early. Tahquamenon Falls is about a half hour's drive.

WHITEFISH POINT

Andrus Lake Campground

906-293-5131

6 miles north of Paradise via Wire Rd. and Vermillion Rd.

Amenities: Sandy beach, good fishing, vault toilets, potable water from hand pump

Fee: $15 a night

Reservations: Not accepted; campground is very popular in summer

Sites: 25

Open: May–Nov.

Large, rustic campsites are spread through a pleasant hemlock and birch grove near Whitefish Point, with a large sandy beach on Andrus Lake. A boat launch and fishing pier are available at the lake. Fishing for bass, bluegill, and perch is good at Andrus, while the nearby wetlands created by the Sheldrake Dam are excellent for rock bass, pike, perch, and bluegill, and the section of Lake Superior 1 mile east of the campground is known for trout. The nearby Whitefish Point Bird Observatory is a landing place for various migratory and other birds, including hawks, owls, blue jays, and loons.

RESTAURANTS AND FOOD PURVEYORS

Dining options remain pretty limited in this largely undeveloped area, but there are still a few good meals to be had, all of which revolve around fish. Dining is even more focused on fish in this region than it is in the rest of the U.P. Here, every night feels like a Friday fish fry, but with great fresh local trout, that's not a bad thing. In more developed Sault Ste. Marie there are more restaurants to choose from and an eclectic mix of cuisines.

Dining Price Codes

Restaurant prices are described as Inexpensive, Moderate, Expensive, or Very Expensive in each of the dining reviews. These tags refer to the average price of a dinner consisting of an entrée, appetizer or dessert, and glass of wine or beer (tax and gratuities not included). Following is a breakdown of the dining price code:

Inexpensive	Up to $15
Moderate	$15-$30
Expensive	$30-$50
Very Expensive	$50 or more

Credit Cards

AE: American Express
D: Discover
MC: MasterCard
V: Visa

GRAND MARAIS

Lake Superior Brewing Company at the Dunes Saloon

906-494-2337
Lake Ave., Grand Marais, MI 49839
Open: Daily
Price: Inexpensive
Cuisine: American
Serving: L, D
Credit Cards: Not accepted
Handicapped Access: Yes
Special Features: Beer brewed on-site; old-fashioned cream sodas and root beer also brewed on-site; beer available "to go"

Really the only place consistently open for dinner, the LSBC is the hub of Grand Marais' nightlife and restaurant scene. Fortunately, the beer and the food are both really good. The beer sampler is a good bet for newcomers unfamiliar with the brewery's beer, which includes both standard (stout, pilsner, pale ale) and unique new recipes (Jasper Cherry, Cattail Ale). The brewpub also sells growlers of beer for those who want to take some back to their cabin or room. On the food front, pizza is the go-to here, but the fresh fish is very good in the summer, and homemade soups are hearty and warming in winter.

SAULT STE. MARIE

The Antlers

906-632-3571
804 E. Portage Ave., Sault Ste. Marie, MI 49783
Open: Daily, 11 AM till late; closed Sunday and Monday Oct.–May
Price: Inexpensive to Moderate
Cuisine: American, Irish
Serving: L, D
Credit Cards: MC, V
Handicapped Access: Yes

The name says it all. Hundreds of pairs of antlers adorn the walls of this family restaurant, interspersed with a variety of stuffed hunting game, including polar bears, deer, and beaver. Probably not the best place to take your committed vegetarian friends, the Antlers is nonetheless a good laugh, and its quirky decor and wisecracking menu have made it one of the most popular restaurants in town. The menu is your typical pub menu, with burgers, sandwiches, whitefish-and-chips, soups, steaks, chicken, and seafood options, with a few Mexican dishes thrown in. It's as much a bar as a restaurant, so head here for a fun and noisy night out, not a quiet sit-down dinner.

Clyde's Drive-In

906-632-2581
1425 Riverside Dr., Sault Ste. Marie, MI
    49783
Open: Daily, Apr. to mid–Oct.
Price: Inexpensive
Cuisine: American
Serving: B, L, D
Credit Cards: Not accepted
Handicapped Access: Limited (curbside)
Special Features: Drive-in service

Clyde's has a lot going for it before you even get to the food. First off, it's a fully functional drive-in, which is rare these days. Second, it's a local institution, which makes it a great place to get a feel for the town and meet some locals. The giant, tasty C-burgers are just icing on the cake. If you're not in the mood for a burger, the chili's decent, as is the fried whitefish. Clyde's also serves a good greasy-spoon breakfast, perfect for fueling up before a drive around Sugar Island (the ferry dock is right next door).

★ Freighters

906-632-4100
240 W. Portage Ave. (at Ramada Plaza Hotel
    Ojibway), Sault Ste. Marie, MI 49783
Open: Daily
Price: Moderate

Cuisine: Continental
Serving: B, L, D
Credit Cards: AE, D, MC, V
Handicapped Access: Yes

You wouldn't expect that a city's nicest restaurant would be in its local Ramada Inn, but Freighters, in the Ramada Plaza Hotel Ojibway, surpasses all expectations. An entire wall of the restaurant is windows looking out onto the Soo Locks, which makes for a spectacular view any time of day and an especially beautiful sunset. Fortunately, the food here is also good. Aside from the wall of windows, the dining room looks like most hotel dining rooms—small wooden tables with green and white cloth tablecloths and rounded upholstered chairs—but the kitchen puts its own spin on a variety of popular dishes to produce an excellent menu. Standouts include gumbo and, of course, whitefish. Seafood specials are always great, and breakfast is popular here with locals and visitors alike. One complaint the restaurant gets often—the service is a tad on the slow side, so don't plan on eating here if you've got to be somewhere else at any particular time. The Captain's Pub & Grill next door is a good spot to grab an after-or-before-dinner cocktail.

★ The Lockview

906-632-2772
329 W. Portage Ave., Sault Ste. Marie, MI
Open: Late Apr. to mid–Oct., daily 7 AM–
    8 PM
Price: Inexpensive
Cuisine: Seafood, American
Serving: B, L, D
Credit Cards: MC, V
Handicapped Access: Yes

A two-story 1950s-style restaurant directly across from the locks, the Lockview is known far and wide for its delicious whitefish, which is caught in the morning and served up any way you like it for lunch or dinner. The restaurant is also open for breakfast, which consists of hearty

The Lockview Restaurant is popular for whitefish and views of the Soo Locks. Matt Girvan

American standards, although a few HeartSmart options are also available. In addition to the whitefish, folks come here for the views. It's pretty cool to enjoy a meal while an enormous ship goes floating by the window right next to you. The second story of the restaurant remains closed unless it's busy, but even from up there you get a nice view of the locks through the trees.

Penny's Kitchen

906-632-1232

112 W. Spruce St., Sault Ste. Marie, MI 49783

Open: Mon.–Fri. 7 AM–6 PM, Sat. 8–5

Price: Inexpensive

Cuisine: Deli

Serving: B, L

Credit Cards: MC, V

Handicapped Access: Yes

Tucked onto a tiny side street, Penny's Kitchen serves the best sandwiches and possibly the best breakfast in the Soo. Penny started out catering but grew her business into this small and always-busy café. Lunch consists of gourmet deli sandwiches (try one of the croissant sandwiches on Penny's homemade croissants), soups, and a variety of delicious salads. Penny's also operates as a bakery, a fact that is obvious at breakfast when the perfume of freshly baked pastries, cookies, croissants, and breads fills the air and Penny's staff serves up moist coffee cake, muffin tops stuffed with fruit and nuts, sourdough pancakes, cinnamon French toast, and delicious French *boules*—fresh sourdough bread bowls filled with eggs, cheese, and your choice of a variety of other toppings—or stuffed morning croissants. If you're looking for a place to stock up on goodies for a road trip or a picnic lunch on the beach, this is it.

TAHQUAMENON FALLS

Beary Patch
906-477-6214
W14740 US 2, Engadine, MI 49827
Price: Inexpensive
Cuisine: American
Serving: B, L
Credit Cards: Not accepted
Handicapped Access: Yes
Special Features: On snowmobile trail

Frequented by snowmobilers in the winter and hungry motorists the rest of the year, this small bear-themed restaurant has built a reputation for hearty breakfasts, sandwiches piled high, and friendly service. Homemade jam from chef-owner Ethel Thoms is served with all toast and it's delicious. Homemade soup also gets rave reviews, as do the Beary Patch's burgers.

Brown Fish House
906-492-3901
MI 123, west edge of Paradise, MI
Open: Mon.–Sat. in summer, Fri. and Sat. only the rest of the year
Price: Inexpensive
Cuisine: American
Serving: L, D
Credit Cards: Not accepted
Handicapped Access: Yes
Special Features: Erratic hours

The tiny restaurant of a local commercial fisherman opens up when he gets a good catch and remains shut otherwise. While the schedule may be a bit unreliable, this policy ensures that Brown's consistently delivers the freshest fish around. A smoker in the back makes smoked whitefish for an outstanding homemade chowder.

★ Tahquamenon Falls Brewery & Pub
906-492-3341
Upper Falls parking lot, Tahquamenon Falls State Park
Open: Daily
Price: Inexpensive to Moderate
Cuisine: American
Serving: L, D
Credit Cards: MC, V
Handicapped Access: Yes
Special Features: Located in state park; beer brewed on-site; food served on outdoor deck in summer

The food, beer, and entire experience served up here are far, far better than what the average person would expect from a state park concessionaire. Operated by the grandchildren of Jack and Mimi Barrett, who sold the large swath of land next to Tahquamenon Falls to the state in order for the current parking lot and entrance trails to be built, the Tahquamenon Falls brewpub was built on the last two acres of the Barretts' land in a large, handsome log building. The dining room is dominated by windows looking out into the park and a large stone fireplace that keeps the place warm in winter. Microbrews are decent—the brewery sells a wide range of beers, but only four are available at any given time. The menu includes both lunch and dinner items and is served all day. Fresh whitefish—either as an entrée or in a sandwich—is a standout, as are the pasties, entrée-size salads, and beer-battered french fries. Between the setting, the history, the microbrews, and the food, this is the best restaurant available for several miles.

RECREATION

Tahquamenon Falls State Park draws close to 800,000 visitors to this region a year, but it's far from the only site worth visiting. Some of the state's greatest trout streams attract anglers here every year from all over the country, especially to the Fox River and the Two Hearted River. Numerous inland lakes are perfect for swimming and boating, and the numerous wetlands around the area make for prime bird-watching. In the winter, snow-mobilers love the hundreds of miles of trails they have here. Meanwhile, hunters revel in the large, open wilderness expanses and forests full of game.

Beaches

Big Pine Picnic Area, 1 mile east of Bay View Campground, 9 miles northwest of Raco. From this popular and scenic Hiawatha National Forest beach, visitors can see big freighters entering the St. Mary's River from afar. In addition to its sandy strip, the beach offers some pebbly areas that are good for rock hunting.

    Grand Marais Agate Beach. Just to the west of the harbor in Grand Marais is a well-known agate beach where the colorful stones are often found. The mouth of Sable Creek is at one end of the beach, with a path to Sable Falls.

    Grand Marais Harbor Beach, Everett Street, Grand Marais. This crescent-shaped sandy beach provides access to a protected swimming bay and terrific surrounding views of Grand Marais.

The Big Sand

The Grand Sable Dunes (*grand sable* is French for "big sand") are not only interesting to see and fun to walk, they provide some of the only high ground around these parts, affording spectacular views of Lake Superior and the coastline. To reach the dunes, take H58 out of Grand Marais and follow the signs for Sable Falls.

The Grand Sable Dunes provide some of the best Lake Superior views in the region. Matt Girvan

Lake Superior Campground Beach, off H58, 12 miles east of Grand Marais or 7 miles west of Deer Park. Accessed by the North Country Trail, which can be reached through the trails in Muskallonge State Park, this beach is hidden and beautiful, with sand on one side and agate on the other.

Bird-Watching

Whitefish Point Bird Observatory (906-492-3596; 16914 N. Whitefish Point Rd., Paradise) Because of its location in the northeast and the fact that it juts out into Lake Superior, Whitefish Point is a phenomenally popular landing spot for migrating birds. Before heading out to the wetlands or low dunes near the point, birders should check in with the folks manning the observatory gift shop for tips on where to see what.

Canoeing and Kayaking

Guides and Rentals

Mark's Rod & Reel Sport Shop (906-293-5608; 13951 E. CR 462, Newberry) Tahquamenon River and Two-Hearted River

Rainbow Lodge and Canoe Trips (906-658-3357; 32752 CR 423, Newberry) Two-Hearted River

Top Paddles

Blind Sucker #2 (906-293-5131; 33 miles NW of Newberry via MI 123 and CR 407) Six miles of pleasant, easy canoeing from the boat launch at the river's mouth to its source meander through marshlands, forests, and wild blueberry patches.

One of the best ways to see Tahquamenon Falls is from a canoe or kayak. Matt Girvan

Tahquamenon River (906-492-3415) This is a really beautiful canoe trip, particularly on a nice summer day. The park's only canoe livery does two-hour, half-day, and full-day trips starting at the Lower Falls and heading toward the river's mouth.

Two-Hearted River (35 miles NE of Newberry via MI 123 and County Roads 500, 414, 412, and 423. Local canoe liveries (see above) will take paddlers upriver to the Reed & Green Bridge for an all-day paddle back to the river mouth.

Fishing

East Branch of Fox River (906-452-6227; 8 miles north of Seney via MI 77) A very well known and liked brook-trout stream. Like the Two-Hearted, there's no bad spot to fish here. Interestingly, many people believe that the Fox, and not the Two-Hearted, is the river Hemingway was really talking about in his Nick Adams stories.

Two-Hearted River (35 miles NE of Newberry via MI 123 and County Roads 500, 414, 412, and 423) Probably Michigan's best-known trout stream, the Two-Hearted River is buzzing in spring and fall, but even with all the attention it's nowhere near overfished. Most popular spots are the river's mouth and Reed & Green Bridge, but all of the river has good fishing.

Golf

Wild Bluff Golf Course at Bay Mills Resort & Casino (1-877-229-6455; www.4baymills .com; 11386 W. Lakeshore Dr., Brimley) The Bay Mills Sault tribe really upped the ante for U.P. casinos when it built this waterfront championship golf course, which is rated 4 1/2 stars by *Golf Digest*. A challenging but very playable course, Wild Bluff features rolling hills, wild rivers, and large natural ravines in addition to its wooded surroundings and lake views. 18 holes, 7,022 yards, par 72.

Hiking

Lake Superior Nature Sanctuary (517-655-5655; www.michigannature.org) This wild, undeveloped piece of Lake Superior shoreline is currently under the protection of the Michigan Nature Association. Visitors are welcome in the sanctuary, but chances of getting horribly lost are high, which is why the Nature Association began training volunteer guides to take people around.

Lime Island (906-635-5281) Michigan's "other" car-free island is as rustic as Mackinac is Victorian and prim. Visitors need to bring their own boat or charter a boat to get here, but once they do, they have access to 980 acres of wilderness, surrounded by the St. Mary's River. Wilderness hikes, or walks through an abandoned company town, with the river's huge freighters in the background, are one-of-a-kind.

Tahquamenon Falls State Park. North of MI 123 in the park are several inland lakes surrounded by forests, marshes, bogs, and other wetlands and a half dozen or so hiking trails that connect them all. Hikers can catch the Giant Pines Loop from Upper Falls, follow it to Wolf Lake, and catch the Wilderness Loop, which connects to a 16-mile section of the North Country Trail that passes through the park. With everyone focused on the falls, these trails are usually empty and quiet, making them prime wildlife viewing areas.

Blueberry Bonanza

Wild blueberries grow unchecked in much of the land surrounding this area, and everyone is allowed to pick those found in national forest land. Blueberries are in season from the end of July to the end of August. Following are some good spots to find them:

Blind Sucker River—In Deer Park, the south banks of the Blind Sucker River

Lac La Belle—On the south shore of the Keweenaw Peninsula, along US 41 between Lac La Belle and Gay

Muskallonge Lake State Park—Along the section of the North Country Trail that runs through the park

Raco—Near the old missile base off MI 28 between Brimley and Raco

Cross-Country Skiing

Algonquin Pathway (906-635-5281; 20th St. West & 16th Ave. West, Sault Ste. Marie; take I-75 north from Sault Ste. Marie and exit at 3 Mile Rd.) This 9.3-mile groomed trail is part of the Lake Superior State Forest. The first loop is also lit for those out at sundown or early morning.

    Chi Mukwa (Big Bear) Community Recreation Facility (906-635-7465; 2 Ice Circle Dr., Sault Ste. Marie) This large rec. center operated by the Sault Ste. Marie Tribe of Ojibwa Indians includes a groomed cross-country ski trail in addition to a public skating rink, in-line skating, and various other activities open to the public.

    Pine Bowl Pathway (906-635-5281; 19 miles SW of Sault Ste Marie. Take I-75 to the Kinross/Tone Rd. exit; turn east on Tone Rd., then south on Wilson Rd.) Also part of the Lake Superior State Forest, Pine Bowl includes over 7 miles of secluded groomed cross-country ski trails over rolling terrain.

Hunting

Game/Season

White-tailed deer—Bow: Oct. 1–Nov. 14 and Dec. 1–Jan. 2; regular firearm: Nov. 15–30; muzzle loaders: Dec. 2–18

Russian boar—Year-round (hunters can hunt boar with any valid hunting license)

Black bear—Sep. 10–Oct. 26

Elk—Aug. 25–29; Sep. 15–18; Dec. 11–18

Wild turkey—Oct. 8–Nov. 14

American woodcock—Sep. 22–Nov. 5

Pheasant—(Males only) Oct. 10–Nov. 14

Ruffed grouse—Sep. 15–Nov. 14; Dec. 1–Jan. 1

Ducks and mergansers—Sep. 29–Nov. 27

Canada geese—Sep. 18–Nov. 1

Private Land Hunting Locations

Antler Bay Trophy Whitetail Ranch (906-647-2018; www.antlerbay.net, 16532 S. Scenic Dr., Barbeau) White-tailed-deer hunts on a 1,700-acre private hunting preserve.

Public Land Hunting Locations

Monocle Lake Recreation Area (From Brimley take Lakeshore Dr. north about 6 miles to Monocle Lake Recreation Area on the left side of the road.) The campground area at Monocle Lake is closed to hunters, but elsewhere in the park visitors can hunt for deer, beaver, and waterfowl in season.

Muskallonge Lake (From Newberry take MI 123 north toward Tahquamenon and turn west onto CR 407. Muskallonge Lake is 30 miles northwest of Newberry on CR 407.) Although hunting is not allowed in Muskallonge State Park, duck and goose hunting is allowed on the portion of the lake that is not within the park's boundaries, as well as on the nearby section of Lake Superior not within the confines of the park.

Pictured Rocks National Lakeshore near Grand Marais (906-387-2607; E22030 Coast Guard Point Rd., Grand Marais) Hunting for deer, grouse, and bear is allowed in Pictured Rocks National Lakeshore, which stretches from Munising to Grand Marais. Hunting areas are restricted, however. Area closure maps are available at the Grand Marais Ranger Station.

Tahquamenon Falls State Park (906-492-3415; 41382 W. MI 123, Paradise) No-hunting signs are clearly posted throughout areas of the park restricted to hunting. The rest of the 50,000-acre park is open to hunters who visit annually in search of deer, bear, fox, beaver, and grouse in season.

Snowmobiling

Rentals
Gallagher's Windy Corners (1-888-491-8808; Wolf Inn area north of Newberry)
North Shore Lodge (906-494-2361; 22020 Coast Guard Point, Grand Marais)

Trails
Falls Trail. Beginning in Newberry, the Falls Trail heads northeast to Paradise, Whitefish Point, and Tahquamenon Falls, where it meets up with the Grand Marais Trail.

Grand Marais Trail. This long trail stretches from Grand Marais all the way east to Tahquamenon and finally south to loop around Hulbert Lake.

FAMILY FUN

Agawa Canyon Tour Train (1-800-242-9287; www.agawacanyontourtrain.com) An old railroad that used to haul lumber and iron ore from Canada's interior to the industrial port of Sault Ste. Marie, Ontario, the Algoma Central Railroad is now best known for its Agawa Canyon Tour, a railway trek into the Canadian wilderness. The trains are much nicer than those old lumber trains, with large picture windows and comfortable seats, and the ride into the dense wilderness is pretty amazing, especially when the train dips and shoots down to the canyon floor, where visitors can get out for a couple of hours and hike or walk around the canyon, which contains the Agawa River and a handful of waterfalls. The trip takes one full day and is especially beautiful during fall color season, or in the winter when it's referred to as the "Snow Train."

Great Lakes Shipwreck Museum and Whitefish Point (MI 123 north to Paradise, then follow N. Whitefish Point Rd. to its end) This very well-organized museum has become increasingly popular over the years. In addition to the museum, which tells the stories of some of the better-known wrecks and gives the general background of Lake Superior, the bird observatory is fantastic, and the lighthouse exhibits do a great job painting a picture of a lighthouse keeper's life as it really was.

Despite the slow speed, riding through the locks in a boat is a big rush. Matt Girvan

Oswald's Bear Ranch (906-293-3147) From Newberry take MI 123 toward Tahquamenon Falls. Turn left at 4 Mile Corner (Deer Park Rd., Muskallonge Lake, H37 H407) and continue on straight for 4 1/2 miles to the ranch. A fantastic ranchland home for 30 rescued American black bears invites visitors to walk through its four large habitats. The bears are enclosed, for the safety of visitors, but their enclosures are very large, and the Oswalds have made a real effort to provide a natural habitat. Viewing platforms provide the perfect angle for pictures of the bears playing or lounging. Many of the bears have been raised here, as people and the DNR bring rescued cubs here every year. The ranch provides golf carts and a trolley for those who can't walk the premises. Admission is $10 per car.

Soo Locks Boat Cruise (906-632-6301; Dock #1, 1157 E. Portage Ave., Sault Ste. Marie) See the locks and the freighters up close and personal.

Tahquamenon Falls Riverboat Tour and Toonerville Trolley (906-876-2311; www.superiorsights.com/toonerville/; Soo Junction) A great combination of trips all wrapped into one that concludes with Tahquamenon means that everyone will be tired but happy by the end of this all-day excursion. Visitors take a narrow-gauge train through dense forests to the Tahquamenon River, then disembark from the train and hop on a riverboat for a 21-mile cruise down the river, ending a half mile above Upper Falls.

Sunday Drive on Sugar Island

Sugar Island, the ancestral home of the Ojibwa, is a lovely place to visit, both for its views of the St. Mary's River and beyond, and for the profound sense of history felt upon its shores. Covered in sugar maple (hence the name), it's also a fantastic place to see fall color. The Sugar Island Ferry (906-635-5421; $6/car) leaves from the dock at the end of Portage Ave. in Soo Locks Park in Sault Ste. Marie twice an hour all year long.

Waterfalls

Sable Falls. Take H58 east from Grand Marais and follow signs to falls. Some of the most picturesque waterfalls in the U.P.—which is saying a lot, considering there are hundreds of them—Sable Falls is often overlooked in favor of larger, more powerful falls. Power or not, you can't beat the absolutely perfect composition of these falls—water cascades down the middle of centuries-old black rocks, bordered by bright green moss and hemlock and cedar groves.

Tahquamenon Falls State Park (906-492-3415) Just under 200 feet wide, the Tahquamenon Falls are by far the largest in Michigan, sending up to 50,000 gallons of water per second hurling nearly 50 feet into the canyon below. There are two prime viewing spots in the park for both falls—Upper Falls and Lower Falls—and a great 4-mile loop hike (8 miles round trip) between them that follows the river. The Lower Falls, while not as tall and thundering as the Upper Falls, are no less beautiful. The river gets very wide here and the water comes stumbling along several rock shelves. In addition to hiking between the two, visitors can rent canoes to paddle the river, being very careful, of course, not to get sucked into the rapids.

Scenic Route: Tahquamenon to Sault Ste. Marie via Lake Shore Drive

Lake Shore Drive, running from MI 123 at Tahquamenon Falls east to Sault Ste. Marie, passes by several scenic vistas and worthy stops, including, from west to east, Whitefish Bay, the Hiawatha National Forest (especially pretty during the fall color season), Mission Hill views of the Lake Superior shipping lanes, Point Iroquois Lighthouse, Monocle Lake, Bay Mills Indian community and Bay Mills Casino, and the scenic and popular Bay Mills section of the North Country Trail with its panoramic views and swinging bridge.

Lower Tahquamenon Falls is just one of the water-centered attractions in this part of the U.P. Matt Girvan

Tucked away in a hemlock forest, Sable Falls are among the U.P.'s most picturesque. Matt Girvan

Shopping

There aren't all that many shops here, but in general those that open up and manage to stay in business are of very high quality.

Grand Marais

Campbell Street Gallery (906-494-2252; www.maevecroghan.com; 14281 Campbell St., Grand Marais) Housed in a historic Grand Marais frame building, built in 1881 as a lumber company office, Maeve Croghan's gallery sells her own paintings as well as crafts and artwork from a select few Grand Marais artists. Croghan's Mackinac Island gallery is well known, and her work has gained some level of recognition nationally, particularly her vineyard paintings, some of which have been turned into labels for vineyards in Paso Robles, California.

The Marketplace (906-494-2438; N14268 Lake Ave., Grand Marais) Open daily in July and August, weekends in May, June, and Sep., closed Oct.–Apr.) Housed in another Grand Marais historic frame building, the Marketplace sells the work of 20-some local artists and craftspeople collectively known as Grand Marais Cottage Industries. Merchandise ranges from needlepoint to original watercolors to incredibly beautiful wood carvings, and all of it is made in Grand Marais.

Sault Ste. Marie

Alberta House (906-635-1312; 217 Ferris St., Sault Ste. Marie) Part exhibition gallery, part shop, Alberta House is the nonprofit arts center of the Sault Area Arts Council. Housed in a former railroad hotel built in 1903, Alberta House now contains the Olive

Craig Gallery, the Alberta House Shop, and the Arts Council office on the first floor. Artist studios and a growing art library are housed on the upper floors. The shop is a place for local artists to showcase and sell their work. Generally staffed by the artists themselves, the shop contains everything from photographs and oil paintings to more gift-oriented items like clocks made from old Michigan license plates.

Culture

Unlike other areas in the U.P., this region was not affected by the closing of any mines, but by the downturn of the lumber industry. Unlike the iron and copper mining companies, however, the lumber companies didn't spend a lot of money building up towns or donating libraries and theaters. While the abandoned mining towns were able to carry on or at least left some trace of their history, most people can't tell that a town ever existed on the site of former logging towns like Deer Park and Bay Mills. Other towns, like Grand Marais—which was left isolated and abandoned when its lumber company hightailed it out of town and took its railroad tracks with it—have been able to make use of their scenic locations to become tourist draws.

The ups and downs of lumber aside, in general this area has historically been economically depressed, routinely posting Michigan's highest unemployment and poverty numbers. Recently, however, thanks mostly to the local Ojibwa, the economy has been on an upswing as the area's tourism numbers surged, thanks to the popularity of the Sault tribe's Kewadin Casinos and the Bay Mills tribe's Bay Mills Resort and Casino, which also includes a scenic golf course.

Sault Ste. Marie, at the Lake Superior end of the St. Mary's River, has always been a little hub of industry in a sea of inactivity. When the Ojibwa lived predominantly on Sugar Island, the rapids of the St. Mary's provided a constant flow of fish, and eventually the name for the town: "the rapids," which is *sault* in French and *bawating* in Ojibwa. Later, as European settlers filtered in, the river retained its importance, becoming a major hub of the fur trade. As the fur trade began dying out in the 1800s, the success of other industries made it increasingly important for ships to be able to travel from one lake to the next, and the river again became a focal point, this time of the shipping industry and, eventually, the tourism industry.

Historic Buildings and Sites

Sault Ste. Marie

Bay Mills Township (Lake Shore Drive / MI 123 west of Sault Ste. Marie, on the waterfront) The historic center of the Bay Mills Ojibwa tribe, Bay Mills was also at one point a smoking, lurching factory town. Evidence of those days are long gone, but the Bay Mills Ojibwa are currently thriving in this small town, and pieces of their history have been preserved at the Mission Church and Bay Mills Indian Cemetery on lovely Lake Shore Drive. The Bay Mills tribe has since gone into the gambling business, building the first casino to take advantage of the area's natural beauty by incorporating a golf course into its plans. Though more remote than the Kewadin Casino near Sault Ste. Marie, the Bay Mills casino is equally as popular.

Chippewa County Courthouse (Corner of E. Portage Ave. and Bingham Ave., Sault Ste. Marie) In 1877 this beautiful rambling building of limestone trimmed with Jacobsville sandstone was erected on the site of one of the area's first missions, built in the early

Built in 1877, the Chippewa County Courthouse is one of Sault Ste. Marie's landmarks. Marjorie O'Brien

1820s. The courthouse is now listed on the National Register of Historic Places. Designed in the Second Empire style, the courthouse is composed of four bays, highlighted by a large central bay capped with clock and bell towers. The building is topped with a wooden statue of "Lady Justice." Four clock faces above the four main bays light up at night.

Riverfront Walk (E. Water St. between Ashmun St. and Soo Locks Park, Sault Ste. Marie) In Brady Park, the site of the first Fort Brady in 1823, a historic walkway between Water Street and the St. Mary's River is marked with various plaques and monuments commemorating different times in the town's history. A bust of Chase Osborn, Michigan's only U.P. governor and the former publisher of the *Sault Evening News*, is displayed alongside various scenes depicting the highlights of his entertaining career, and an obelisk monument commemorating the locks' 50th birthday (they're now over 150 years old) looks out over the park. The monument was designed by Charles McKim of the renowned New York architecture firm McKim, Mead and White.

Soo Locks Park (906-632-3311; from I-75 take either of the I-75 business loop exits to Ashmun St.; at T-intersection turn left onto Portage Ave. and you'll see the locks in a block) Built in 1855, the Soo Locks really brought the Industrial Revolution to bear in the Upper Peninsula. In addition to the money spent on the locks, the government invested heavily in several lighthouses throughout the Great Lakes to keep up with the increased shipping traffic. The St. Mary's River, which connects Lake Superior to Lake Huron, was the obvious shipping route when engineers first started looking at how to get big ships from up north out to the rest of the world. The problem, however, was a well-known stretch of rapids that dropped over 20 feet, which no commercial freighter would be able to navigate. The locks—four in total—solved that problem. Of course as boats continue to get larger and larger, some of the largest have outgrown the older locks. The only lock able to handle the giant 1,000-foot freighters is the Poe Lock, farthest away from the docks. There is always talk of building another lock to keep up with the big ships. Standing in the viewing area at the docks and watching one of the big ones roll through is amazing. It's easy to see why this spot attracts boat fans from all over the world. Note: Shipping season closes in winter when the lakes freeze. The date varies every year but is generally around the end of January to mid-March.

Tower of History (326 E. Portage Ave., Sault Ste. Marie; tickets, $6 adults, $3 children) A 210-foot-tall sculptural tower provides visitors with terrific views of the

The Soo Locks opened up a major shipping trade in the U.P. and became a popular tourist destination.

Matt Girvan

locks, St. Mary's River, the Canadian city and surrounding wilderness across the river, and the town of Sault Ste. Marie directly below the platform. Originally built by the Catholic Church in 1968 as a shrine to the U.P.'s early missionaries, the tower was donated to Sault Historic Sites in 1980 and has been the "Tower of History" ever since. Enclosed within the tower are exhibits about local and Native American history, which do still include some mention of the missionaries the tower was initially built to honor. The exhibits are actually pretty interesting, but most people take the express elevator to the viewing platform and miss them altogether.

Water Street Historic Block (Water St. west of George Kemp Marina, parallel to Portage Ave.) Several historic homes are located in this block, two of which are fully on display, inside and out, with artifacts from their original owners. The John Johnston house is the home of one of the first European settlers to the area, an early fur trader from Ireland. Johnston immigrated to Canada in 1785 and met with early success in the fur trade. He married Ozhahguscodaywayquay, daughter of Waubojeeg, the leader of the Ojibwa, in 1793, after which the couple moved to Sault Ste. Marie and built this house. During the War of 1812 Johnston helped the British take Fort Mackinac, and his house was burned in retaliation. He rebuilt what he could, and this is what is left. The Henry Rowe Schoolcraft Office was the home and office of Henry Schoolcraft, the area's first Indian agent and Johnston's son-in-law. Schoolcraft compiled a book of the history and legends of the Ojibwa that Longfellow eventually used to write his celebrated narrative poem "Hiawatha." Though not open to the public, the home of Bishop Baraga, one of the first and most influential Catholic missionaries in the U.P., is also included in this block.

The Cranberry Capital

In 1876 a farmer named John Clarke bought a farm on Whitefish Point and began growing cranberries, mimicking the processes he had seen the local Ojibwa use to grow blueberries and cranberries here and sell them. As the year marked the nation's centennial, he called his farm Centennial Cranberry Farm, and it is still in operation today. The current farmers have opened up the farms to self-guided tours and set up a gift store and picnic tables to attract tourists on their way to the Shipwreck Museum. It makes for an interesting pit stop, if only to check out a farm that's over 200 years old, and the cranberries make for a good emergency snack break for those who forget that Whitefish Point is isolated and without stores or restaurants. (Centennial Cranberry Farm, 1-877-333-1822; www.centennialcranberry.com. From Paradise, take Whitefish Point Rd. 10 miles north to Wildcat Rd., then turn left at the big cranberry farm sign and head west 2 miles.)

Lighthouses
Au Sable Point Lighthouse, near Grand Marais. From Grand Marais take H58 to the Hurricane River Campground to catch the trail out to the lighthouse. Built atop red sandstone cliffs, the redbrick Au Sable Lighthouse, with its white tower, was restored earlier this decade to its original 1910 state, including the Fresnel lens. The lighthouse can be accessed only on foot, requiring about a 3-mile round-trip hike. From the top of the tower the Grand Sable Dunes are spectacular. Just down the beach are the remnants of two shipwrecks poking out of the sand, an interesting, if slightly jarring, reminder that lighthouses like this one were built to help cut down on the large amount of wrecks occurring in Lake Superior.

Point Iroquois Lighthouse (906-437-5272; Lake Shore Dr., 5 miles west of Brimley) Perched on Point Iroquois, a strategic point for the Ojibwa as a gateway to the St. Mary's River—a place they battled with the Iroquois over and won—Point Iroquois Lighthouse was

Point Iroquois Lighthouse. James Phelps

built in 1870 and decommissioned in 1963. Visitors can climb to the top and use the tele-scope there to see broadly across the channel.

Museums

GRAND MARAIS

Gitche Gumee Agate & History Museum
906-494-2590
www.agatelady.com
E21739 Brazel St., Grand Marais
Open: Oct.–May by appointment, arranged in advance; Memorial Day weekend Thu.–Sun.
5–8 PM; June, Thu.–Sat. 5–8 PM; July and Aug., Mon.–Sat. 1–8 PM, Sun. 5–8 PM; Sep.,
Thu.–Sat. 5–8 PM
Admission: $1

Housed in a little green house with yellow trim, the Gitche Gumee is a fantastic little place full of reverence for history and the land, and for the museum's founder, Axel Niemi. A large display of agates, many of them Lake Superior specimens gathered by Niemi over 71 years, is the centerpiece of the museum, but there are also a few great historical exhibits delving into how Grand Marais was formed, what happened when lumber came and went, and how the town's people survived it all. The current owner spent childhood summers visiting the museum constantly, and she has boundless enthusiasm for her two subjects: agates and local history. Impromptu classes on agate hunting are not uncommon, and the museum also schedules longer workshops for those who really want to get into it.

Pickle Barrel Museum

906-494-2404
Corner of H58 and Main St., Grand Marais
Open: June and Sep., Thu.–Sun. 1–4; July and Aug., daily 1–4
Admission: Donations gladly accepted

The Teenie Weenies comic strip, popular from 1914 to 1970, was created by William Donahey, who along with his wife, Mary, used to spend summers in Grand Marais. In addition to the comic strip, the Teenie Weenies showed up in children's books, toys, and advertisements throughout their career, including regular ads for Monarch food products, a line that included popcorn, pickles, and toffee. One of the ads, depicting the Teenie Weenies in a tiny pickle barrel, was so successful that the Monarch owner decided to build the Donaheys a summer home in Grand Marais to show his thanks. The home was built in the shape of a pickle barrel, naturally— or rather, two pickle barrels. The large barrel housed a living room/dining room, bedroom, and work areas, while a smaller barrel enclosed the kitchen. The house became such a tourist attraction that the couple found it difficult to work in, so they moved it into town as a souvenir shop and visitor center. It was eventually abandoned and fell into disrepair, but the Grand Marais Historical Society purchased it in 2003 and restored it, opening it to the public in 2005 as a museum commemorating the Donaheys, their funny little cabin, and the Teenie Weenies.

SAULT STE. MARIE

Museum Ship *Valley Camp*

906-632-3658
www.thevalleycamp.com
Corner of Johnston and Water Sts., Sault Ste. Marie
Open: Mid-May to June, daily 10–5; July to late Aug. daily 10–7; late Aug.–Sep., daily 10–6;
    Oct. 1–15, daily 10–5
Admission: Adults $10, children $5

This 20,000-square-foot maritime museum is housed in an old Great Lakes freighter. It's fun to visit the *Valley Camp* just to get onboard the ship, but the exhibits are fairly interesting as well, ranging from a crew's quarters, to an *Edmund Fitzgerald* memorial complete with the salvaged lifeboats from the infamous wreck, to four 1,200-gallon aquariums holding various fish found in the Great Lakes.

River of History Museum

906-632-1999
www.thevalleycamp.com
209 E. Portage Ave., Sault Ste. Marie
Open: Mid-May to mid-Oct., Mon.–Sat. 11–5
Admission: Adults $6, children $3

The large Beaux Arts building on Portage Avenue is often overlooked when people assume it's still the post office it was built to be. In fact it is now a large and impressive local history museum, taking visitors through the history of the local people vis-à-vis the St. Mary's River. Some 8,000 years of history are captured in 11 galleries through various life-size dioramas and a guided tour (a motion sensor plays the soundtrack when people enter each room).

TAHQUAMENON FALLS

Luce County Historical Museum
906-293-5709
411 W. Harrie St., Newberry
Open: Fourth of July to Labor Day, Tue.–Thu. 2-4
Admission: Free

Housed in the 1894 sheriff's residence and county jail, the Luce County Historical Museum exhibits clothing and home furnishings from a bygone era, as well as photographs and newspaper clippings of the early days of the county. The museum also houses important archaeological findings from the 1960s, when pottery fragments washed up on the beach by Whitefish Bay proved to date from 200 BC to AD 800. The building itself, in an ornate Queen Anne style in brick and red sandstone with stained-glass windows, is worth a visit. Its interior parlors have been restored, and the museum kept the old jail cell too, which is fun to check out.

WHITEFISH POINT

Great Lakes Shipwreck Museum
1-888-492-3747
wwww.shipwreckmuseum.com
18335 N. Whitefish Point Rd., Paradise
Open: Daily 10–6, May–Oct.; closed Nov.–Apr.
Admission: Adults $10, children and seniors $7

Downtown Sault Ste. Marie is a lively spot with a 1950s-vintage vibe. Matt Girvan

Built next to the oldest Great Lakes lighthouse—Whitefish Point—just outside the stretch of Lake Superior's coast known alternately as the "Graveyard of the Great Lakes" and "Lake Superior's Shipwreck Coast," the Shipwreck Museum is full of evidence of the dangers of sailing on the Great Lakes. Exhibits include historic diving equipment used to investigate early shipwrecks, and various artifacts from the hundreds of ships that have met with untimely ends in the Great Lakes, including the bell from the *Edmund Fitzgerald*. A guided tour of the 1861 light keeper's quarters is included in the museum admission fee and delves into the personal stories of the various keepers who manned Whitefish Point. Outside, paths leading to Lake Superior pass through the Whitefish Point Bird Observatory, where several species of migratory birds stop every fall and spring. These three activities together make it easy to see why the Shipwreck Museum is one of the most popular tourist attractions in the region.

Casino Country

The Sault Ste. Marie area is home to two huge casinos—Kewadin and Bay Mills—that have recently revived the area's economy. The two casinos attract visitors from all over the state for gambling in their Vegas-like game rooms. Both have also taken a page from Vegas's book and added additional entertainment options to their facilities. Country music star Loretta Lynn, comedian Roseanne Barr, and the '80s rock band Poison have all played at the 1,500-seat theater at Kewadin, and Bay Mills built a highly acclaimed 18-hole waterfront golf course and opened a comedy club to keep gamblers entertained. Most of the hotels in Sault Ste. Marie offer free shuttle service to the Kewadin, and some will take guests to Bay Mills (farther away) as well. To sweeten the deal Bay Mills has started offering free drinks to gamblers, one of the Vegas standbys that none of the other U.P. casinos have adopted. Both casinos also have restaurants and a couple of bars, featuring live music, a DJ, or karaoke every night of the week. In addition to the Sault Ste. Marie casino, Kewadin operates casinos in St. Ignace, Manistique, Hessel, and Christmas.

Bay Mills Resort & Casino, 11386 W. Lakeshore Dr., Brimley; 1-888-422-9645
Kewadin Casino, 2186 Shunk Rd., Sault Ste. Marie; 1-800-539-2346

SEASONAL EVENTS

JANUARY
500-mile Snowmobile Endurance Run, Grand Marais; 906-494-2729
Dog-Sled Races, Newberry; 906-658-3464

FEBRUARY
Cabin Fever St. Patrick's Celebration, Grand Marais; 906-494-2447
I-500 Snowmobile Race, Sault Ste. Marie; 906-635-1500
Sled Dog Championship and Midnight Run, Grand Marais; 906-748-0513
Tahquamenon Falls Winter Fest, Tahquamenon Falls State Park; 906-293-5562

MARCH
MUSH Two-Hearted River Dogsled Races, Newberry; 906-658-3464
Woodchoppers Ball, Newberry; 906-293-3816

APRIL
Annual Easter Egg Hunt, Grand Marais; 906-494-2447

Whitefish Point Bird Observatory Spring Fling

MAY
Michigan Week, Sault Ste. Marie; 517-373-5578

JUNE
Annual International Bridge Walk, Sault Ste. Marie; 906-632-3366
Bay Mills Indian Community Annual Pow-Wow, Bay Mills; 906-248-3705
Splash-In on the Bay, Grand Marais; 906-494-2700

JULY
Fourth of July Celebrations, Grand Marais, Newberry, Sault Ste. Marie
Grand Marais Fly-In at Burt Township Airport, Grand Marais; 906-494-2447
Great Lakes Sea Kayak Symposium, Grand Marais; 906-494-2447

AUGUST
Annual Wild Blueberry Festival, Paradise; 906-492-3219
Grand Marais Music & Arts Festival, Grand Marais; 906-494-2447
Sugar Island Old Time Music Festival, Sault Ste. Marie; 906-632-8750

SEPTEMBER
Annual Fish Boil, Whitefish Point; 1-888-492-3747
Chippewa County Fair, Kinross; 906-632-3952
Cooper Classic Golf Tournament, Sault St. Marie; 906-635-6670
Grand Marais Triathlon, Grand Marais; 906-494-2700
Luce and Western Mackinac County Fair, Newberry; 906-293-8785
Salmon Slam Fishing Competition, Sault Ste. Marie; 906-495-7084
Wilderness Canoe Race, Tahquamenon Lower Falls; 906-492-3351

OCTOBER
Annual Barn Dance, Grand Marais; 906-494-2447
Oktoberfest, Sault Ste. Marie; 906-635-6973
Tahquamenon Harvest Festival, Tahquamenon Falls State Park; 906-293-5562

NOVEMBER
Annual Christmas Parade of Lights, Sault Ste. Marie; 906-635-6973
Edmund Fitzgerald Annual Memorial Ceremony, Whitefish Point; 1-888-492-3747
Starry, Starry Night Holiday Shopping Event, Grand Marais; 906-494-2447
Sweet Soo Invitational Hockey Tournament, Sault Ste. Marie; 906-440-4994

DECEMBER
New Year on the Bay, Grand Marais; 906-494-2447

Ferries leave to Mackinac Island from the St. Ignace docks several times a day, making it a popular home base for visitors to the area. Matt Girvan

Lake Huron and the Straits of Mackinac

Islands of the East—Beaches, Boats, and Bike Rides

The Straits of Mackinac link Lake Huron to Lake Michigan and separate Michigan's Lower Peninsula from its Upper Peninsula, with the Mackinac Bridge over the Straits acting as a gateway to the eastern U.P.

The land bordering these waterways to the north makes up the easternmost part of the U.P. and comprises more islands than any other region in Michigan. The high concentration of islands has historically made boating, paddling, and fishing both popular and necessary in the region, and the islands themselves have long been socially important, first as meeting places for the Ojibwa and then as vacation destinations for downstaters.

There is great variety among the islands of the eastern U.P.—car-free, Victorian-inspired Mackinac Island and modern, elegant Drummond Island offer four-star lodging and dining, while the islands that make up Les Cheneaux (French for "The Channels" and often referred to as "the Snows") are dotted with unpretentious resorts, rugged fishing camps, parks, and woodland campgrounds. Beyond the islands, the shores of Lake Huron are home to waterfront towns that range from charming (St. Ignace) to touristy (Mackinaw City).

The primary regions and towns surrounding Lake Huron and the Straits of Mackinac are, in alphabetical order: Drummond Island, Les Cheneaux, Mackinac Island, Mackinaw City (on the northernmost tip of the Lower Peninsula), and St. Ignace. Each is described in greater detail below.

Drummond Island

At 36 miles long, Drummond ranks as the largest island in Michigan, but it remains one of its lesser known, despite efforts in the last two decades to put Drummond on the map as a travel destination.

Once home to a small logging and fishing community, Drummond has almost always had vacation cottages and lodges built to accommodate visiting hunters, boaters, and fishermen in the summer, and adventurous snowmobilers in the winter. In the last 20 years or so, though, a fair amount of development has taken place on Drummond, elevating it to a sort of high-end vacation destination, at least by U.P. standards.

The island first came to some prominence in the 1980s when Domino's Pizza founder (and then-owner of the Detroit Tigers) Tom Monahan bought a large portion of it with the

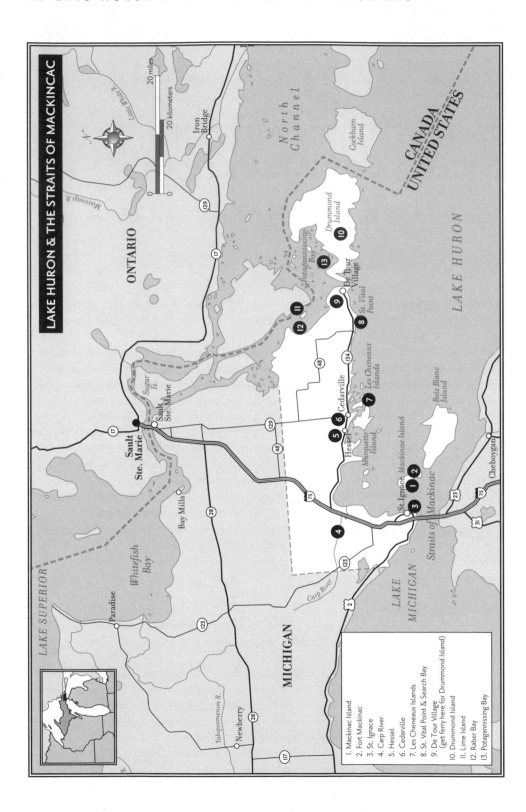

LAKE HURON & THE STRAITS OF MACKINAC

1. Mackinac Island
2. Fort Mackinac
3. St. Ignace
4. Carp River
5. Hessel
6. Cedarville
7. Les Cheneaux Islands
8. St. Vital Point & Search Bay
9. De Tour Village
   (get ferry here for Drummond Island)
10. Drummond Island
11. Lime Island
12. Raber Bay
13. Potagannissing Bay

intention of turning the island into an upscale executive retreat. Monahan built a large and swanky lodge, lakefront cottages, a fine-dining restaurant, a golf course, tennis courts, and a huge 20-person sauna. In the process of building out the resort, Monahan found God in the woods of Drummond Island. The last thing he built was a beautiful and serene outdoor chapel in a peaceful glen overlooking the water—sitting here on a clear morning it's not hard to see how Monahan might have felt touched by a higher power. After selling the resort, his baseball team, and his business and toiling for a time in Mexico as a missionary, Monahan resurfaced in Florida where he made waves with the design and development of a town and Catholic university, both named Ave Maria. Ave Maria, Florida, is run in accordance with Roman Catholic principles and has been the subject of much debate since it appeared in 2006.

Whatever the fate of Ave Maria, the Drummond Island Resort is here to stay, and since Monahan's departure it has become a popular destination for those looking for a bit of wilderness without giving up the comforts of home. Above and beyond the resort, Drummond Island is an outdoor enthusiast's paradise, with 40 inland lakes, 50 outlying islands, several protected coves, hiking and biking trails, golf, a variety of birdlife, fantastic hunting and fishing, and morel mushrooms just waiting to be scooped up and added to your next recipe.

Les Cheneaux

At one time (the late 1800s, to be more precise) nearly every wealthy Midwest family had a summer home on one of the 36 small islands that make up Les Cheneaux. These people had money, but they were looking for modest family summer homes rather than elaborate retreats. So, though some of these houses (built by the likes of Eli Lilly) are large enough to qualify as mansions, and a few of the boats skimming between the islands could cost as

When the Mackinac Bridge was built in 1957 it opened the U.P. up to a whole new tourism industry. Matt Girvan

Big Shoal Beach is just one of several secluded beaches on Drummond Island. Matt Girvan

much as you paid for your house, Les Cheneaux remains a quiet and unpretentious place to enjoy a bit of the great outdoors.

Hessel and Cedarville are two small villages on the shore of the main peninsula nearest Les Cheneaux. In addition to a handful of restaurants and lodging options, these former Indian fishing villages are home to an annual antique wooden boat show that brings boating fans from throughout the Northeast.

Mackinac Island

Yoopers have a love-hate relationship with Mackinac Island. It's both a point of pride ("Have you been to Mackinac? It's beautiful, you should go!") and the butt of local jokes ("Stay away from Mackinac for a couple of months, the fudgies are in town!")

Mackinac is known for a few key things: It's a car-free island, so you'll see horses, carriages, bikes, and skateboards, but no automobiles, which is extremely rare in Michigan; there are more fudge shops than restaurants on the island (hence the term "fudgies" for summer tourists to Mackinac); lilac blooms like crazy in the spring and summer, just in time for the annual Lilac Festival; and all the buildings are Victorian-inspired, from the celebrated Grand Hotel up on the hill (another one of Mackinac's attractions) to the few residences scattered around the island.

Whether you find its Victorian residences and vintage downtown quaint or tacky, you must visit Mackinac at least once—it's a unique experience.

Mackinaw City

Unlike Mackinac Island, no one has a hard time forming an opinion of Mackinaw City—this northernmost outpost of the Lower Peninsula is pure tourist tack. That said, it's the sort of tacky that is totally enjoyable if you're in the right mood, and kids tend to really dig it. It's also much cheaper than nearby Mackinac Island, which is why many visiting families opt to stay here and just ferry back and forth to the island. In addition to its proximity to Mackinac Island and the rest of the eastern U.P., Mackinaw City is minutes away from one of the nation's longest-running archaeological digs—Colonial Michilimackinac Historic State Park.

St. Ignace

With its wooden boardwalk, waterfront restaurants, and charming old homes, St. Ignace offers the same affordable prices and proximity to Mackinac Island as Mackinaw City, but without the tacky tourist vibe. You'll meet friendly locals in the restaurants and bars here, or riding their bikes along the waterfront. The ferry to Mackinac picks up from the St. Ignace docks, across from which are a number of affordable B&Bs. From St. Ignace, a short drive on US 2 west will take you through silent woods and along pretty stretches of shoreline.

LODGING

Lodging varies greatly in the eastern U.P., from over-the-top luxury hotels to romantic B&Bs to rugged fishing lodges. As with all the lodging establishments in this book, please be sure to call ahead before getting on the road. Though I have tried to make a note of any winter closings, that information can always change, and you don't want to be stuck in the snow with no place to sleep.

Mackinac Island hotels and B&Bs tend to book up very quickly for the summer months, so it's best to book as far in advance as possible if you plan to stay on the island. On-island lodging is also the most expensive in the U.P. Budget hotels have sprung up in Mackinaw City and St. Ignace, but even they can fill up during the summer. If you're planning a trip to Mackinac and decide that staying on-island isn't for you, St. Ignace is the better plan B of the two; you're actually more likely to find a good deal at one of the waterfront town's charming B&Bs than at Mackinaw City's chain budget hotels.

All the properties included here are recommended, but those that are particularly special have been marked with a star.

Lodging Prices

Prices listed are based on a per-room, double-occupancy rate. Price ranges run from low off-season rates to higher summer rates.

Credit Cards

AE: American Express
D: Discover
MC: MasterCard
V: Visa

DRUMMOND ISLAND

Drummond Island Hotel

906-493-6799 or 906-493-5799
www.drummondislandhotel.com
sleep@drummondislandhotel.com
34834 S. Townline Rd., Drummond Island, MI 49726
Take the ferry from De Tour Village; from the Drummond ferry dock take MI 134 east (left), , turn left onto Townline Rd
Price: $59–$79 a night
Credit Cards: AE, D, MC, V
Handicapped Access: Yes
Open: Year-round
Special Features: Pets welcome

The newest lodging option on the island, the Drummond Island Hotel offers affordable, large rooms with one king or two queen beds and cable TV, and a complimentary continental breakfast every morning. Rooms are neither charming nor rustic, just simple, clean, and comfortable. The hotel is located near Four Corners, the only thing close to a "downtown" on Drummond Island, and is within walking distance or close driving distance to the lakeshore, a marina, restaurants, and the island's only grocery store. Discounts are available for senior citizens and for stays of three or more nights.

★ Drummond Island Resort and Conference Center

Owner: G. Dennis (Denny) Bailey
906-493-1000 or 1-800-999-6343
www.drummondisland.com
woodmoor@drummondisland.com
33494 S. Maxton Rd., Drummond Island, MI 49726
Take the ferry from De Tour Village; off the ferry, turn onto MI 134, turn left at stoplight at four-way stop (Four Corners), then right onto Maxton Rd. and follow it to the resort entrance on your left.
Price: Summer, $154 a night for lodge room, $201 for private one-bedroom apartment or cabin; winter, $118 a night for lodge, $136 a night for the Boathouse, and $146 a night for cabin
Credit Cards: AE, MC, V
Handicapped Access: Limited
Open: Year-round

This is the resort that put Drummond Island on the map. Locals are still a bit wary of it—the resort's golf course, "The Rock," has won awards and brings more visitors to the island, but residents can't decide if that's a good thing. Visitors are usually pleasantly surprised by all the resort has to offer, though, and no one disputes the fact that it's a beautiful place. Founder and Domino's Pizza exec Tom Monahan was a huge Frank Lloyd Wright fan, and it shows in the design of the main lodge and various cottages scattered throughout the property. With high ceilings and lots of windows and wood, it's a look that blends well with the natural surroundings. The main hotel (Woodmoor Lodge at Drummond Island) is a 40-room log cabin; additional lodging options include a '50s-style private bedroom in the Boathouse down on the lake, a private one-bedroom log cabin called the Hermitage that's perfect for couples, a dozen or so Craftsman-style cottages along the bay, and a handful of other log cabins suitable for families and larger groups spread throughout the rest of the property (2,000 acres of woods, wetlands, and that famous golf course). In addition to golf, there are tennis courts, an outdoor pool, even a bowling alley. Decor is tastefully rustic—like the log cabin that Banana Republic would design—and there are two on-site dining options: Bayside Dining, which is a fine-dining restaurant specializing in seafood and grilled meat, and Pins, a casual dining restaurant with an assortment of salads, pastas, pizzas, sandwiches, and surprisingly good Mexican food. There is a large sauna next to the lodge, a full bowling alley, and complimentary bikes and kayaks for guests. Golf and cooking-class packages are available.

You can rent this boathouse through the Drummond Island Resort for total privacy and 360-degree views.
Matt Girvan

Drummond Island Yacht Haven

Owner: G. Dennis (Denny) Bailey
906-493-5232 or 1-800-543-4743;
    fax 906-493-5229
www.diyachthaven.com
yachthaven@lighthouse.net
33185 S. Water St.
Drummond Island, MI 49726
Take the ferry to Drummond Island from De
    Tour Village. Once on the island, follow
    MI 134, turn left onto Townline Rd., then
    left onto Maxton Rd., then right onto
    Water St. and follow the road until it ends
    at the Drummond Island Yacht Haven.
Price: $90 a night for one-bedroom cot-
    tage; $160 a night for two-bedroom cot-
    tage on water; $125 a night for
    second-row two-bedroom cottage (no
    water view); $230 a night for three-bed-
    room cottage; $349 a night for four-
    bedroom cottage
Credit Cards: AE, MC, V
Handicapped Access: Limited
Open: Year-round

A sister property to the Drummond Island
Resort, the Yacht Haven offers more modest
lodging but unbeatable views. Cottages (19
of them, one-, two-, three-, and four-bedroom) sit right on Potagannissing Bay, and
visitors with boats are welcome to dock at
the Yacht Haven's guests-only docks. The
cottages themselves are roomy and comfortable, though the interiors haven't had a
design update since the 1970s. Still, linens
and towels are clean and new, and dishes,
silverware, pots, pans, and other cooking
utensils are provided for those who want to
eat in. Many of the units have great limestone fireplaces with kindling and wood
provided. Boat rentals and a fish-cleaning
station are available at the nearby marina.
In addition to cottages, the Yacht Haven has
a small campground located in the wooded
area next to the lake; campers can choose
between a "rustic" site with no water or
electricity and a "modern" site with both.

Northern Properties

Managers: Michael and Amy Bailey
906-493-5930 or 1-800-292-5064
www.northernproperties.com
amy@northernproperties.com
29507 E. Channel Rd.
Drummond Island, MI 49726
Price: From $150 a night for a small cabin
    during low season to $1,955 a night for a
    large, luxury waterfront home during
    high season
Credit Cards: Varies
Handicapped Access: Varies

This company handles private vacation
rentals ranging from affordable cottages in
the woods to luxury waterfront stunners with
hot tubs and private docks. More than half
their rental properties are on the water, and
a surprising number are available for rent
year-round, but be sure to double-check
with an agent before booking.

LES CHENEAUX

Cedarville Inn

906-484-2266 or 1-800-222-2949;
    fax 906-484-3066
www.cedarvilleinn.net
cedarinn@lighthouse.net
106 W MI 134, PO Box 189
Cedarville, MI 49719
Stay on I-75 across Mackinac Bridge, take
    exit 359, turn right off the ramp, and
    head east on MI 134. The hotel is approx-
    imately 17 miles from the exit, on the left
    (north) side of MI 134 in Cedarville.
Price: $79–$99 a night
Credit Cards: MC, V
Handicapped Access: Yes
Open: Year-round

Formerly a Comfort Inn, the Cedarville Inn
still looks like a chain motel, with nondescript floral-print bedspreads and dark
green carpeting, but it has a few unique and
attractive features going for it—several
rooms have Jacuzzi tubs, the hotel has a 40-

foot indoor heated swimming pool and a small fitness room, a handful of pet-friendly rooms cater to guests traveling with their furry friends, and a complimentary deluxe continental breakfast is served daily. The motel also rents snowmobiles and provides access to over 100 miles of snowmobile trails.

Hessel Bay Sunset Cabins

Owner/Managers: Perry and Becky
    Kogelschatz
906-484-3913 or 616-365-2035
www.hesselsunsetcabins.com
info@hesselsunsetcabins.com
3347 W. Lake St., P.O. Box 87
Hessel, MI 49745
From I-75 take MI 134 east to Hessel.
    Sunset Cabins are at the west end of
    Lake St. in Hessel.
Price: $70–$95 a night
Credit Cards: No
Handicapped Access: Yes
Open: May 1–Sep. 30

Six simple, clean cabins are set on a grassy acre of lakefront with nearly 300 feet of sandy shoreline access, just two blocks from the Hessel Marina. Full-size kitchens with fairly new appliances are great for a family vacation, and each cabin has a porch, a lake view, a charcoal grill, and a picnic table, as well as a TV/VCR. Guests are responsible for their own towels. Kayaks, fishing boats, and a paddleboat are available for a small rental fee, as is dockage.

Lakeview Motel & Cottages

Manager: Paula Chafins
906-484-2474
lakeviewhessel@easternup.net
3078 W. Lake St., Hessel, MI 49745
Price: Motel from $48.50; cabins from $75
    a night
Credit Cards: V
Handicapped Access: Limited
Open: Year-round.

Choose between 10 homey log cabins (two or three bedrooms) or one of eight tidy motel rooms in this pleasant waterfront family-friendly complex. All cabins have covered porches and at least a partial water view, and the property includes a lakefront sandy beach for the exclusive use of guests. This is a terrific spot for kayakers, who can get in and out of the lake easily from the beach. Furnishings vary from cabin to cabin but generally have a rustic feel, with some important modern updates like coffeepots and satellite TV. A major bonus: A 14-foot aluminum boat is available for use with any of the cabins, and Lakeview has a 250-foot private dock.

Spring Lodge & Cottages

906-484-2282 or 1-800-480-2282;
    fax 906-484-2165
www.springlodge.com
springlodge@springlodge.com
916 Park Ave., Cedarville, MI 49719
From I-75 take MI 134 east and look for the
    big group sign. Spring Lodge & Cottages
    is on 4 Mile Block Rd. / Park Rd.
    between Hessel and Cedarville.
Price: $50–$65 a night for two-person log
    cabins; $57–$70 a night for four-person
    cottages with no view; $93–$115 a night
    for four-person cottages with view
Credit Cards: Not accepted
Handicapped Access: Yes
Open: June 1–Nov. 1.

The cottages at Spring Lodge offer the sort of all-American family fun Norman Rockwell paintings are made of. Most of the cottages have views from both decks and glass-and-screened-in living rooms, there's a large sandy swimming beach with bonfire pits, various boats are available for rent, and a number of trees provide a bit of pleasant shade on warm summer days. The cottages have been built at different times and with different looks—some were painted dark brown and white, others were left a natural knotty pine, some are fairly new, others have been around since the late 1920s—but all have been well maintained through the years and are equipped with microwaves, coffeemakers, cable TV, and deck furniture. Golfers can boat to the nearby public Les Cheneaux Golf Course and play nine holes along the waterfront, and guests not in the mood to cook can walk across the street to the popular Snows Bar & Restaurant.

★ **Tobesofree Waterfront Cottage**
Owners: Robert Stefanski and Lynn Brown
650-269-0919 or 650-269-3269
www.tobesofree.com
stefanski81@yahoo.com
4799 W. Cedar Rd., Hessel, MI 49745
From I-75 take MI 134 east to Hessel.
Price: $125–$150 a night
Credit Cards: MC, V
Handicapped Access: Limited

This crisp, white charmer is set on 200 feet of private waterfront with refinished hardwood floors, a large deck facing the water, plenty of windows, high ceilings, a woodburning fireplace, cable TV with DVD player, and a large kitchen with contemporary appliances, including a washer and dryer. The main cottage has a master bedroom and a bunk room, and a small bunkhouse on the property includes two bunk beds with pull-out trundles and a half-bath. The size of the cottage and the lot, its waterfront location, and its recent spruce-up make Tobesofree a bit more expensive than some of the other family resorts in the area, but the upgrades are well worth it.

MACKINAC ISLAND

Getting to Mackinac Island
Three ferry companies offer trips to Mackinac and back:
Arnold Transit (906-847-3351 or 1-800-542-8528; www.arnoldline.com) This is the oldest company, but they have the fastest boats, which leave from both St. Ignace and Mackinaw City. They also offer a slower, traditional ferry.
Shepler's (1-800-828-6157; www.sheplersferry.com; 556 E. Central Ave., Mackinaw City) Shepler's leaves from both St. Ignace and Mackinaw City, but its hub is Mackinaw City. Customers can print their own tickets online. Shepler's also sells tickets to the Mackinac Historical State Park attractions on the island.
Star Line (1-800-638-9892; www.mackinawferry.com) Star runs hydro-jet ferries that produce a 35-foot rooster-tail spray, which is fun for kids to see. Leaves from both St. Ignace and Mackinaw City. Keep in mind that in the early spring and later fall the companies taper their schedules back a bit and don't offer service every day. Not that it would be such a bad thing to be "stuck" on Mackinac! If you head over in April, you'll see all the folks on their way to Mackinac for "the season" with trunks of clothing and food, not unlike the way things were back in the 19th century.

Bogan Lane Inn
Manager: Trish Martin
906-847-3439
P.O. Box 482, Mackinac Island, MI 49757
From the ferry dock on Mackinac, turn right (east) on Huron St. (Main St.). Bogan Lane is tucked away on a quiet street near Ste. Anne's Catholic Church. Hint: Follow the tall white steeple of Ste. Anne's.
Price: $85–$125
Credit Cards: Not accepted
Handicapped Access: No
Open: Year-round

View of Mackinac Island from an approaching ferry. Matt Girvan

Unlike the majority of resorts on Mackinac, the small and charming Bogan Lane Inn is open year-round. It also doesn't take Internet reservations, all rooms share bathrooms, and its prices are shockingly reasonable for this part of the U.P. Innkeeper Trish Martin has lived on Mackinac all her life; she grew up in what is now the inn, a lovely family home built in 1859 with a spacious front porch and a fireplace in the living room. In addition to running the inn, Trish writes a column for the weekly newspaper about plant life on Mackinac (she has a master's in field botany), serves on the local school board, spins wool in the living room on occasion, and looks after her 83-year-old mother, who still helps out around the inn. Staying at the Bogan Lane Inn is so cozy and comfortable, it feels like visiting your favorite grandmother. It's also a fabulous place to stay if you're looking to really feel at home on Mackinac and get an insider's take on the island. Plan on booking early if you're looking to stay at Bogan Lane during the summer, as it books up quickly.

★ Grand Hotel

906-847-3331 or 1-800-334-7263
www.grandhotel.com
Grand Hotel, Mackinac Island, MI 49757
From the ferry docks on Mackinac, walk
    past "downtown" and up the hill (10
    minutes) to the hotel, or take a horse-
    drawn taxi.
Price: $440–$600(meals included)
Credit Cards: AE, D, MC, V
Handicapped Access: No
Open: May–Oct.

The most expensive hotel on the island by a long shot, and by far the best known, the Grand Hotel has hosted presidents and been used in a handful of Hollywood films. Esther Williams swam in the pool here, and President Harry S. Truman relaxed on the front porch, as did four other U.S. presidents and countless presidential hopefuls. Its huge white columns, manicured rose gardens, and hushed, deferential service hark back to a long-gone era of gentility and refinement. In an effort to keep that air

The Grand Hotel is Mackinac Island's most famous hotel. Matt Girvan

of glamour, the hotel has a fairly strict dress code, requiring guests to wear evening wear every night (coats and ties for men, dresses or pantsuits for women). If you're going to splurge on a room here, it's worth a few extra dollars to get a slightly larger one with a view; the interior rooms can feel like you've been trapped in your grandmother's attic. As you may have guessed, the decor is Victorian-influenced, with four-poster beds and plenty of flowers everywhere—on the wallpaper, the bedspreads, curtains, end tables, and chairs—while windows and lake views help to break it all up a bit. A daily full breakfast, lunch, and five-course dinner are included in the hotel's rates and served in the Main Dining Room, a large and charming restaurant with cheery yellow walls, white linen tablecloths, dark green chairs, and dozens of large windows looking out over the Straits of Mackinac. In lieu of the five-course meal, guests can opt for a more casual grill menu at Fort Mackinac, where they can also watch historical reenactments of Mackinac's military history and a cannon-firing demonstration. For lunch, guests can choose between a variety of casual options (the Jockey Club at the Jewel golf course, the Gatehouse, the Pool Grill, Carlton's Tea Store), a proper afternoon tea at the Fort Mackinac Tea Room, a picnic packed by the staff, a Bavarian-inspired lunch at Woods Restaurant, or indulge in the Grand Luncheon Buffet—a smorgasbord of roasted meats, imported cheeses, hot and cold entrées, seafood, salads, and handmade pastries served in the Main Dining Room. In keeping with the hotel's Great Gatsby vibe, its Terrace Room offers live Big Band music in a swanky formal ballroom—it's worth a visit if only for the fun of pretending you're Esther Williams, cutting a rug to some white-hot swing music and sipping champagne like it's what you were born to do.

Mackinaw or Mackinac?

Both, actually. The Native American tribes in the area called it Michinni-makinong, but the name was shortened over the years by French and British settlers. In the 1600s the French pronounced the ending as "aw" and spelled it as "ac," which is why today Michilimackinac, Fort Mackinac, Mackinac Island, the Straits of Mackinac, and the Mackinac Bridge are all spelled with an "ac" but pronounced "aw." Upon the arrival of the British, a village established as Mackinaw (now Mackinaw City) was pronounced as "aw" and also spelled that way.

Haan's 1830 Inn Bed & Breakfast

906-847-6244 or 847-526-2662 (if calling in winter)
www.mackinac.com/haans/
P.O. Box 123, Mackinac Island, MI 49757
From the docks on Mackinac, turn right onto Huron St. (Main St.) and walk through town. Haan's is three blocks outside downtown on your left.
Price: $115–$150 a night
Credit Cards: MC, V
Handicapped Access: No
Open: Year-round

With its stately white-with-black-trim paint job and large, imposing columns, Haan's looks like something straight out of *Gone with the Wind*, and in fact it was once the home of one of the island's better-known military men—Colonel Preston, one of the last officers at Fort Mackinac and first mayor of the island at the turn of the twentieth century. Today the stately old home is a quiet and peaceful getaway for out-of-town guests. Just past downtown, Haan's is surrounded by green lawn and blooming lilac. Because it's across the street from the waterfront, there are not the same waterfront views you'll find at some of the other inns, but the large front porch is still a pleasant place to while away an afternoon. It's hard not to feel like you've stepped into a bygone era here. The rooms are lovely—each is named for a different island hero and features an antique bed of some kind (sleigh, four-poster, Victorian)—and breakfast is served in front of the fireplace at a long wooden table dotted with antique oil lamps.

Harbour View Inn

Innkeepers: Nancy and Nick Haan
906-847-0101; fax 906 847-3998
www.harbourviewinn.com
PO Box 1207, Mackinac Island, MI 49757
From the ferry dock on Mackinac, turn
    right (east) on Huron St. (Main St.).
    Harbour View Inn is about three blocks
    up, on the corner of Huron and Church
    Sts. next to Ste. Anne's Catholic Church.
    Hint: Follow the tall white steeple of Ste.
    Anne's.
Price: $89–$199
Credit Cards: AE, D, MC, V
Handicapped Access: Limited
Open: May 4– Oct. 31

A bit more reasonably priced than some of the other inns on the island, the Harbour View is walking distance to downtown but far enough away to keep summer guests from the busy tourist bustle. The inn consists of three separate buildings—the Chateau, the Carriage House, and the Guest House. The Chateau houses the lobby and several guest rooms; suites, many with private balconies, are located in the Carriage House and Guest House, which sit on opposite sides of a quiet courtyard with an outdoor spa, gazebo, and floral gardens. Though the rooms in the Chateau are smaller and may not have views, the decor is far more pleasant, with crisp white bedspreads and French-inspired striped wallpaper. The rooms and suites in the Carriage House and Guest House, though spacious and comfortable, tend to have busy, flowery wallpaper and dark carpet. Not all of the rooms have air conditioning, so be sure to ask if you're booking during the summer.

Although there is no restaurant on-site, a complimentary continental breakfast (pastries, fruit, yogurt, cereal, coffee, juices, tea) is served daily, and the extremely helpful, friendly staff will be happy to point you in the direction of a great restaurant.

★ Iroquois Hotel

Owner/Manager: Margaret McIntire
906-847-3321 or 616-247-5675 (in winter)
www.iroquoishotel.com
Main St., Mackinac Island, MI 49757
From the ferry docks on Mackinac, turn
    right onto Main St.; the hotel is just one
    block from downtown.
Price: $205–$405
Credit Cards: AE, D, MC, V
Handicapped Access: No
Open mid-May to Oct. 22

Its great location, close to both the water and "downtown" but not too close to either for noise to be a problem, makes the Hotel Iroquois popular with regular visitors and newbies alike. The grounds are beautiful, with manicured lawns butting up against jagged rocks that fall off into the ocean. Rooms in the back of the hotel have views of the water and the lighthouse, while rooms at the front have pleasant views of the Main St. boardwalk—good for people watching—so there's not really a bad room in the house. The decor is "Victorian-inspired" like the rest of the properties on the island, so expect a lot of flowers. That said, they've done a fairly good job of modernizing the Victorian look with the addition of white space and some softer colors, plus everything is spotlessly clean, so the rooms feel bright and cheery as opposed to frumpy. The only drawbacks are some of the little details: toiletries are cheap, TVs are tiny (the hotel should update them or get rid of them and focus on the view), that sort of thing. Overall, this is a great spot for a couple's or friends' weekend away; though children are welcome here, it's much better suited to adults.

★ The Island House Hotel
906-847-3347 or 1-800-626-6304;
    fax 906-847-3819
www.theislandhouse.com
P.O. Box 1410, Mackinac Island, MI 49757
Upon arrival on Mackinac Island, guests are
    greeted by Island House porters and
    escorted to the resort.
Price: $229–$339
Credit Cards: AE, D, MC, V
Handicapped Access: Limited
Open: Early May into late Oct.

Mackinac's first hotel is still one of its finest. Perched above Main Street near Marquette Park, the rambling crisp white-with-red-roof house boasts one of the island's best locations, close to downtown (two blocks) but far enough away to be peaceful and quiet even during the summer rush, with unobstructed views of the marina, the lighthouse, and the shipping lanes. Rocking chairs line the expansive front porch, and it's not uncommon for guests to spend the better part of a day here, staring out at the water. The rooms themselves are a little "Grandma's Rose Garden," with plenty of floral prints and pastel walls, but you're likely to spend more time in the large, bright lobby, one of the popular restaurants (1852 Dining Room, with its stellar water view, or the local favorite Ice House Bar & Grill), or on the front porch than in your room.

Mission Point Resort
866-851-9499 or 1-800-833-7711
www.missionpoint.com
One Lakeshore Dr., Mackinac Island, MI
    49757
Once on Mackinac Island, guests are
    greeted by Mission Point porters and
    escorted to the resort.
Price: $109–$179

Credit Cards: AE, D, MC, V
Handicapped Access: Yes
Open: May to Oct.

Sitting on its own quiet corner of the island, the Mission Point Resort offers a wide variety of resort activities without an ounce of stuffiness. This is a popular destination for visiting families—children under 18 stay free, children under 12 eat for free, and the resort offers numerous planned activities for kids, ranging from the all-day Kid's Club to regularly scheduled field trips, all for free. It manages to strike a nice balance between family-friendly and upscale that lets parents relax with amenities like a full-service spa, 18-hole putting course, outdoor pool and hot tubs with beautiful Lake Huron views, and fine-dining restaurants, while the kids can run around and be kids without getting the evil eye they might get at the island's more adult-focused hotels and inns. As an added bonus for parents and kids, movies are screened nightly in the resort's theater. Room rates vary depending on the view—and since all of the hotel's public spaces take full advantage of its location right on the lakeshore, if having a view from bed isn't of great importance to you, opt for one of the interior rooms and plan on spending most of your vacation exploring.

Murray Hotel & The Inn on Mackinac
1-800-462-2546
www.4mackinac.com
mackinac@mich.com
P.O. Box 476, Mackinac Island, MI 49757
From the docks on Mackinac, turn right to
    head downtown. The Murray Hotel is
    located in the yellow and lavender
    building on your left.
Price: $69–$179
Credit Cards: AE, MC, V
Handicapped Access: Limited

While the Murray Hotel is smack in the middle of Main Street and has a cool old

ISLAND HOUSE

Constructed for Charles O'Malley about 1852, this building was one of the first summer hotels on Mackinac Island. Captain Henry Van Allen, a Great Lakes skipper, purchased the hotel in 1865. He later moved it from the beach to its present location. By the 1880s the Island House was known as "The best family hotel on the island." Following the death of her parents, Mrs. Rose Van Allen Webster...

The Island House was the first hotel on the island to cater to families visiting in the summertime. Matt Girvan

mining town saloon feel—you halfway expect to see women in bustles and someone in a top hat playing the piano when you walk in—the Inn on Mackinac is tucked away in a residential neighborhood above Main Street and embodies everything the words "Victorian Inn" bring to mind: tall, round turrets, an elaborate and colorful paint job, a large wraparound veranda. Both B&Bs have been recently remodeled, complete with outdoor sundecks, pools, and hot tubs. Rooms are spacious and comfortable, with modern bathrooms and Victorian-decorated bedrooms (floral wallpaper, elaborate headboards, antique bedside tables), and home-baked bedtime cookies are offered nightly at both hotels.

Mackinac Resort Management Condos & Vacation Rentals

1-800-473-6960
www.mackinacislandvacationrentals.com
P.O. Box 849
Mackinac Island, MI 49757
Price: Moderate–Very Expensive
Credit Cards: Varies
Handicapped Access: Varies
Open: Year-round

For a bit more privacy than a B&B or a hotel, and the option of cooking some of your own meals, this property management company offers a variety of vacation rentals ranging from the Sunset Condos, tucked into the woods on the lakeshore about a 20-minute walk from downtown (but close to a restaurant, a nine-hole golf course, and an inn) to the two downtown Harbor Suites to an assortment of private historic homes for rent that sleep 8 to 14 people.

MACKINAW CITY

Brigadoon Bed & Breakfast

Owner: Sherree Hyde
231-436-8882
www.mackinawbrigadoon.com

207 Langlade St., Mackinaw City, MI 49701
Take the Jamet St. exit 339 off I-75, the last northbound exit before you reach the Mackinac Bridge. Go east on Jamet through four stop signs, turn right on Langlade, and Brigadoon will be the second house on your right.
Price: $165–$255
Credit Cards: AE, D, MC, V
Handicapped Access: Some (Suite 101)
Open: Apr.–late Oct.

A bright and cheery yellow Victorian home a block north of downtown Mackinaw City and walking distance to the ferry docks, Brigadoon offers eight large, elegant suites, all with fireplaces. The prices aren't cheap, but you get much more than you would for the same price on Mackinac Island. In addition to the fireplaces, all suites have sitting rooms, and bathrooms feature Gilchrist & Soames bath products, heated marble floors, and whirlpool tubs. Breakfast is a hot, full, home-cooked affair served on the veranda and paired with really good locally roasted coffee.

Deer Head Inn

231-436-3337
www.deerhead.com
109 Henry St., Mackinaw City, MI 49701
Price: $100–$225
Credit Cards: AE, D, MC, V
Handicapped Access: No
Open: Year-round

The Deer Head Inn really does have a number of deer heads lining its walls. Done up in traditional northern hunting lodge style, the inn features bear rugs, fireplaces, and lots of cozy exposed wooden walls and beams inside, and a pleasant brick facade outside. All rooms have beautiful remodeled private bathrooms, fireplaces, and sitting areas. The inn is in the heart of downtown Mackinaw City, steps away from shopping, restaurants, and theaters, and walking distance from the ferry docks.

Northpointe Inn

231-436-9812

www.northpointeinn.com

1027 S. Huron St., Mackinaw City, MI 49701

Take I-75 North to exit 337, turn right off the exit, go to the first stoplight and turn right on US 23. The hotel is a quarter-mile on the left.

Price: $80–$130

Handicapped Access: Yes

Open: May 15–Oct. 31

The Northpointe is a great deal for families visiting the area. Rooms are simple and clean, with basic Best Western–style furnishings and decor. The hotel has its own sandy private beach on the lake, and many of the rooms have views of Mackinac Island. A hot breakfast is included in the room rates, and the indoor pool is very kid-friendly, with several water slides and a hydro tower. The hotel also has a large video arcade to keep the little critics happy, and for adults there are Jacuzzi rooms, a gym, and free shuttles to downtown Mackinaw City and the ferry docks.

ST. IGNACE

The Balsams Resort

906-643-9121

www.balsamsresort.com

1464 W. US 2, St. Ignace, MI 49781

From I-75 take exit 344B to US 2 West. Go 4 miles west of the bridge and look for the Balsams Resort sign.

Price: $45–$110

Handicapped Access: Some

Nine separate cabins and a small motel are tucked into 40 acres of woods along Lake Michigan's shore. With its own private sandy beach, surrounded by the forest and a handful of streams, the Balsams is tough to beat for those looking to get away from it all and enjoy nature. The charming little log cabins are nonetheless spacious, each with its own fully equipped kitchen and many

with wood-burning fireplaces. About half of them are secluded in their own little part of the woods, while the others were built in more of a communal setting. The cheery little yellow motel's six rooms are a shockingly good deal, especially considering that all rooms have a view of Lake Michigan.

★ Colonial House Inn Bed & Breakfast

906-643-6900

www.colonial-house-inn.com

90 N. State St., St. Ignace, MI 49781

From I-75 take US 2 toward St. Ignace and follow it down to State St. The Colonial House Inn is the large yellow Victorian across from the waterfront and next to Bentley's B-n-L.

Price: $69–$135

Credit Cards: D, MC, V

Handicapped Access: No

A charming restored Victorian on the waterfront, directly across from the ferry docks, the Colonial House is painted a cheerful yellow with white trim. It's easy to imagine the original owners rocking in chairs on the wraparound veranda and watching ships sail in and out of the harbor. The seven rooms manage to escape the Grandma feel of so many similar establishments and pull off tasteful Victorian. Two rooms (the Verandah and the Antique) have fireplaces, and all have private baths. A full, hot breakfast is cooked by your gracious host Phil and served by his lovely wife, Elizabeth, from 8 to 9:30 daily. An adjacent motel offers basic rooms with private baths; breakfast is not included but can be purchased separately in the restaurant. For summer bookings it's best to call at least two months in advance.

CAMPING

Much of the undeveloped forestland in this region belongs to the state, and camping is almost always allowed with a backcountry permit. Following are recommendations for specific sites.

DRUMMOND ISLAND

Glen Cove

About 15 miles from the ferry on the main interior road, at Johnswood, turn northeast onto Kreetan Rd., which becomes Sheep Ranch Rd. (these two are sometimes collectively called Glen Cove Rd.), turn left at Corned Beef Junction to reach the cove.
Amenities: None (backcountry camping)

Fee: Free
Reservations: Not available
Open: May–Oct.

Popular with kayakers for its easy water access, Glen Cove provides backcountry camping, no permit required.

H&H Resort and Campground

906-493-5195
33185 S. Water St., adjacent to the Yacht Haven Marina
Amenities: Water and electrical hookups, flush toilets, hot showers
Fee: $15
Reservations: www.diyachthaven.com
Sites: 16
Open: Year-round

St. Ignace offers a handful of charming, affordable B&Bs like the Colonial House that provide easy access to Mackinac without the expense. Matt Girvan

Though sites are fairly close together, location is convenient, with easy access to the marina for both kayakers and boaters.

Township Park
906-493-5089
Channel Rd. (MI 134)
Amenities: Fire pits, electrical hookups, water wells, boat launch. No flush toilets.
Fee: $15
Reservations: Not accepted
Sites: 48
Open: May–Oct.

These large sites, over half of which have electrical hookups, are nestled in the woods, with access to a sandy beach.

LES CHENEAUX

De Tour State Park
906-635-5281
5 miles west of De Tour Village via MI 134
Amenities: Fire pits, no flush toilets
Fee: $15
Reservations: Not accepted
Sites: 21
Open: May–Oct.

This first-come, first-served campground has 21 rustic sites in the woods on Lake Huron. This is a dynamite spot—great fishing on-site in Lake Huron and nearby at Caribou Lake and the St. Mary's River, hiking trails through the Cranberry Lake Flooding area 1 mile north, wetlands and marshlands that attract various birds and wildlife, easy boat access to the lake via De Tour Passage.

Government Island
906-387-3700
Off Les Cheneaux' La Salle Island
Amenities: None (backcountry camping)
Fee: None
Reservations: Not accepted
Open: May–Oct.

Hiawatha Forest backcountry camping; permit required. A beautiful, uninhabited island with a sandy beach and pleasant forest walks.

Search Bay
906-643-7900
From MI 134, 6 miles west of Hessel and 7 miles east of I-75, look for "Ski Trail" sign. Take FR 3436 / Search Bay Rd. to the water, about 1 1/2 miles south of MI 134
Amenities: Boat launch, fire pit. No flush toilets.
Fee: None
Reservations: Not accepted
Sites: 10
Open: May–Oct.

This section of the Hiawatha Forest allows for backcountry camping with a permit and no fee. Two sites around Search Bay are ideal, with access to a sandy beach, a boat launch, and terrific birding opportunities.

ST. MARY'S RIVER

Lime Island
906-635-5281
Amenities: Cottages, fire pits, picnic tables, showers, solar-powered electricity, shared restrooms with flush toilets
Fee: $15 for camping, $65 for cottages
Reservations: Call 906-635-5281
Sites: 20
Open: Memorial Day to mid-Sep.

This is a great place to fish, hike, lounge on the beach, watch the freighters in St. Mary's River, and just get away from it all. Rustic cottages and campsites are maintained here by the state park system, but in order to get to the island you'll need to have your own boat or charter a boat. It's only 3 miles across from De Tour, but the channel is too rough to kayak over. See "Recreation—Fishing" for boat charter information.

RESTAURANTS

There are arguably more restaurants to choose from in this small section of the U.P. than anywhere else in the peninsula. All the large Mackinac resorts take pride in hiring top-tier chefs from around the world to prepare inventive, delicious meals for island guests. Mackinac tourism also supports a number of stand-alone restaurants, each with its own theme and culinary focus, from comfort food to Mexican and Middle Eastern specialties. And, while Drummond Island doesn't boast quite the variety of Mackinac, there are a surprising number of options there as well, from a top-notch New York–style deli to fine dining at the Drummond Island Resort. Meanwhile, throughout Les Cheneaux and St. Ignace, the U.P. classics—whitefish, pasties, and apple dumplings—are done as well or better than anywhere else in the peninsula. Whether you're in the mood for a four-course meal or just a good old-fashioned fish fry, you'll find it here.

Dining Price Codes

Restaurant prices are described as Inexpensive, Moderate, Expensive, or Very Expensive in each of the dining reviews. These tags refer to the average price of a dinner consisting of an entrée, appetizer or dessert, and glass of wine or beer (tax and gratuities not included). Following is a breakdown of the dining price code:

Inexpensive	Up to $15
Moderate	$15-$30
Expensive	$30-$50
Very Expensive	$50 or more

Credit Cards

AE: American Express
D: Discover
MC: MasterCard
V: Visa

DRUMMOND ISLAND

★ Bayside Dining

906-493-1014
www.drummondisland.com
33494 S. Maxton Rd. (at the Drummond Island Resort), Drummond Island, MI
Open: Daily, Apr.–late Oct.
Price: Inexpensive–Moderate
Cuisine: American, international
Serving: D
Credit Cards: MC, V
Handicapped Access: Yes
Special Features: Outdoor seating available; reservations recommended

The Bayside stands out among the area's seafood restaurants for two reasons: its serious attention to the wine list, and the addition of several fresh fish entrées that don't include whitefish. Of course local fish has a spot on the menu as well, but the management has made a point of flying in harder-to-find tuna, swordfish, and halibut fresh every morning. The original owner (Tom Monahan, CEO of Domino's Pizza) designed the Bayside in the style of his hero, Frank Lloyd Wright, and had it built overlooking Potagannassing Bay. Though seafood is the star, Bayside's menu includes aged beef, spring lamb, and homemade pastas. Ask about wine dinners.

LES CHENEAUX

Dockside Café

906-297-5165
100 Ontario St., De Tour Village, MI 49725
Open: Daily
Price: Inexpensive
Cuisine: American
Serving: B, L, dinner on Friday
Credit Cards: MC, V
Handicapped Access: Yes
Open: Year-round

Every U.P. town has its local Friday fish fry spot, and the Dockside is De Tour's, staying open for dinner only on Friday to serve its popular all-you-can-eat fish fry. During the rest of the week, the Dockside is a favorite breakfast and lunch destination, where the old-timers head for coffee every morning. The huge omelets and crispy hash browns are popular, and the Dockside is where most people in De Tour head when they're in the mood for a burger. The restaurant also offers a number of healthier options, including salads, homemade soups, and wraps.

★ Hessel Bay Inn

906-484-2460
387 Lake St., Hessel, MI 49745
Open: Daily
Price: Inexpensive–Moderate
Cuisine: American
Serving: B, L, D
Credit Cards: MC, V
Handicapped Access: Yes
Open: Year-round
Special Features: Outdoor dining; water view; reservations required for parties of six or more

A great little family restaurant prized for its whitefish, perch, and water views, the Hessel Bay Inn has been serving both locals and summer visitors for going on 10 years now. In addition to the super-fresh fish specials, the menu includes several soups and pastas made from scratch by chef James Romanuk. And Romanuk even does Mexican food well, cooking up a delicious and enormous "wet" burrito smothered in cheese. For lunch, the fresh whitefish makes a great sandwich, and the popular Friday fish fry features all-you-can-eat whitefish. Breakfast includes the usual assortment of pancakes and omelets, with a better-than-average eggs Benedict and a Sunday morning breakfast buffet. During the summer, diners can eat outside on the deck, with a pleasant view of the water.

Islander Bar

906-484-3359
134 S. Pickford Ave., Hessel, MI 49745
Open: Daily
Price: Inexpensive–Moderate
Cuisine: American
Serving: B, L, D
Credit Cards: MC, V
Handicapped Access: Yes

A local institution, the Islander Bar is great fun for a burger and a beer on a sunny summer day . . . or a frozen winter night, for that matter. The Islander is a central meeting place for locals and a beloved tradition for regular visitors who look forward to a week or two of fishing Les Cheneaux during the day followed by burgers and beers at the Islander. Located in downtown Hessel, and easily found by its huge kitschy pirate-ship sign, this place is lively all year round, with a jukebox, live music some nights, and mammoth half-pound burgers.

Pammi's Restaurant

906-484-7844
54 W. MI 134, Cedarville, MI 49719 (corner of MI 134 and MI 129)
Open: Daily
Price: Inexpensive
Cuisine: American
Serving: B, L, D
Credit Cards: MC, V
Handicapped Access: Yes
Special Features: Takeout

What started as a popular local coffee place with good espresso drinks and fresh baked goods has blossomed into one of the area's best restaurants, serving three meals a day. Lunch baskets with your choice of fish and fries are fantastic, particularly the super-fresh local perch. Homemade soups and sandwiches are good too, with lots of creative combinations plus a killer Reuben, and Pammi's menu includes more wraps than you'll find anywhere in the U.P., including her popular California Wrap—

chicken, bacon, tomato, avocado, and ranch dressing. All sandwiches and wraps are served with one of Pammi's famous deviled eggs, which has the effect of making every lunch here feel like a summer picnic. The Friday fish fry is a local favorite, but Pammi's dinner menu has other standouts as well, including a very good steak, melt-in-your-mouth ribs, crispy fried chicken, and an assortment of pastas. Pammi's is still making those good espresso drinks, paired with her famous breakfast specials—the sausage-and-cheese omelet topped with a biscuit and gravy (yes, you read correctly) is a popular way to prepare for a cold day or recover from a late night in Cedarville. Baked treats like apple bread fresh from the oven for breakfast or decadent brownies for dessert round out the menu.

★ Raber Bay Bar & Grill

906-297-5701
28826 S. Raber Rd., Goetzville, MI 49736
Open: Daily
Price: Inexpensive–Moderate
Cuisine: American, seafood
Serving: L, D
Credit Cards: MC, V
Handicapped Access: Yes

People make the trek out to Raber Bay for super-fresh fish, homemade soups, and fantastic views of Lime Island and the St. Mary's River with gigantic freighters passing through its shipping lanes. Some argue that this is actually a better place to see the freighters than the restaurants near the locks in Sault Ste. Marie. The restaurant and bar are located in a well-preserved 1931 saloon in the very tiny one-horse town of Raber. The all-you-can-eat fresh fish dinners, accompanied by a trip to the salad, soup, and

The Islander is a local favorite bar and grill near the Hessel docks. Matt Girvan

dessert bar are a local favorite; diners polish off plate after plate of delicious local perch, whitefish, and walleye. Steaks, burgers, and ribs are also available, but the main draw here is definitely the seafood.

MACKINAC ISLAND

Cannonball

906-847-0932
www.cannonballmackinacisland.com
British Landing Rd., Mackinac Island, MI
    49757
Open: Daily
Price: Inexpensive–Moderate
Cuisine: American, seafood
Serving: L
Credit Cards: Not accepted
Handicapped Access: Yes
Special Features: Patio seating

A fantastic find, halfway around the island from Main Street at British Landing, Cannonball serves seriously good, reasonably priced food on a pleasant, pet-friendly outdoor patio. This is one of the Mackinac Island places that the local residents eat at regularly, which means visitors can trust that it is good and well-priced. The place is famous for its fried pickles, which are far, far better than they sound. The Angus beef burgers are large and juicy and pair nicely with fresh, handmade potato chips. Located along the bike path at the halfway point around the island, Cannonball also sells disposable cameras, batteries, film, and souvenir clothing. The staff is very friendly and helpful here as well. Cannonball is owned by a family that lives on the island year-round, and they are full of good advice for visitors.

The tiny vintage Main Street of "downtown" Mackinac is home to more five-star restaurants than can be found in the entire region. You'll find fudge shops, too. Matt Girvan

Who Has the Best Fudge?

It's an age-old question on Mackinac, but unfortunately it's really up to you. All we can say is that the best fudge shops are those that focus on fudge (in other words, not the hotel fudge shops) and answer a question with a question: Is there such a thing as bad fudge? That said, here are some of our favorites:

Joann's (906-847-3707; 2 Main St.) We like the variety (25 different flavors) and the creamy consistency.

Murdick's (906-847-3530; Main St.) The first fudge shop on Mackinac, Murdick's boasts a recipe that dates back to 1887.

Ryba's (906-847-6324; multiple locations downtown and in the Island House) There's no way to walk past, see the candy-makers, smell the fudge cooking, and not pop in here for a slab.

★ Carriage House at the Iroquois Hotel

906-847-3321
www.iroquoishotel.com
298 Main St., Mackinac Island, MI 49757
Open: Daily
Price: Very expensive
Cuisine: American
Serving: L, D
Credit Cards: AE, D, MC, V
Handicapped Access: Yes
Special Features: Outdoor seating; reservations recommended

Widely considered one of the best splurge restaurants on the island, the Carriage House also affords diners one of the best dinnertime views on Mackinac, including the straits and the lighthouse. All of which does actually make it worth the exorbitant amount of money you'll spend to eat here. Though it's tempting to always order whitefish everywhere in the U.P. because you know it will be really fresh, when you're shelling out for a splurge, go for something you can't get elsewhere. Because whitefish is so fresh, no one really does much to it, which is good, of course, but go to the VI

and spend half what you'll spend here if you're in the mood for whitefish. Here, try the delicious and tender filet mignon with béarnaise sauce, roast prime rib with a ridiculously good blue-cheese bread pudding, the perfectly cooked oven-roasted lamb chop, or the pan-seared diver scallops. The restaurant offers outdoor seating as well, which is worth reserving if you plan ahead. Lunch is priced lower than dinner, of course, but actually it feels like more of a ripoff. As with the whitefish, there's only so much you can do to lunch.

★ Grand Hotel Dining Room

906-847-3331
www.grandhotel.com
286 Grand Ave., Mackinac Island, MI 49757
Open: Daily, May 3–Oct. 31
Price: Very expensive
Cuisine: Continental
Serving: B, L, D
Credit Cards: AE, D, MC, V
Handicapped Access: Yes
Special Features: Prix fixe; formal dress code

During the day nonguests have to pay $10 to get a peak at the stately old Grand Hotel, where presidents have lolled on the porch and Esther Williams has strolled in the gardens. After five, however, anyone is welcome for a dinner or a drink, provided they are dressed in accordance with the hotel's dress code—coat and tie for the gents, dresses or pantsuits for the ladies. Although it is the most expensive place to eat on the island, and probably in the whole U.P., if you're going to dine at the Grand Hotel it seems fitting to be, well, grand. The five-course prix fixe menu ($75 a person) changes every season and offers several choices for each meal (three meals a day are included in the Grand Hotel's room rates, and you can imagine it would get pretty old to have the same five courses for dinner every night). Dinner is served in the hotel's large, opulent dining room by posh tuxedoed and gloved Jamaican waiters. For the record, we're not entirely sure why the waiters, or for that matter the entire Grand Hotel staff, are *all* Jamaican, and honestly feel a bit strange about it. Odd staffing choices notwithstanding, it's hard not to feel giddy dining here. Service is attentive in that perfect way that's neither cloying nor aloof, and the food is absolutely superb, though almost self-consciously "fancy" in a very un-Yooper sort of way—we're pretty sure that the words "jalapeño mint reduction" don't show up on any other U.P. menus. A truly creative chef has cooked up a varied and unique menu that includes almond-crusted local whitefish, an amberjack fillet on lobster risotto that absolutely melts in your mouth, a beautiful prime rib, and a grilled breast of duck with duck confit on black truffle grits with collard greens that may be the best thing ever cooked anywhere. Yes, that's hyperbole, but those are the sorts of statements you want to make in this dining room. If dinner sounds like too much of a splurge, the dining room's lunch buffet is terrific, with a variety of roasted meats, salads, cheeses, fruits, and desserts for $30 a person.

Ice House Bar & Grill

1-800-626-6304
www.theislandhouse.com
6966 Main St., Mackinac Island, MI 49757
Open: Daily, April to late Oct.
Price: Inexpensive
Cuisine: American
Serving: L
Credit Cards: MC, V
Handicapped Access: Yes
Special Features: Patio with straits view

A small pub tucked behind the hotel, the Island House's casual restaurant is literally and figuratively in the shadow of its larger, fancier, more publicized 1852 Grill Room. The 1852 is great, don't get us wrong, but who wants to spend $30 for lunch? Offering outdoor seating with a view of the straits and an affordable but excellent lunch menu, the Ice House is ideal. Hand-cut fresh potato chips accompany every sandwich and are delicious as an appetizer served with warmed blue cheese. Homemade soups change daily, and sandwiches range from simple classics like the sirloin burger to new and delicious creations like the BLT with smoked Gouda and the Steak Sicilian—shaved rib eye with sautéed mushrooms and onions, and provolone cheese, served au jus on a crusty baguette.

Mary's Bistro

906-847-9911
Main St., near Star Line dock, Mackinac Island, MI 49757
Open: Daily, mid-May through Oct.
Price: Moderate
Cuisine: American
Serving: B, L, D
Credit Cards: AE, D, MC, V
Handicapped Access: Yes

Owned and operated by the Island House, though not located at the Island House, Mary's Bistro provides very good, simple food at decent prices with an incredible view; you really can't ask for more than that combination on Mackinac. Spitfire roasted chicken is their specialty, and it is delicious. There are those who say one should never order chicken at a restaurant—it's bland and you could cook chicken at home. Pshaw! Anyone who has ever actually roasted a chicken can tell you how difficult it is to get it just so, and Mary's does it time and again, turning out beautiful roasted chicken that's evenly browned on the outside, tender and juicy inside. Other than the chicken, they serve a great wood-grilled salmon that's got a pleasant and not overbearing smoky taste to it, and a chicken pot pie that's outstanding because it's made with their chicken. Starters are good as well, particularly the shrimp artichoke dip and the baby back ribs. For lunch they offer a smaller version of the pot pie and a half order of the rotisserie chicken, plus a delicious Michigan chicken salad with dried cherries, celery, shallots, and mango chutney, a number of sandwiches and wraps, pizza, and a few extra appetizers including the very-good-but-bad-for-you fried cheese ravioli. The outside deck looks out over the harbor, and Mary's bar stays open as late as customers want it to.

The Round Island Bar and Grill

906-847-3312
www.missionpoint.com
At the Mission Point Resort: 6633 Main St., Mackinac Island, MI 49757
Open: Daily, April to late Oct.
Price: Inexpensive–Moderate
Cuisine: American
Serving: L, D
Credit Cards: AE, D, MC, V
Handicapped Access: Yes
Special Features: Open late

Awesome views of Round Island and the freighters on their way to the locks, combined with a solid, very affordable menu make this an excellent choice for lunch or dinner. An assortment of entrée-size salads (including one with that tasty Michigan combo of dried cherries and cheese), wraps, and sandwiches are available all the time, joined after five by a handful of simple grilled meats and seafood that includes a very good whitefish, steak, and roasted chicken. Round Island is also a popular spot to grab a drink and a late-night snack, and they have developed a very tasty appetizer menu for just that reason, which includes everything from super-greasy favorites such as fondue fries (a cone of fries smothered in cheese, bacon, jalapeño ranch) to light and fresh oyster shooters. A lengthy and well-chosen wine list offers a good range of wines, both in terms of origin and price.

★ Seabiscuit Café

906-847-3611
Main St., Mackinac Island, MI 49757
Open: Daily, April to late Oct.
Price: Inexpensive–Moderate
Cuisine: American, international
Serving: L, D
Credit Cards: MC, V
Handicapped Access: Yes

A former bank, built in the 1800s, has been transformed by two local sisters into this popular, cozy café. There's always a wait for a table in the busiest summer months (July and August), but it's worth it. In addition to the atmosphere—red and exposed brick walls, dim lighting, cavernous booths, a horse-racing theme—the food is outstanding and inventive, from delicious salads like the Michigan Chop Cherry Cob to grilled sandwiches and wraps (the smoked whitefish wrap is a favorite) and a wide variety of dinner entrées that includes some of the best whitefish on the island and ribs roasted so long the meat is falling off the bones. A full bar with a good wine list, a number of specialty cocktails, and excellent bar snacks (macaroni and cheese balls, Guinness cheese dip, hot wings) make this a great place to grab a drink as well. Beer lovers take note: The barman pours a perfect pint of Guinness.

★ Tea Room at Fort Mackinac

906-847-3331
www.mackinacparks.com
Open: Daily, May to late Oct.
Price: Moderate
Cuisine: American
Serving: L, D
Credit Cards: MC, V
Handicapped Access: Yes
Special Features: Reservations recommended

The view and the ambience alone would be enough to bring people here every summer. As an added bonus the food, provided by the Grand Hotel, is also very good. For lunch, assorted salads, soups, and burgers are simple, good, and reasonably priced (a nice surprise, given the fact that the words "Grand Hotel" are involved). The burger is particularly good, made with prime beef and topped with cheddar cheese and bacon. Buffalo chili and PEI mussels in a dip-worthy herb-laden white wine lemon broth are also good choices. For dinner the menu expands a bit to include steak, surf and turf, roasted chicken, and grilled whitefish, all of which are very good. The view from the patio here is absolutely incredible, particularly at sunset. In the evening the fort offers guided tours and stages rifle and cannon demonstrations, which adds to the fun of dining here, particularly for the little ones.

The Village Inn

907-847-3542
www.viofmackinac.com
Hoban Rd., in the Pontiac Lodge, Mackinac Island, MI 49757

(See review in St. Ignace section—the two restaurants are identical in terms of food and service, but the VI on Mackinac is a bit smaller and almost always packed with locals.)

★ Yankee Rebel Tavern

906-847-6249
www.yankeerebeltavern.com
101 Astor St., Mackinac Island, MI 49757
Open: Daily, April to late Oct.
Price: Inexpensive–Moderate
Cuisine: American, international
Serving: L, D
Credit Cards: MC, V
Handicapped Access: Yes
Special Features: Large children's menu; old-fashioned root beer on tap

Just far enough from Main Street to escape a little of the summer bustle, but close enough for convenience, the Yankee Rebel is one of the best restaurants on an island full of good restaurants. In addition to

being one of the only places in the entire U.P. where you can find good sushi, the tavern serves up amazing home-cooked classics, including an incredibly moist and tender pot roast and the famous Rebel Back Ribs, rubbed with brown sugar and spices and roasted for hours. Whitefish is on the menu too, of course, but the Yankee Rebel mixes it up a bit with their pistachio-encrusted whitefish. Their version of chicken pot pie—something that seems to show up on every Mackinac menu for some reason—is also delicious, with a light and flaky pastry crust and fresh roasted chicken. Lunchtime standouts include the Walnut Summer Salad with dried cherries, blue cheese, candied walnuts, and pears, the Tavern burgers, and a sinfully delicious prime rib melt. The lunch menu also includes an omelet option that changes daily in case you're on the lookout for a late breakfast. The dessert menu is the same for lunch and dinner, and the best thing on it is the chocolate bread pudding. In addition to a wide variety of beer, wine, and other liquors, the bar has a 1919 old-fashioned root beer on draft that is absolutely the best drink for a warm summer day.

MACKINAW CITY

★ Audie's Restaurant

231-436-5744
www.audies.com
314 Nicolet St., Mackinaw City, MI 49701
Open: Daily
Price: Inexpensive–Moderate
Cuisine: American
Serving: B, L, D
Credit Cards: AE, D, MC, V
Handicapped Access: Yes
Special Features: Two restaurants to choose from

Audie's is decorated in photographs from when the Mackinac Bridge was being built 50 years ago and the bridge workers used to eat here. The menu probably hasn't changed much since then, and that's why Audie's is so good. Audie's is also divided into two restaurants—the Family Room, which is a good old-fashioned family restaurant with very good prices, and the Chippewa Room, which is a bit more upscale, but still very affordable. The Family Room serves three meals a day, while the Chippewa Room serves only dinner. Meals in both rooms are accompanied by baskets of fresh-baked bread. Lunch and dinner in the Family Room are on the same menu, which includes Audie's fantastic chili, along with a selection of terrific fish sandwiches, a decent Reuben, and burgers. On the entrée side, Audie's offers steaks, pastas, and a really wide variety of seafood preparations, all of which are delicious, especially the walleye. Daily specials are a steal—where else can you get prime rib for $10? In the Chippewa Room the dinner menu includes a similar assortment of seafood specialties with a few additions. The biggest difference is the larger selection of appetizers, the broader selection of meat cuts, and the addition of local seasonal ingredients like morel mushrooms and elk when they're in season. The Chippewa Room also offers a long list of terrific desserts, including a flaming bananas Foster that will put a smile on your face for hours.

St. Ignace

Bentley's B-n-L Café
906-643-7910
62 N. State St., St. Ignace, MI 49781
Open: Daily
Price: Inexpensive
Cuisine: American
Serving: B, L
Credit Cards: Not accepted
Handicapped Access: Yes

Bentley's is a charming '50s diner right across the street from the ferry docks in St. Ignace. Its checkered floor, red booths, and yellow walls are a perfect fit for the time warp that is St. Ignace, and it just happens to be the best breakfast spot in town, to boot. Seating is limited, so you may have to wait for a table in the high season, but it's worth it. Serving up some of the area's best homemade pasties, along with pies, old-fashioned malts and shakes, breakfast, and the perfect grilled cheese sandwich, Bentley's is a favorite among visitors and locals alike. It's a rare morning when the town's old-timers aren't seated along the counter sipping coffee and trading tall tales.

★ Java Joe's
Open: Daily, Memorial Day to Labor Day
Price: Inexpensive
Cuisine: American
Serving: B, L, D
Credit Cards: MC, V
Handicapped Access: Yes
Special Features: Breakfast served all day; large portions

In a bright yellow house with a turquoise awning, Java Joe's serves a huge menu of items that includes pizza, burgers, breakfast served all day, pasties, homemade pies, and legendary enormous sundaes. Though the whole menu is large, the breakfast selection includes a dizzying array of choices, from Joe's delicious crepes to 25 different omelets to over 20 different kinds of pancakes—who knew you could do so many different things to a pancake? They're actually all really good, but the granola pancakes are out of this world. As the name might suggest, Joe's also serves a mean cup of Joe, and they've got an espresso machine if you feel like a cappuccino or latte. In addition to the mammoth ice cream sundaes, Joe's serves an assortment of giant desserts, including a homemade strawberry shortcake, and delicious brownies to add to your giant sundae. Joe himself hangs out at the restaurant most nights and is a total character. From the kitschy decor to the giant menu to the cast of characters, this is one of those places that just make people happy.

The Village Inn

906-643-3364
www.viofmackinac.com
250 S. State St., St. Ignace, MI 49781
Open: Daily
Price: Inexpensive–Moderate
Cuisine: American, seafood
Serving: B, L, D
Credit Cards: MC, V
Handicapped Access: Yes

"The VI" is one of the few restaurants in both St. Ignace and on Mackinac Island to stay open year-round. The menu is all over the place, in terms of both content and quality, but there are plenty of stars to keep you from going hungry if you find yourself in the area during the off-season or are looking for a decent, reasonable meal in summertime. The house specialty, planked whitefish—a huge piece of super-fresh local whitefish, baked and served on a maple plank, surrounded by loads of fluffy duchesse potatoes and a heaping portion of sautéed fresh vegetables—is certainly worth its slightly higher price tag. Other entrées are a bit disappointing (especially pastas), but burgers and pizzas are always a safe bet, and the whitefish-and-chips is excellent, as are the VI's various bar snacks (potato skins, jalapeño poppers, awesome onion rings, and buffalo wings). The bar at both locations is a favorite local hangout and a good place to meet friendly Yoopers at the end of a workday.

Java Joe's draws people in with its colorful exterior and keeps them coming back with good, affordable food and friendly service. Courtesy Java Joes

RECREATION

The islands of the eastern Upper Peninsula make for fantastic kayaking and fishing, and beautiful hiking views as well. Outdoor enthusiasts can really experience the whole gamut here, from an easy bike ride around Mackinac Island to a hard-core backcountry experience on beautiful Drummond Island. In the winter, ice fishing is fantastic, as are cross-country skiing and snowmobiling, thanks to the ice bridges that form between all of the islands.

Bicycling

This is one of the best regions in the U.P. for road cycling—through the Hiawatha National Forest and the Lake Superior State Forest, around little waterfront towns like Hessel and St. Ignace, and everywhere on Mackinac Island.

Rentals

Arnold Transit (906-847-3351; www.arnoldline.com) In addition to ferrying people over to Mackinac all season long, Arnold's rents bikes at the dock upon arrival.
Mackinac Island Bicycle Shop (906-847-6337; Hoban St., Mackinac Island)
Mackinac Wheels (906-847-8022; 1800 Huron Rd., Mackinac Island)

Top Rides

Mackinac Island Circle Tour. An easy ride around the island will take about an hour and a half with no stops, but there are plenty of sights worth pulling over for, and even a tasty snack stop along the way. The bike path starts right next to the ferry docks and follows the coast around the island.

With no cars, Mackinac's wide roads are left solely to bicycles and horses. Matt Girvan

MI 134 between Cedarville and De Tour. This lovely stretch of road affords views of pleasant bays and hushed forests, as well as access to sandy beaches and marshes that are excellent for bird-watching (see below). The road is quite flat, with large, paved shoulders, which makes it ideal for a lazy bike ride. Mountain bikers can take any number of more rough-and-tumble trails off the main road for a more challenging ride.

Bird-Watching

Birge Nature Preserve, about 2 miles west of Hessel. Take MI 134 to Point Brulée Rd. A peaceful 275-acre preserve is home to several eagles and osprey.

MI 134 rest stop, near intersection of MI 48, south of Goetzville. Strange as it may seem, Michigan's Department of Transportation maintains this popular birding site along the highway. The rest stop's shoreline is an excellent place to spot warblers, vireos, and flycatchers, as well as raptors in September and gulls and cormorants offshore.

Neebish Island, in St. Mary's River. Ferry service available from Barbeau. From I-75 take MI 80 east to MI 129. Go north on MI 129 and make a right on 15-Mile Rd. to Barbeau. This largely undeveloped wilderness island is home to a number of unusual birds, includ-ing various owls—great gray, snowy, and northern hawk owls—as well as red- and white-winged crossbills, northern shrike, and rough-legged hawks. Be careful going in off-season unless the ice is frozen solid or melted entirely. The Coast Guard cuts through the ice bridge that forms with the mainland every year in late March, but ice often reforms, not thick enough to walk on, but too thick to allow the small ferry through, essentially stranding people on the island. Don't worry too much, though—although there are no stores on Neebish, there are a handful of residents. In addition to watching the birds, visi-tors to the island can get a close-up view of the big freighters as they pass by on their way to the St. Mary's River and the Soo Locks.

St. Vital Point, near the De Tour State Forest Campground. Part of the Lake Superior State Forest, St. Vital Point is home to large flocks of warblers during the late spring and late summer.

Canoeing and Kayaking

Top Paddles
Kayaking is amazing all the way around **Drummond Island** and betwixt and between **Les Cheneaux,** as well as around the **St. Mary's River** and **Lime Island**. For newcomers it's a good idea to book a guide, particularly to get a handle on the bays and marshes of Les Cheneaux. **Les Cheneaux Water Trail** leads from the Carp River near St. Ignace along the north shore of Lake Huron, through Les Cheneaux to De Tour Village. It's 75 miles in total, almost all of it a stunning coastline paddle.

Rentals
Drummond Island Resort (906-493-1000 or 1-800-999-6343; www.drummondisland .com; 33494 S. Maxton Rd., Drummond Island) The resort and its sister property, Yacht Haven, provide kayaks for free to guests and for a fee to nonguests. The resort's paddling expert leads guided tours along the shoreline and Potagannissing Bay. Longer, full-day trips are also available for those who want to explore the surrounding islands.

Woods and Water EcoTours (906-484-4157; www.woodswaterecotours.com; 20 Pickford Ave., Hessel) This one-woman operation leads kayak trips through Les

Cheneaux and Drummond Island—hands-down the best way to see the shorelines of these islands. Woods and Water also rents boats to those who prefer to go it alone, but requires that you first take their introductory safety course or prove knowledge of the basics covered in it. Maps of the area and rights-of-way maps are provided, and they offer delivery anywhere around the area for an extra $5.

Fishing

Fishing is amazing all throughout the shores and dozens of inland lakes of Les Cheneaux, as well as in Lake Huron and the St. Mary's River, with the local favorite prize being yellow perch. Bass, salmon, pike, herring, smelt, musky, walleye, and splake are all also found in the waters surrounding these 36 tiny islands.

Guides, Charters, Rentals

Dream Seaker Sport Fishing Charters and Guided Tours (1-888-634-3419; www.dreamseaker.com; Hessel Marina) Take exit 359 from I-75 and head east on MI 134 to the blinking light at 3 Mile Rd. Turn right into the Hessel Marina. Les Cheneaux resident and longtime captain Jim Shutt leads visiting fishermen to the northern Lake Huron area and the St. Mary's River system, departing from Hessel, St. Ignace, Cedarville, De Tour, Drummond Island, or Mackinac Island. If you don't catch a fish, Captain Shutt will keep taking you out until you do.

    Les Cheneaux Islands Water Tours and Charter Service (906-484-3776; www.fishing withnorm.com; 117 N. Greenwood Dr., Cedarville) Also known as "Fishing with Norm,"

Almost the entire circumference of Drummond Island is easily navigated by kayak, which makes the island a real paddler's paradise. Amy Westervelt

this local operation offers fishing charters and boating tours throughout Les Cheneaux. Norm has 31 years of experience fishing these waters and guarantees that you'll catch a fish or next time's free.

Sturgeon Bay Charters (906-493-6087; www.sturgeonbaycharters.com; Drummond Island) Lifelong Drummond Island resident Captain Ivan Gable knows this island and its waters like the back of his hand. He sticks to what he knows—Drummond Island and its environs—and leads fishermen to perch, salmon, walleye, trout, and herring.

Places to Fish

Caribou Lake, 3.5 miles west of De Tour Village off MI 134. Caribou Lake is a popular local fishing lake, known for smallmouth bass, rock bass, walleye, yellow perch, northern pike, pumpkinseed sunfish, brown bullhead, and white sucker.

De Tour State Forest Campground, 5 miles west of De Tour Village on MI 134. The De Tour campground provides direct access to prime Lake Huron fishing for walleye, bass, pike, and musky.

Mackinac Island. Fishing is decent right off the shoreline rocks, especially on the back side of the island, away from the crowds. Fishermen catch perch, salmon, walleye, musky, steelhead, pike, and whitefish here.

Golf

The Rock at Drummond Island Resort (906-493-1000; www.drummondisland.com; 33494 S. Maxton Rd., Drummond Island) It's not many golf courses that list deer and geese as regular course obstacles. In addition to the local wildlife, the Rock boasts challenging long, tree-lined fairways and water obstacles, earning a four-star rating from *Golf Digest*. 18 holes, 6,830 yards, par 71.

Scottish Links (906-847-3871; www.wawashkamo.com; British Landing Dr., Mackinac Island) A nine-hole course where golfers can still use classic Scottish hickory sticks if they choose, Scottish Links, or Wawashkamo ("walk a crooked trail"), as the Ojibwa called it, is the oldest continuously played course in Michigan and offers visitors a truly unique experience. Played on nine greens from 18 tees, par 72. No metal spikes allowed.

The Jewel at the Grand Hotel (906-847-3331; www.grandhotel.com; Mackinac Island) Expanded to 18 holes by Jerry Matthews in the mid 1990s, the Jewel is a fantastic course that mixes long, open fairways near the hotel with tougher, tree-lined fairways on the back nine in the woods. A special horse-drawn carriage takes golfers between the front and back nine. 18 holes, 5,500 yards, par 67.

Hiking

Birge Nature Preserve, off MI 134 west of Hessel on Point Brulée Rd. Vibrant wildflowers run riot over this 275-acre preserve at the base of Point Brulée about 2 miles west of Hessel. Its wetlands and forests also provide prime wildlife viewing, including regular sightings of eagles, beavers, and osprey.

Government Island, off La Salle Island, Les Cheneaux. This pretty, 2-mile-long uninhabited island with hardwood forests and sandy beaches is a short boat ride from Hessel.

Marble Head, eastern shore Drummond Island. Take MI 134, turn east on Glen Cove Rd., then east again on the unmarked road after Fourth Lake Rd., and follow that road until it ends at Marble Head. A path along 200-foot-high dolomite cliffs leads down to the North Channel, with breathtaking views of the water and Cockburn Island, Ontario.

Search Bay Beach and St. Martin Hiking Trail (906-643-7900) From MI 134, 6 miles west of Hessel and 7 miles east of I-75, look for "Ski Trail" sign. Take FR 3436 / Search Bay Rd. to the water, about 1 1/2 miles south of MI 134. A sleepy little out-of-the-way spot tucked into the Hiawatha National Forest, the beach at Search Bay is mostly sand, and small boats can launch from the shore. In winter two groomed cross-country ski loops take skiers through the woods and wetlands. One of the loops makes for an excellent hike in the spring and summer, with plenty of opportunities to spy on the local wildlife—deer, grouse, bald eagles, hawks, and sometimes even porcupine or bear.

Hunting

Both the deer and bear populations in this region of the U.P. have decreased in recent years, which has made some locals criticize Michigan DNR for not regulating hunts more in this region. That said, it remains a popular sport, and, as in other regions, land located in the Hiawatha National Forest (much of the land around Hessel and Les Cheneaux Islands) and the Lake Superior State Forest is open to hunters. See www.fs.fed.us/ r9/forests/hiawatha/ for details on hunting in the Hiawatha Forest, and www.michigan.gov/dnr for information on hunting in Lake Superior National Forest.

Game/Season

White-tailed deer—Bow: Oct. 1–Nov. 14 and Dec. 1– Jan.2; regular firearm: Nov. 15–30; muzzle loaders: Dec. 2–18

Russian boar—Year-round (hunters can hunt boar with any valid hunting license)

Black bear—Sep. 10–Oct. 26

Elk—Aug. 25–29; Sep.15–18; Dec. 11–18

Wild turkey—Oct. 8–Nov. 14

American woodcock—Sep. 22–Nov. 5

Pheasant—(Males only) Oct. 10–Nov. 14

Ruffed grouse—Sep. 15–Nov.14.; Dec. 1–Jan. 1

Ducks and mergansers—Sep. 29–Nov. 27

Canada geese—Sep. 18–Nov. 1

Guides and Private Hunting Land

Lucky Strike, Drummond Island (906- 493-5455, www.michigan-outdoors.com/ LSguide.htm) Guided bear, deer, and duck hunts on Drummond Island with all hunts guaranteed.

Cross-Country Skiing

DeTour Pathway, 5 miles west of De Tour Village on MI 134. There are spectacular views on this 4-mile groomed, marked trail leading through the woods to St. Vital Point on the shores of Lake Huron.

Drummond Island Ski Trails. Several miles of groomed trails cut through the trees and around the shores of Drummond Island. Access trails in the woods near the Drummond Island Lodge; trail maps are available at the lodge.

Mackinac Island. All roads and trails are open to cross-country skiing; back of island is reserved for cross-country skiing and snowshoeing, with no snowmobiling allowed.

Sand Dunes Ski Trail, 11 miles west of St. Ignace on US 2, 0.5 mile north of CR H57. Marked and groomed trails along the sand dunes in the Hiawatha National Forest; there are five trails, 1.5 to 6.2 miles (2.4 km to 10 km).

St. Martin Cross-Country Ski Trail, 6–7 miles west of Hessel. Two groomed cross-country ski loops take skiers through the woods and wetlands near Search Bay.

Snowmobiling

Ice bridges between the islands are one of the biggest draws of snowmobiling in this area. Particularly popular is the **International Ice Bridge to Canada on Drummond Island**. Near Christmastime, when the ice has frozen solid, snowmobilers bring Christmas trees to outline an ice highway from Drummond over to the nearest Canadian island. As winter progresses, another tree-lined bridge opens up to mainland Canada, giving access to a whole new network of trails. In addition to the ice bridge, Drummond has over 100 miles of groomed snowmobiling trails. The popular **St. Ignace Snowmobile Trail** leads east to Hessel and Les Cheneaux, where it meets up with several more miles of groomed trails.

Snowmobile rentals

The Country Store (906-493-5455; Four Corners, Drummond Island)
Quality Inn of St. Ignace Snowmobile Rental (1-800-906-4656; 913 Boulevard Dr.)

FAMILY FUN

Fort Mackinac (www.mackinacparks.com; fort overlooks downtown Mackinac Island) Walk up the front ramp just west of the ferry docks for a harbor view, or take a carriage or taxi to the back entrance; adults $10, children $6; children 5 and under free). Kids get a kick out of

Arch Rock has been a Mackinac attraction since the late 1800s; this photo dates to around 1900.
Library of Congress

the interactive children's museum, and the cannon and rifle demonstrations as well.

Great Turtle Toys (906-847-6118; www.greatturtletoys.com; located in the Lilac Tree Hotel Mall on Main St. downtown) A fun and interactive toy shop carrying vintage toys, board games, flying toys, all sorts of items with a physical or educational element, and no video games or electronic toys. The staff are great with kids and love to do demonstrations of the various toys.

Mackinac Island Bike Ride. A paved bike path circles the island, providing fun for the whole family. There are convenient stops along the way at British Landing, Arch Rock, and Mission Point, and you can always take a breather anywhere along the path and stare at the lake for a while. At the end of the ride, treat the kids to a slab of fudge at one of downtown Mackinac's dozens of fudge shops.

Totem Village Museum (906-643-8888; 1230 W. US 2, Moran) While purists will point out that totem poles aren't indigenous to this region, the man who carved these totem poles had nothing but a deep reverence for the local Ojibwa, and they in turn took a liking to him. Kids love to wander around the village and pick out gifts like fur hats and mini totem poles in the gift shop.

Fossil Hunting

Fossils are abundant in this part of the U.P. and especially so on Drummond Island's north shore. Fossil Beach is obviously known for its fossils, and the Maxton Plains, best known for their protected alvar grasses, are also a decent place to spot fossils. The folks at the Drummond Island Chamber of Commerce are very helpful. They're happy to plan out a fossil-hunting trip for visitors, depending on whether they have four-wheel-drive or not or whether they want to deal with hiking in. Call 906-493-5245 for more information.

SHOPPING

As with the rest of the U.P., shopping is not the reason that people visit this region. That said, the large numbers of Mackinac Island visitors support the existence of more shops here than you would expect in such small towns, although the region lacks the bookstores and antiques stores common in the rest of the U.P., where a greater number of year-round residents can keep such businesses afloat. Gifts unique to the area include Mackinac Island fudge and traditional Native American art.

LES CHENEAUX

Creekside Herbs and Art (906-484-2415; 752 N. Blindline Rd., Cedarville) A truly unique place comprising a renovated barn with an art gallery, a kayak shop, nature trails, and display gardens, Creekside Herbs is a must for anyone staying in the area. Owned by two local sisters who strive to introduce visitors to local and Native American arts and culture, this place feels more like a community center than a store, which is exactly the desired effect. That said, the items for sale here are interesting too, especially Native American art and crafts, handblown glass items, unique pottery, beads, and jewelry. There is a lot to see here, and plenty of unique items to take home for yourself or loved ones. And the "herbs" part of the name isn't just a reference to the herb gardens in back; the sisters sell hundreds of herbal remedies and delight in passing on their knowledge.

MACKINAC ISLAND

Fudge Shops. See sidebar in "Restaurants" section.

Mackinac State Historic Parks Gift Shops. A shop at the Visitors Center as you land on Mackinac, and two shops at Fort Mackinac—one at the soldiers' barracks, and a kids' shop at the children's exhibit—sell an assortment of historically themed items unique to Mackinac and its stories.

ST. IGNACE

John Herbon Pottery and Ceramics Studio (906-643-8196; 99 Stockbridge St., St. Ignace) Very beautiful handcrafted ceramics, all with subtle touches and allusions to the surrounding nature that make them distinctly north woods, but not in a touristy way. It's worth stopping in here just to have a look.

Native Expressions Ojibwa Museum Store (906-643-9161; 566 N. State St., St. Ignace) This great little store in the Ojibwa Museum sells a large selection of Native American books and music and a very high-quality assortment of locally made Native American art and crafts. It's worth a visit even if you're not going to the museum.

Totem Village Museum (906-643-8888; 1230 W. US 2, Moran) The totem village itself is great fun, but its museum shop is really something else. A clearinghouse for delightfully kitschy Native American–inspired items that look like the same souvenirs the shop might have sold in the 1950s, the shop and the museum do actually hold a deep reverence for the Ojibwa, and the shop's original owner was held in high esteem by the local tribes.

The Indian Village souvenir shop is almost as much fun to visit as the attached museum. Brett Schutzman

CULTURE

As with the rest of the eastern U.P., there's a lot of history in this region. Long before Mackinac was a Victorian island enticing celebrities and presidents, it figured into the Ojibwa creation myth. Similarly, more than a hundred years before St. Ignace became a good low-cost alternative to the lavish hotels on Mackinac, the town was a key meeting place between the native Ojibwa and the new Europeans, with French fur trappers and missionaries like Father Marquette brokering a cultural truce far more honest and powerful than any subsequent treaties. It was here that the British defeated the French and the Americans in turn defeated the British, taking Fort Mackinac. Much of this history is preserved today through various monuments and museums throughout the area, as well as through ongoing celebrations and rituals.

Historic Buildings and Sites

Carriage Tours (906-847-3307; www.mict.com) One of the best ways to be immediately swept up in the history of Mackinac is to book a carriage tour, a tradition that has been on the island since 1869, according to Mackinac Island Carriage Tours, the company formed by the island's carriagemen in 1948. The tour covers all the major Mackinac sights—Main Street, the Grand Hotel, Fort Mackinac, Arch Rock—as well as some sights cooked up by the carriage company, seemingly to make more money. Their butterfly conservatory is very pretty, but it can feel a bit like they just picked you up and now they want more money. Still, the horses are lovely, the carriagemen are generally knowledgeable about the island, and it's a pleasant way to get a brief overview.

Grand Hotel (906-847-3331 or 1-800-334-7263; Grand Hotel, Mackinac Island, MI

Horse-drawn carriage is still a primary mode of transport on Victorian Mackinac Island.
Courtesy Mackinac Island Tourism Bureau

49757) Up on the hill, away from the bustle of Main Street, the Grand Hotel is the picture of 19th-century elegance, a majestic white structure with a mammoth porch sweeping around huge columns. Everything about the Grand is extreme. The gardens aren't just lovely, they're prize-winning. The pool isn't just refreshing, it once enticed Esther Williams for a swim. And that huge porch? Several U.S. presidents have sat on it. Though some might bristle at the idea of a hotel charging an entrance fee to nonguests, it is both worth it and probably necessary. Without the fee, the hotel would very likely be completely overrun with tourists, making it hard to justify the astronomical room rates to guests. Once inside it's like walking into the past—this is as close to time travel as you can get.

> ### Somewhere in Time
> Mackinac Island was further immortalized by the film *Somewhere in Time*, starring Christopher Reeve and Jane Seymour. The Chamber of Commerce actually hands out maps to the various filming locations for interested visitors. Even if you're not interested in the film, the map can be a handy guide to the Grand Hotel, where much of the film was shot.

Historic Downtown Mackinac. Several of Mackinac's historic buildings stretch to the east of where people congregate now, toward Mission Point from Main Street. The walk is beautiful and should be done regardless, but the story behind some of these buildings is very interesting as well, including the Indian Dormitory, a three-story white building with black shutters that housed the American Indian Agency. Though the building was once open to the public with tours, the Mackinac Island State Historic Park has closed it in recent years while preparing a new exhibit focused on the impact of the agency and its founder, Henry Schoolcraft. Also included in this stretch of the island are the Protestant Mission Church, which is a charming New England–style chapel, bright white with a tall steeple, and St. Anne's Catholic Church, which dates to colonial Michilimackinac days.

Mackinac Bridge. "Big Mac" turned 50 in 2007 with many celebrations statewide. Until it was built, the only way to the U.P. from the Lower Peninsula was by car-ferry, which took 45 minutes. During the summer and hunting season, when there were more cars wanting to get across than there were ferries to take them, people often waited for several hours for their turn to cross. The completion of the bridge really introduced the two parts of the state to each other, and provided the U.P. with a new industry—tourism—just in the nick of time. The third-longest suspension bridge in the world, this is one of those great bridges to cross, with Lake Huron off to one side and Lake Michigan to the other, and great, arching spans above. The idea of a bridge had been broached numerous times beginning in the late 1800s, but plans were always thwarted for some reason or another—money, wars, and bad publicity from other bridge disasters among them. In 1954 former U.S. senator Prentiss Brown from St. Ignace, Michigan's then-governor G. William "Soapy" Williams, and W. Stewart Woodfill, the owner of the Grand Hotel, joined forces to help get the bridge up. It took them a long time to get enough support and funding for such a large suspension bridge. It was bridge designer David B. Steinman's willingness to eat the cost of preparing plans for the bridge, should the funding have fallen through, that got him the design job. The bridge was the highlight of his career. At the time, it was the largest bridge-construction project ever undertaken, and the whole state was fascinated by it. The Bridge Authority hired one photographer, Herman Ellis, to document the construction, and he did an extraordinary job. Unfortunately, the museum that contained the bulk of his photographs burned to the ground in 2005, leaving behind only reproductions of the images in numerous books.

Market Street on Mackinac (906-847-3328; Market St., from Fort St. south, Mackinac Island) The white clapboard buildings at the head of Astor Street that now house the island's city hall, community center, fire hall, police department, and courthouse were warehouses for John Jacob Astor's American Fur Trade Company back in the early 1800s. Down the street, four of Market Street's historic structures, including Michigan's oldest house, the McGulpin House, are part of the Mackinac State Historic Park—entry to them is included with admission to Fort Mackinac.

Marquette Mission Park, St. Ignace. This great little park surrounds the Museum of Ojibwa Culture and commemorates French missionary Father Jacques Marquette, who built several missions throughout the U.P. and was widely respected by the Ojibwa and the U.P.'s early settlers. In addition to his missionary work, Marquette was a skilled cartographer and was responsible for helping to map the river network that leads from the U.P. all the way down to the Mississippi. Unfortunately it was that exploratory trip that eventually did him in. He died on his way back to St. Ignace, most likely near present-day Ludington, according to

This white obelisk in Marquette Mission Park commemorates the culturally and historically significant life of Father Jacques Marquette. Matt Girvan

historians. A fountain and a plaque paying tribute to Marquette are placed at the center of the park on the spot that some believed to be his grave when they found a limestone slab there in 1877. A nearby plaque entitled "Black Robes of the Wilderness" explains the basic beliefs of the Jesuits and the role they played in the region. A subsequent panel, "Priest, Missionary, Explorer," delves into Marquette's own history, tracing his route from France to Quebec, and eventually to the U.P. in "New France." Finally "A Gathering Place" details what was going on in the area and between the tribes during the time Marquette was here. Though Marquette spent most of his time in Sault Ste. Marie and then here in St. Ignace, the famous Father Marquette statue is on Mackinac Island in the park in front of Fort Mackinac.

Paging Doctor Crain

Thought not a Mackinac Island native, "Doc" Crain has been an island resident for several years and has made it his goal to learn as much as he can about Mackinac. His lust for life and boundless enthusiasm quickly endeared Doc to locals, and once he began his "Doc Crain's natural and human history tours by foot and bike," he developed a loyal following among visitors as well. Doc started his tours purely to help people discover that there was more to Mackinac than fudge and horse-drawn carriages, and his tales of Native American legends and how the wildflowers bloom here have inspired many, many people to learn more about the island and to treat it with respect, as more than just a tourist destination. Doc's Web site says it all: "I am a father and grandfather and remember when my children were smaller often having to make hard decisions about what our family could afford to do on vacation. There is no charge for my tours. No tickets required. All are welcome all the time. I have been doing this for a decade and find that people are naturally generous enough with tips and gratuities. Bring your family. Give what you can—if you can. 'Nuff said." For information about Doc and his tours, visit www.mackinacislandhikebike.com.

West Bluff, Mackinac Island. The Grand Hotel sits at the entrance to a neighborhood full of 19th-century cottage mansions for the well-to-do, including the ornate Queen Anne–style Cudahy Mansion, once the governor's summer residence. It's fascinating to stroll through this neighborhood and see how the wealthy lived back then. As the road turns along the bluff, curious visitors can continue on to another neighborhood of cottages, Hubbard's Cove, which are not as ornate, but still very beautiful.

Museums
Colonial Michilimackinac Historic State Park
231-436-4100
www.mackinacparks.com/parks/colonial-michilimackinac_7/
Enter at the Colonial Michilimackinac Visitor Center near the south end of the Mackinac
   Bridge (exit 339 from I-75) and follow signs.
Open: May 3–June 9, daily 9–4; June 10–Aug. 20, 9–6; Aug. 21–Oct. 8, 9–4
Admission: Adults $9.50; youths (6–17) $6.00; children 5 and under free

This 1715 French fur-trading village and military outpost, which was later occupied by British military and traders, has been reconstructed and features reenactments of native life, the French fur trade, and the 1761 British takeover, along with a surprisingly interesting archaeological tunnel exhibit entitled "Treasures from the Sand." Those planning to visit either of the other two sites making up the Mackinac State Parks (the nearby Historic Mill Creek State Park or Fort Mackinac on Mackinac Island) can buy a combination ticket that allows them into all three for $20 (adult) or $12.50 (children).

Mackinac Island: Home of the Spirits

Mackinac Island holds a sacred place in the Ojibwa tradition. Because of its shape—not unlike a turtle's back—the Ojibwa named the island Michilimackinac, or "Land of the Great Turtle." They believed the island was where the first people lived and that it was home to the Great Spirit Gitche Manitou. Located in the center of the Great Lakes, Mackinac became a tribal gathering place, where celebrations were held and offerings to Gitche Manitou were made, and where chiefs were buried in order to honor the Great Spirit. Not unlike today, spring was a time for the Ojibwa to gather together on the island, relax after the long winter, celebrate the Great Spirit, hunt, fish, and spend time with their families. Ojibwa legend has it that the arrival of the Europeans scared Gitche Manitou off; the Great Spirit fled the island to dwell instead in the northern lights.

Fort Mackinac

906-847-3328
www.mackinacparks.com
Mackinac Island, MI; overlooking downtown
Open: May to early June, 9–4:30; June to Aug., 9:30–8; late Aug. to Oct., 9:30–4:30
Admission: Adults $10, children $6

The imposing fort overlooking Mackinac's harbor was built by the British in 1780 during the American Revolution. Within 14 of its original buildings visitors can explore various history exhibits, see how a military hospital operated back in the early 1800s, visit the old officers' quarters, which are furnished as they would have been during the late 1700s and early 1800s, or have lunch or dinner in the Tea Room (see "Restaurants"), all while enjoying incredible views of the island and the straits. A large interactive exhibit for kids lets

Fort Mackinac was built by the British during the American Revolution and wasn't turned over until long after the war. Matt Girvan

them play a giant fife or "fire" a pretend cannon, among other things. The museum's largest exhibit, a tribute to Mackinac Island as a whole, is ironically sponsored by Ford, whose cars are not allowed on the island! In addition to the exhibits, the fort offers three guided tours a day, two cannon firings, and various other informational tours, including "A Soldier's Life" and a reenactment of a court-martial. There's a *lot* going on at the fort. You could easily spend all day there, but most people would rather spend the whole day biking around the island, eating fudge, or hanging out at the beach. To make the most of your time, take the fort's guided tour to see almost everything; it's followed by the cannon firing, which you can enjoy from the Tea Room patio while grabbing a bite to eat or a cup of coffee; finish up with the giant Ford exhibit, which is very interesting and well produced. If you've still got burning unanswered questions or you're a military history buff, carry on and visit the specific exhibits that interest you. One thing to note: There are many, many stairs leading up to the fort, but you're rewarded with terrific views for all that climbing.

The Museum of Ojibwa Culture
906-643-9161
500–566 N. State St., St. Ignace, MI
Open Memorial Day weekend through late June, daily 11–5; late June through Labor Day,
    Mon.–Sat. 10–8 and Sun. noon–8; Labor Day through early Oct., 11–6.
Admission: Family $5; adults/teens $2; elementary school students $1; free for preschool and younger children

This small but well-done museum is housed, interestingly, in a former Catholic church built on the site of Father Marquette's original Jesuit mission, which was erected in 1671 and burned down in 1701. The front gallery of the museum focuses on the precolonial history of the Ojibwa people and how they survived those early harsh winters. The back gallery deals with the arrival of other tribes (the Huron and the Ottawa) and of French fur traders in the 17th and 18th centuries. The exhibit depicts a camaraderie between the Ojibwa and the French as they joined together against their common enemy, the British. A park surrounds the museum, with a memorial to Father Marquette, a Huron longhouse, and various outdoor exhibits related to the Ottawa and Huron cultures.

NIGHTLIFE

Nightlife in St. Ignace, Mackinaw City, and Les Cheneaux is relatively sleepy, with the exception of the nearby **Kewadin Casinos**. Mackinac, however, is a hotbed of nighttime activity, with live music at several venues.

Cupola at Grand Hotel (906-847-3331 or 1-800-334-7263; www.grandhotel.com; Grand Hotel, Mackinac Island) This old-fashioned piano bar feels like something out of *The Great Gatsby*. The ambience, coupled with phenomenal views of the bridge, make it a popular cocktail spot, particularly for couples on a romantic weekend away.

Horn's Gaslight Bar & Restaurant (906-847-6154; 101 Main St., Mackinac Island) One of the more popular bars on the island, Horn's is known for its nachos, its margaritas, and its live rock and roll.

Mustang Lounge (906-847-9916; 8 Astor St., Mackinac Island) A favorite hangout for locals and summer workers, the Mustang is a pleasantly divey bar, good for beer and greasy snacks, and open year-round.

In spite of, or perhaps because of, its lack of cars, Mackinac is abuzz with nightlife during the summer.
Matt Girvan

Patrick Sinclair's Irish Pub (906-847-8255; Main St., Mackinac Island) One of the few places to stay open year-round (usually trading off with the VI and/or the Mustang so that there's always at least one bar open), Patrick Sinclair's is beloved by everyone on the island—locals and visitors alike. With various beers on tap and pretty decent pub grub, Sinclair's is always a good bet, but it gets especially lively when there's an Irish band playing.

Pink Pony Bar and Grill (906-847-3341; 250 Main St., Mackinac Island) The Pink Pony in the Chippewa Hotel is a celebrated Mackinac bar, restaurant, and entertainment venue. The deck is a great place to hang out for the night, and there is almost always live music playing, plus a pool table and darts.

SEASONAL EVENTS

FEBRUARY
Annual Winter Festival, Mackinac Island; 907-847-3542
Chili Cook-Off, Mackinac Island; 907-847-3542
MIRA Blizzard on the Bay, Cedarville; 906-484-3935
MIRA Snowmobile Races, Drummond Island; 906-493-5245
Siberian Husky Dogsled Race, Drummond Island; 906-493-5245
Snows Fest, Les Cheneaux; 906-484-3935
Winterfest, Mackinac Island; 1-800-454-5227

In early June Mackinac Island celebrates its annual lilac festival. Courtesy Mackinac Island Tourism Bureau

MAY
Frogfest, Cedarville and Hessel; 906-484-3935
Memorial Day Celebration at Fort Mackinac, Mackinac Island; 231-436-4100

JUNE
Antiques and Classics on the Bay, St. Ignace; 906-643-9402
Mackinac Island Lilac Festival, Mackinac Island; 1-800-454-5227

JULY
Fourth of July Celebrations, Les Cheneaux, Mackinac Island, St. Ignace
Mackinac Island Yacht Races, Mackinac Island; 313-822-1853

AUGUST
Antique Wooden Boat Show, Hessel; 906-484-2821
Drummond Island Salmon Derby, Drummond Island; 906-493-5245
Mackinac Island Fudge Festival, Mackinac Island; 1-800-454-5227
Rendezvous at the Straits Pow-Wow, St. Ignace; 906-635-6050

SEPTEMBER
Annual Labor Day Regatta, Mackinac Island; 906-847-3363
Annual Mackinac Bridge Walk, Mackinac Island; 1-800-454-5227
Carleton Varney's Antique & Design Fall Festival, Mackinac Island; 906-847-3331
Grand Hotel Labor Day Jazz Festival, Mackinac Island; 906-847-3331
Hiawatha Paddling Festival, Lake Huron Cedar Campus; 906-484-4157
Mackinac Island Horsemen's Association Formal Ride, Mackinac Island; 1-800-454-5227

OCTOBER
Autumn Apple Days and Great Pumpkin Roll, St. Ignace; 1-800-970-8717
Geocaching Autumn Adventure, Mackinac Island; 906-847-3355
Somewhere in Time Weekend, Mackinac Island; 906-847-3331

NOVEMBER
Car Parade and Tree Lighting, Mackinaw City; 231-436-5664

DECEMBER
New Year's Eve Celebrations, Mackinac Island, St. Ignace, Drummond Island

INFORMATION

This chapter is a quick and handy guide to the essential details. Compiled with both the local and the visitor in mind, information is presented on the following subjects:

Ambulance/Fire/Police
Area Codes
Banks
Bibliography
Climate, Weather, What to Wear
Fishing and Hunting Regulations
Handicapped Services
Hospitals and Emergency Medical Service
Media
Tourist Information

AMBULANCE/FIRE/POLICE

Always dial **911** in an emergency situation—to report a fire or request an ambulance or immediate police response. For police assistance that doesn't require an emergency response, contact the number listed below for the city closest to your location.

AREA CODES

The entire U.P. uses the **906** area code. Mackinaw City, in Cheboygan County on the Lower Peninsula, uses **231**.

TOWN POLICE

Ahmeek 337-2211
Allouez 337-2211
Alpha 875-3465
Amasa 875-3012
Arnold 346-9224
Atlantic Mine 482-3102
Au Train 387-2275
Aura 524-6161
Baraga 353-7181

TOWN POLICE

Bark River 466-7441
Bay Mills 248-3244
Bergland 787-2300
Bessemer 667-0203
Big Bay 485-1888
Brampton 428-3131
Brevort 643-8383
Brimley 248-3251
Bruce Crossing 884-4901
Calumet 337-2345
Carney 497-5511
Caspian 265-3223
Cedarville 495-5889
Champion 485-1888
Channing 875-3012
Chassell 482-4411
Chatham 387-2275
Christmas 387-2275
Cooks 341-2133
Copper City 337-0528
Copper Harbor 337-0528
Cornell 428-4411
Covington 524-6950
Crystal Falls 875-3012
Curtis 293-5151
Dafter 495-5889
Daggett 753-2275
De Tour Village 495-5889
Deer Park 293-5236
Deerton 249-4040
Dodgeville 482-4411
Dollar Bay 482-2121
Drummond Island 495-5889
Eagle Harbor 337-0528
Eagle River 337-2345
Eben Junction 387-2275
Eckerman 293-5151
Engadine 293-5151
Ensign 428-3131
Epoufette 293-5151
Escanaba 786-5911
Ewen 787-2300
Faithorn 774-2121
Fayette 428-4411

TOWN POLICE

Felch 563-5801
Ford River 497-5511
Foster City 774-2121
Gaastra 265-3223
Garden 341-2133
Garden Corners 341-2133
Germfask 293-5151
Gladstone 428-3131
Goetzville 632-2216
Gould City 293-5151
Grand Island 387-2275
Grand Marais 293-5236
Greenland 884-4901
Gulliver 341-2133
Gwinn 346-9224
Hancock 482-3102
Harris 466-2911
Helmer 293-5236
Hendricks 293-5151
Herman 524-6161
Hermansville 497-5511
Hessel 643-8877
Houghton 482-2121
Hubbell 296-9911
Hulbert 293-5236
Ingalls 753-2275
Ingallston 863-4441
Iron Mountain 774-1234
Iron River 265-4321
Ironwood 932-1234
Ishpeming 486-4416
Jacobsville 337-2345
Kearsarge 337-2345
Kingsford 774-2525
Kinross 495-5889
L'Anse 524-6050
Lac La Belle 482-3102
Lake Gogebic Area 787-2300
Lake Linden 296-9911
Laurium 337-4000
Limestone 387-2275
Loretto 563-5801
Mackinac Island 847-3300
Mackinaw City 231-436-7861

TOWN POLICE

Manistique 341-2133
Marenisco 787-2300
Marquette 228-0400
Mass City 884-4901
Matchwood 787-2300
McMillan 293-5151
Melstrand 387-4540
Menominee 863-5568
Michigamme 485-1888
Mineral Hills 265-4321
Mohawk 337-0528
Moran 643-8877
Munising 387-2275
Nadeau 497-5511
Nahma 428-4411
Nahma Junction 428-4411
Naubinway 643-8877
Negaunee 475-4154
Newberry 293-5236
Nisula 524-6161
Norway 563-5801
Ontonagon 884-4901
Osceola 482-3102
Painesdale 482-3102
Palmer 475-4154
Paradise 248-3244
Pelkie 524-6161
Pequaming 524-6161
Perkins 428-4411
Pickford 495-5889
Powers 497-5511
Quinnesec 774-2121
Raco 248-3251
Ralph 346-9224
Ramsay 667-0313
Rapid River 428-4411
Republic 376-8800
Rock 428-4411
Rockland 884-4901
Rudyard 495-5889
Sagola 875-3012
Sand River 249-4040
Sault Ste. Marie 632-3344
Seney 293-5151

TOWN POLICE

Shingleton 387-2275
Sidnaw 524-6161
Silver City 884-4901
Skandia 249-4040
Skanee 353-7181
Soo Junction 293-5236
South Range 482-3102
Spalding 497-5511
St. Ignace 643-8877
Stambaugh 265-3223
Stephenson 753-4006
Stonington 428-4411

TOWN POLICE

Strongs 248-3244
Sugar Island 632-3344
Tamarack 337-4000
Thompson 341-2133
Three Lakes 524-6161
Toivola 482-3102
Traunik 387-2275
Trenary 387-2275Trout
Lake 293-5236
Vulcan 563-5801
Wakefield 667-0313
Wallace 863-5568

TOWN POLICE

Watton 524-6950
Waucedah 774-6262
Watersmeet 358-4313
Wells 786-5911
Wetmore 387-2275
White Pine 884-4901
Whitefish Point 632-2216
Wilson 466-7441

BANKS

Branches for major banks are located in Escanaba, Hancock, Houghton, Iron Mountain, Ironwood, Mackinaw City, Marquette, Menominee, Munising, Newberry, Sault Ste. Marie, and St. Ignace. All banks have ATMs. In smaller towns without a major bank, ATMs are usually available on the street or in grocery and convenience stores.

BIBLIOGRAPHY

The U.P. has inspired many a poet, naturalist, and historian. A growing number of fictional works have also been based in the U.P., a handful of which—like *Anatomy of a Murder*, which was made into a film in 1959—have gained national fame. There are thankfully several independent bookstores throughout the U.P. that carry regional books, covering both the U.P. in its entirety and specific regions. These bookshops are worth a visit while you're in town. In the meantime, following is a reading list to get you started.

Biography and Reminiscence

Crowe, William S. *Lumberjack: Inside an Era in the Upper Peninsula of Michigan*. Skandia, MI: North Country Publishing, 2002. 144 pp., photos. A 1950s classic that has recently been reprinted, *Lumberjack* is a firsthand account of the logging industry in the U.P., particularly around the Manistique area, when the industry was booming.

Emerick, Lon L. *Going Back to Central: On the Road in Search of the Past in Michigan's Upper Peninsula*. Skandia, MI: North Country Publishing, 2003. 160 pp., photos. Very well researched and written travelogue through the U.P., full of rich characters, local folklore, and beautiful landscapes.

———. *The Superior Peninsula: Seasons in the Upper Peninsula of Michigan*. Skandia, MI: North Country Publishing, 1996. 216 pp. Emerick, a retired professor, pens a moving love letter to the U.P., organized by seasons. If anything could make you fall in love with six-month winters, it's this book.

Harju, Jerry. *Northern Reflections: A Lighthearted Account of "Growing Up North."* Marquette, MI: North Harbor Publishing, 1999. 123 pp. A fun and funny collection of stories about growing up in the U.P. in the 1940s, during a time when iron and lumber, though on a major decline, were still big business in the U.P., and the Mackinac Bridge hadn't yet been built.

Zechlin, Carol Brisson. *Growing Up Yooper: Childhood Memories of Michigan's Upper Peninsula.* St. Germain, WI: The Guest Cottage, Inc., 2004. 91 pp. A collection of charming short stories about being a kid in the U.P. in the 1950s.

Fiction

Anderson, Lauri. *Misery Bay and Other Stories from Michigan's Upper Peninsula.* St. Cloud, MN: North Star Press, 2002. 160 pp. A collection of short stories that celebrate the Finnish heritage of the U.P., especially in the Copper Country era. Lots of local customs and legends are introduced here.

Traver, Robert. *Anatomy of a Murder.* New York: St. Martin's Press, 1958. 448 pp. A novel based on a real murder and court case in Big Bay, Michigan, *Anatomy of a Murder* was highly praised for its character development and skillful description of courtroom drama. A film was made out of the book in 1959, bringing a bit of notoriety to the U.P.

History & Cultural Studies

Bohnak, Karl. *So Cold a Sky: Upper Michigan Weather Stories.* Negaunee, MI: Cold Sky Publishing, 2006. 350 pp., illus. A series of true tales chronicling Yooper weather battles from the pioneers to the present day.

Dodge, Roy L. *Michigan Ghost Towns: The Upper Peninsula.* San Diego, CA: Thunder Bay Press, 1994. 300 pp., photos. A detailed account of the many ghost towns in the U.P. The background of each town is given, how it was built, what it was like, what happened to it, and what's left of it today. A must for anyone interested in exploring the U.P.'s many ghost towns.

Graham, Loren R. *A Face in the Rock: The Tale of a Grand Island Chippewa.* Berkeley: University of California Press, 1998. 172 pp. Winner of the Follo Award of the Michigan Historical Society for its contribution to Michigan history, Graham's book details the plight of the Chippewa on Grand Island, from battles with other tribes to white encroachment and a loss of culture, language, and land. Graham finishes on a positive note, looking at the preservation of Grand Island and recent efforts to honor the Chippewa culture.

Lankton, Larry. *Cradle to Grave: Life, Work, and Death at the Lake Superior Copper Mines.* New York: Oxford University Press, 1993. 352 pp., illus., photos. An academic work, written by a Michigan Tech history professor, focused on both the technical side of the mining world (how technological advancements in mining affected the mining business) and what was happening socially and culturally both above and below ground during the Keweenaw's copper boom. It's a great precursor to a Copper Country visit.

Osborn, Chase S. *The Iron Hunter.* Detroit: Wayne State University Press, 2002. 248 pp., photos. A reprint of the fascinating autobiography of Chase Salmon Osborn, the eccentric publisher-turned-governor, who remains the only Michigan state governor to hail from the U.P. There are several monuments to Osborn in his hometown of Sault Ste. Marie.

Piljac, Thomas. *Mackinac Island: Historic Frontier, Vacation Resort, Timeless Wonderland*. Chicago: Chicago Review Press, 1996. 320 pp., photos. A very informative and comprehensive look at Mackinac's long and varied history.

Nature Guides
Dufresne, Jim. *Isle Royale Foot Trails and Water Routes*. Seattle, WA: Mountaineers Books, 2002. 144 pp., photos, illus. An indispensable guide to what can be a very confusing island to navigate. Dufresne does an excellent job of unlocking the mystery of Isle Royale for visitors.

Glime, Janice. *The Elfin World of Mosses and Liverworts of Michigan's Upper Peninsula and Isle Royale*. Houghton, MI: Isle Royale Natural History Association, 1993. 154 pp., photo, illus. A field guide to mosses and liverworts, written for the layperson.

Hansen, Eric. *Hiking Michigan's Upper Peninsula*. Guilford, CT: Falcon, 2005. Hands-down the best hiking guide to the area. Hansen gives vivid descriptions and very detailed directions to hikes ranging from easy to challenging, popular to hidden.

Huggler, Tom. *Fish Michigan: 100 Upper Peninsula Lakes*. Davison, MI: Friede Publications, 1994. 112 pp., photos. A detailed guide to the best fishing lakes in the U.P., with information on when and where to find the fish you're looking for.

Photographic Studies
Phipps, Terry. *Seasons of Mackinac*. Ann Arbor: University of Michigan Press, 2004. 128 pp., photos. A lovely introduction to Mackinac in all four seasons, this is a great book for visitors to check out to see that there's more to the island than just summertime.

CLIMATE, WEATHER, WHAT TO WEAR
There's a popular saying in Michigan that if you don't like the weather, just wait five minutes. Nowhere in the state is this more the case than in the U.P., where a warm summer day can turn into a thunderstorm and back again in minutes. Obviously, in winter it's winter and that's not going to change until April, but even in the snow season, the wind can whip up and die down at a moment's notice, drastically increasing and decreasing the amount of bundling needed throughout the day. That said, in broad strokes, the weather is very seasonal—it's hot in the summer, cold in the winter, rainy in the fall, and sunny but cool in the spring. June brings blackfly season, so be prepared with bug spray, long sleeves, and pants. By August the lakes are warm enough to swim in; more shallow, inland lakes warm up a bit earlier.

On Isle Royale, in the middle of Lake Superior, it can be cold even in August, so be sure to pack warm clothes if you're making the trip to the island. It does warm up there during the day, especially in August, but even on the warmest of days it cools down at night and in the morning.

In the winter you absolutely must have a warm winter jacket, gloves, a hat, and boots at a minimum. Certain areas get more snow than others, but in general you're looking at around 150–200 inches of snow a season. If you're driving in the U.P. it's best to have a four-wheel-drive vehicle. Snow chains aren't allowed in Michigan.

In the fall the colors here are absolutely spectacular, especially in the Porcupine Mountains. The leaves generally start to turn at the end of September and early October, when the U.P. gets its last surge of visitors before the winter sets in.

FISHING AND HUNTING REGULATIONS

A fishing or hunting license is required for all fishing and hunting in Michigan, and they are available from the state's Department of Natural Resources (906-228-6561; www.michigan.gov/dnr). Different regulations apply to different species in different areas, so be sure to check the DNR's Web site before planning your trip. Every year the DNR picks a weekend in June to be Michigan's Free Fishing Weekend—no fees are required on these days, but licenses are. To find out about the next free weekend, check the DNR's Web site. Applications may also be filed on-line for permits, and reservations can be made for most state park campgrounds through the site as well.

Persons with mental disabilities may fish or hunt in Michigan without a license, provided they are accompanied by an adult with a valid license. Senior citizens are offered a discounted rate on licenses, and legally blind persons are also eligible for the discount.

HANDICAPPED SERVICES

A surprising number of hotels and restaurants in the U.P. are handicapped accessible, and the DNR has a great program to provide information and assistance to disabled fishermen, hunters, and campers. Still, many of the buildings up here were built long before ADA regulations became law, and the historic buildings are not required to upgrade, so there are still some buildings with very narrow doorways and large staircases that are not easily accessed by the disabled.

The state and national parks and forests all have information regarding campsites for the disabled (most campgrounds have at least one accessible campsite) and handicapped access to parks and facilities, as well as TDD phone numbers to call for the hearing impaired. For an accessibility guide to Fort Mackinac and other Mackinac State Historic Parks properties, call 231-436-4100 or fax 231-436-4210.

HOSPITALS AND EMERGENCY MEDICAL SERVICE

All the hospitals listed here have 24-hour emergency care. The level of care tends to be better at the larger hospitals, purely because they have more money for equipment and staff. The good news is that once you're in the U.P., it doesn't take all that long to get from one place to the next, so no matter where you are you're generally close to a good emergency facility. Because this is a wilderness area, there are trained search and rescue teams throughout the peninsula.

Baraga County Memorial Hospital, 770 Main St., L'Anse; 906-524-3300
Bell Hospital, 101 S. 4th St., Ishpeming; 906-486-4431
Dickinson County Healthcare System, 1721 S. Stephenson Ave.
Iron Mountain; 906-774-1313
Grand View Health System, 10561 N. Grand View Lane, Ironwood; 906-932-2525
Helen Newberry Joy Hospital, 502 W. Harrie St., Newberry; 906-293-9200 or
1-800-743-3093
Iron County Community Hospital, 1400 W. Ice Lake Rd., Iron River; 906-265-6121
Keweenaw Memorial Hospital, 205 Osceola St., Laurium; 906-337-6500
Mackinac Straits Hospital, 200 Burdette St., St. Ignace; 906-643-8585

Marquette General Health System, 580 W. College Ave., Marquette; 906-228-9440
Munising Memorial Hospital System, 1500 Sand Point Rd., Rte. #1 Box 501,
Munising; 906-387-4110
Ontonagon Memorial Hospital, 601 S. 7th St., Suite 1, Ontonagon; 906-884-4134
OSF St. Francis Hospital, 3401 Ludington St., Escanaba; 906-786-5707
Portage Health System, 500 Campus Dr., Hancock; 906-483-1000 or 1-800-573-5001
Schoolcraft Memorial Hospital, 500 Main St., Manistique; 906-341-3200
War Memorial Hospital, 500 Osborn Blvd., Sault Ste. Marie; 906-635-4460

MEDIA

Fiercely independent and proud of their home and cultural heritage, U.P. residents boast a
lively and entertaining publishing and radio scene. On the music front, the radio stations
skew heavily toward country and oldies, and every once in a while you'll hear some classic
Yooper folk songs as well. Following are some of the best local papers and stations—one of
the best ways for visitors to truly immerse themselves in U.P. culture.

Newspapers and Magazines

The Daily Mining Gazette (906-482-1500, www.miningazette.com; offices in Houghton
and Calumet) Serving Houghton, Keweenaw, Baraga, and Ontonagon Counties since 1858,
the paper obviously started in the mining days and has continued to cover what's near and
dear to the locals ever since. This is a great place to find out about what's going on in local
politics, both in this region and U.P.-wide.

The Eagle Herald (715-735-6611 or 1-800-777-0345; www.eagleherald.com) A great little
paper serving Menominee and Marinette (interesting, given that the towns are in two different states!), the *Eagle Herald* focuses on local news and runs national and world news
from the Associated Press. The paper also produces a Sunday edition with more features,
classifieds, and entertainment listings.

The Finnish-American Reporter (906-487-7549; www.finnishamericanreporter.com;
Hancock) This is a great, only-in-the-U.P. paper out of Finnish-centric Hancock. It's
printed in English but covers Finnish and Finnish American news, as well as human-
interest stories that are of interest to Finnish Americans.

Marquette Monthly (906-226-6500; www.mmnow.com, Marquette) Just the sort of magazine you'd expect to find in a college town like Marquette, jam-packed with cultural news,
events, and commentary as well as local entertainment listings. This is a good place to find
out about local art exhibits and upcoming concerts in the Marquette area.

Soo Evening News (906-632-2235; www.sooeveningnews.com; Sault Ste. Marie) Not an
amazing paper for news coverage, but the *Soo Evening News* is a great slice-of-life read and
offers excellent local sports coverage.

Upper Peninsula Magazine (906-789-7710; www.upperpeninsula.biz; 1007 Ludington
St., Escanaba) The magazine mostly covers its advertisers, but its advertisers are mostly all
businesses that visitors will be interested in, so it's not so bad. Its event listings are always
very good.

Radio

AM

590 **WJMS,** Ironwood; Country
600 **WCHT,** Escanaba; News
680 **WDBC,** Escanaba; Adult contemporary
920 **WMPL,** Hancock; Talk
940 **WIDG,** St. Ignace; Sports
970 **WZAM,** Ishpeming; News
1230 **WIKB,** Iron River; Oldies
1230 **WSOO,** Sault Ste. Marie; Adult contemporary
1240 **WIAN,** Ishpeming; Talk
1320 **WDMJ,** Marquette; News/talk
1400 **WKNW,** Sault Ste. Marie; Talk
1400 **WQXO,** Munising; Nostalgia
1400 **WCCY,** Houghton; Nostalgia
1450 **WMIQ,** Iron Mountain; Talk
1490 **WTIQ,** Manistique; Oldies

FM

88.5 **WOAS,** Ontonagon; Variety
90.1 **WNMU,** Marquette; Public Radio / classical
90.1 **WLSO,** Sault Ste. Marie Variety
91.1 **WGGL,** Houghton; Classical/news/talk
91.5 **WUPX,** Marquette; Alternative
91.5 **WVCM,** Iron Mountain; Religious
91.9 **WMTU,** Houghton; College
92.3 **WJPD,** Ishpeming; Country
93.1 **WIMK,** Iron Mountain; Classic rock
93.5 **WKMJ,** Hancock; Adult contemporary
94.1 **WUPK,** Marquette; Classic rock
94.3 **WZNL,** Norway; Adult contemporary
95.7 **WHWL,** Marquette; Religious
97.1 **WGLQ,** Escanaba; Top 40
99.1 **WIKB,** Iron River; Oldies
99.7 **WIMI,** Ironwood; Adult contemporary
97.7 **WOLV,** Houghton; Classic rock
97.9 **WIHC,** Newberry; Classic rock
98.3 **WHCH,** Munising Oldies
98.3 **WCNF,** Sault Ste. Marie Public Radio
99.5 **WYSS,** Sault Ste. Marie Top 40
99.5 **WNGE,** Negaunee; Oldies
100.7 **WOBE,** Crystal Falls; Oldies
101.1 **WUPY,** Ontonagon; Country
101.3 **WSUE,** Sault Ste. Marie Rock
101.5 **WJNR,** Iron Mountain; Country
101.9 **WKQS,** Negaunee; Adult contemporary

102.3 **WHKB,** Houghton; Country
102.5 **WCMM,** Gulliver; Country
102.9 **WMKC,** St. Ignace; Country
103.3 **WFXD,** Marquette; Country
103.7 **WHYB,** Menominee; Country
104.3 **WVCN,** Baraga; Religious
104.7 **WYKX,** Escanaba; Country
105.7 **WCUP,** L'Anse; Country
106.9 **WUPM,** Ironwood; Top 40
107.7 **WMQT,** Ishpeming; Adult contemporary

Tourist Information

Lake Michigan and Environs
Delta County Chamber of Commerce (Escanaba, Manistique, Bays de Noc)
230 Ludington St., Escanaba; 906-786-2192; www.deltami.org
Delta County Tourism Bureau (Escanaba, Gladstone, Rapid River, Fayette)
230 Ludington St., Escanaba; 906-789-7710 or 1-800-533-4FUN; www.deltafun.com
Escanaba and Bays de Noc Tourism Bureau, 230 Ludington St., Escanaba;
906-789-7862; www.travelbaysdenoc.com
Hiawatha National Forest Office, 449 E. Lakeshore Dr. / US 2, Manistique;
906-341-5666
Iron County Chamber of Commerce, east of downtown Iron River on US 2;
906-265-3822; www.iron.org
Manistique Area Tourist Council, Manistique; 1-800-342-4282; www.onlynorth.com
River Cities Chamber of Commerce, Menominee and Marinette; 906-863-2679;
www.rivercities.net/tourism

Lake Superior and Environs
Alger County Chamber of Commerce; 906-387-2138
**Baraga County Tourist & Recreation Association (L'Anse-Baraga-Skanee-Huron
Mountains/Covington)**, 755 E. Broad St. at US 41, L'Anse; 906-524-7444 or
1-800-743-4908; www.baragacountytourism.com
Keweenaw Convention & Visitors Bureau; 906-337-4579 or 1-800-338-7982;
www.keweenaw.info
Lake Gogebic Chamber of Commerce; 906-842-3611
Ironwood Chamber of Commerce, 116 N. Lowell St., Ironwood; 906-932-1122
Marquette Country Convention & Visitors Bureau; 1-800-544-4321;
www.marquettecountry.org
Ontonagon Chamber of Commerce; 906-884-4735 www.ontonagonmi.com
Pictured Rocks/Hiawatha National Forest Visitor Center, H58 just east of MI 28, where
the main highway turns west to follow the lakeshore in Munising; 906-387-3700;
www.nps.gov/piro
Western U.P. Tourism and Convention Bureau; 1-800-522-5657; www.westernup.com

Eastern Lake Superior and Whitefish Bay
Grand Marais Visitors Bureau; 906-494-2447; www.grandmaraismichigan.com
Newberry Chamber of Commerce; 906-293-5562; www.newberrychamber.net
Sault Ste. Marie Convention & Visitors Bureau; 906-632-3301; www.saultstemarie.com
Tahquamenon Falls State Park; 906-492-3415; www.michigan.gov/dnr

Straits of Mackinac and Environs
Drummond Island Tourism Bureau, Drummond Island; 906-493-5245;
www.drummondislandchamber.com
Les Cheneaux Tourism Bureau, Cedarville; 1-888-364-7526; www.lescheneaux.org
Mackinac Island Visitors Bureau; 1-800-454-5227; www.mackinacisland.org
Mackinaw City Chamber of Commerce, 214 E. Central St., Mackinaw City; 231-436-5574;
www.mackinawcity.com
Michigan Welcome Center, Mackinac Bridge exit, St. Ignace; 906-863-6496
St. Ignace Chamber of Commerce, 560 N. State St., St. Ignace; 906-643-8717 or 1-800-
970-8717; www.stignace.com

General Index

Dining by Price